X RAYS

TABLES OF PHYSICAL AND CHEMICAL CONSTANTS AND SOME MATHEMATICAL FUNCTIONS

BY

G. W. C. KAYE
O.B.E., M.A., D.Sc.

AND

T. H. LABY, M.A.

Royal 8vo, 14s. net

LONGMANS, GREEN, AND CO.

LONDON, NEW YORK, BOMBAY, CALCUTTA, AND MADRAS

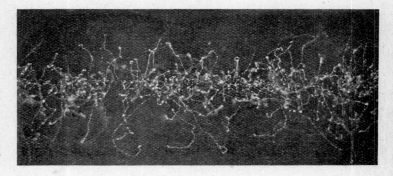

FIG. 1.—Photograph obtained by C. T. R. Wilson of the path of a beam of X rays in supersaturated air. The beam of rays, some 2 mm. in diameter, was sent through the moist air (from left to right in the figure) immediately after the expansion which produced the supersaturation (see p. 156). The axis of the camera was horizontal, and the magnification of the photograph is about 2½ times.

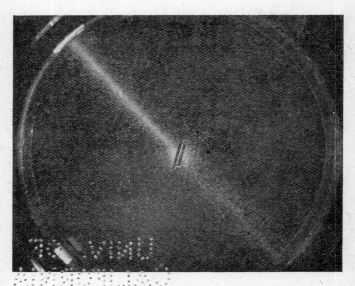

FIG. 2.—Photograph obtained by C. T. R. Wilson showing the passage of X rays (from left to right) through a thin copper plate (see p. 159).

X RAYS

BY

G. W. C. KAYE, O.B.E., M.A., D.Sc. F.Inst.P.

SUPERINTENDENT OF THE PHYSICS DEPARTMENT, THE NATIONAL PHYSICAL LABORATORY
PAST PRESIDENT OF THE RÖNTGEN SOCIETY
EDITOR OF THE JOURNAL OF THE RÖNTGEN SOCIETY
HON. MEMBER, THE SOCIETY OF RADIOGRAPHERS

FOURTH EDITION

WITH ILLUSTRATIONS

LONGMANS, GREEN, AND CO.
39 PATERNOSTER ROW, LONDON
FOURTH AVENUE & 30TH STREET, NEW YORK
BOMBAY, CALCUTTA, AND MADRAS
1923

Made in Great Britain

EXTRACT FROM PREFACE TO FIRST EDITION.

THIS little book does not profess to be a treatise or hand-book on X rays. It aims at giving an account of such of the present-day methods and apparatus as appear valuable or novel, and which, in many cases, can only be found scattered throughout many journals; it deals with the physics of a number of the main principles of radiology being concerned with the development of theory as well as of experiment; and it attempts to convey a notion of the historical trend of events from Professor Röntgen's world-famous discovery in 1895 down to the present year.

The author trusts that the form of the book will be accept-able, not only to the student of physics, but to the man of general scientific interests, and particularly to the members of the medical profession. He is aware from experience as teacher and examiner of medical students of their need of a book on the subject which is neither recondite nor mathematical.

To two of his colleagues at the National Physical Labora-tory, the writer wishes to record his grateful thanks. Dr. E. A. Owen has co-operated in the treatment of the Diffraction of X Rays by Crystals. Mr. W. F. Higgins has given freely of his time and energies, and rendered in-valuable aid. He has executed a large proportion of the diagrams, and is responsible for the preparation of the index and some of the tables.

Finally, the author would wish to thank his wife for general assistance, and Dr. A. A. Robb, F.R.S., of St John's College, Cambridge, for permission to include his verses on Maxwell's famous equations and the birth of an X ray. Dr. Robb's " Revolution of the Corpuscle " first saw light in the Post-Prandial Proceedings of the Cavendish Laboratory.

The writer will be content if his work can be regarded as one of the many tokens of esteem with which old students of the Cavendish School of Research have delighted to honour their distinguished professor, Sir J. J. Thomson.

February 1914.

PREFACE TO SECOND EDITION.

IN this edition the writer, so far as his military duties would permit, has subjected the book to a thorough revision. He would again record the help of Mr. W. F. Higgins who has written an additional chapter on X-Ray Equipment and Technique. The author is happy to think that his little book has been of service to the many X-ray workers now labouring in the common cause of humanity in our hospitals both at home and overseas.

September 1916.

PREFACE TO FOURTH EDITION.

THE rapid and enormous growth of the subject of X rays in a great variety of directions, has made the task of revision arduous, and rendered it difficult to discriminate between the mass of material available, so as to avoid substantially increasing the size of the book.

A good deal of revision has been attempted throughout the text, and the substance of the writer's recent lectures at the Royal Institution, the Royal Society of Arts, and the Royal Society of Medicine has been drawn on, particularly with reference to the applications of X rays.

The author wishes to thank his wife for unfailing assistance.

March 1922.

CONTENTS.

CHAPTER III.
X RAYS.

CHAPTER IV.
AN X-RAY BULB.

CHAPTER V.
HIGH-POTENTIAL GENERATORS.

CHAPTER VI.

THE "HARDNESS" OF A GAS X-RAY BULB.

CHAPTER VII.

THE BLACKENING OF AN X-RAY BULB.

CHAPTER VIII.

THE MEASUREMENT OF X RAYS.

CHAPTER IX.

SCATTERED, CHARACTERISTIC AND SECONDARY CORPUSCULAR RAYS.

CHAPTER X.

FURTHER PROPERTIES OF THE X RAYS.

CHAPTER XI.

PRACTICAL APPLICATIONS OF X RAYS.

CHAPTER XII.

X-RAY EQUIPMENT AND TECHNIQUE.

CHAPTER XIII.

DIFFRACTION OF X RAYS BY CRYSTALS.

CHAPTER XIV.

THE NATURE OF THE X RAYS.

APPENDIX I.

APPENDIX II.

APPENDIX III.

APPENDIX IV.

APPENDIX V.

APPENDIX VI.

e = unit of electricity $\begin{cases} = \text{charge carried by hydrogen ion in electrolysis,} \\ = 4\cdot77 \times 10^{-10} \text{ electrostatic units (E.S.U.),} \\ = 1\cdot59 \times 10^{-20} \text{ electromagnetic units (E.M.U.)} \end{cases}$

...ATURE.	RAYS.	RATIO OF CHARGE TO MASS, (e/m), ETC.		VELOCITY. cms./sec.	RANGE, ETC.
		E.M.U.grm.$^{-1}$	E.S.U.grm.$^{-1}$		
...CTRI- ...LY ...TRAL.	Hertzian waves. Infra-red rays. Visible light rays. Ultra-violet light. Entladung-strahlen.	2×10^6 to $0\cdot2$ cm. $0\cdot031$ to $7\cdot7 \times 10^{-5}$ $\begin{cases} 7\cdot2 \times 10^{-5} \text{ to} \\ 4 \times 10^{-5} \end{cases}$ $\begin{cases} 4 \times 10^{-5} \text{ to} \\ 2 \times 10^{-6} \end{cases}$ Wave length About 10^{-6} ?		3×10^{10}.	From a few mm. of air to infinity.
	X rays	Wave length : 5×10^{-6} to 6×10^{-10} cm.		3×10^{10}.	From a few mms. to over 100 metres in air at N.T.P.
	γ rays of Ra, U, Ac, Th, etc.	Wave length : $1\cdot4 \times 10^{-8}$ to 1×10^{-10} cm.		3×10^{10}.	Reduced to 1 per cent. by $\frac{1}{2}$ mile of air at N.T.P.
	Ordinary atoms and molecules.	H_2 atom $m = 1\cdot66 \times 10^{-24}$ grm. Diam. $= 2\cdot2 \times 10^{-8}$ cm.		$H_2 : 18\cdot4 \times 10^4$ } at $O_2 : 4\cdot6 \times 10^4$ } $0°$ C.	Mean free path of H_2 at $0°$ C., $1\cdot8 \times 10^{-5}$ cm.
...RIERS OF ...ATIVE ...CTRI-...Y.	Electrons. Corpuscles. Cathode rays. Lenard rays. Negative ion at low pressures.	(For small velocities.) $1\cdot77 \times 10^7$	$5\cdot31 \times 10^{17}$	Photoelectrons 10^7 to 10^8. Wehnelt cathode rays 10^8 to 10^9. Cathode rays 10^9 to 10^{10}.	Very small. Very small. Range in air a few mms.
	β rays of Ra, U, Th, Ac, K, etc.	$\begin{bmatrix} m_0 = 1/1850\ H_2 \text{ atom.} \\ \text{Diam.} = 4 \times 10^{-13} \text{ cm.} \end{bmatrix}$		β rays of Ra 10^{10} to $2\cdot99 \times 10^{10}$.	Stopped by about 1 cm. of lead.
	δ rays (slow β rays).			As low as $3\cdot2 \times 10^8$.	Too slow to ionise.
	Negative ion.	May have several charges (though usually one) and up to 30 molecules.		In air ; $1\cdot8$ for unit electric field.	—
	Negatively charged atoms and molecules in discharge tubes.	10^4 (for H_2).	3×10^{14} (for H_2).	Up to 10^8.	—
...RIERS OF ...ITIVE ...TRI-...	α rays of Ra, U, Th, Ac, etc. (helium atoms with charge $2e$).	$4\cdot8 \times 10^3$ $[m = 6\cdot56 \times 10^{-24}]$	$1\cdot4 \times 10^{14}$.	Initial value $1\cdot6 \times 10^9$ to $2\cdot2 \times 10^9$ (depending on source).	3 to 8 cms. in air at N.T.P.
	Recoil atoms.	47 (RaB).	$1\cdot4 \times 10^{12}$.	5×10^4 (RaC).	1/10 mm. in air at N.T.P.
	Positively charged atoms and molecules (Kanalstrahlen) in discharge tubes.	10^4 (for H_2).	3×10^{14} (for H_2).	Up to 10^8.	—
	Positive ion.	May have several charges (though usually one) and up to 30 molecules.		In air ; $1\cdot5$ for unit electric field.	—

THE REVOLUTION OF THE CORPUSCLE.[1]

A CORPUSCLE once did oscillate so quickly to and fro,
He always raised disturbances wherever he did go.
He struggled hard for freedom against a powerful foe—
An atom—who would not let him go.
The aether trembled at his agitations
In a manner so familiar that I only need to say,
In accordance with Clerk Maxwell's six equations
It tickled people's optics far away.
　　　You can feel the way it's done,
　　　You may trace them as they run—
$d\gamma$ by dy less $d\beta$ by dz is equal $K \cdot dX/dt$.

While the curl of (X, Y, Z) is the minus d/dt of the vector (a, b, c).

Some professional agitators only holler till they're hoarse,
But this plucky little corpuscle pursued another course,
And finally resorted to electromotive force,
Resorted to electromotive force.
The medium quaked in dread anticipation,
It feared that its equations might be somewhat too abstruse,
And not admit of finite integration
In case the little corpuscle got loose.
　　　For there was a lot of gas
　　　Through which he had to pass,
　　　And in case he was too rash,
　　　There was sure to be a smash,
　　　Resulting in a flash.
Then $d\gamma$ by dy less $d\beta$ by dz would equal $K \cdot dX/dt$.

While the curl of (X, Y, Z) would be minus d/dt of the vector (a, b, c).

The corpuscle radiated until he had conceived
A plan by which his freedom might be easily achieved,
I'll not go into details, for I might not be believed,
Indeed I'm sure I should not be believed.
However, there was one decisive action,
The atom and the corpuscle each made a single charge,
But the atom could not hold him in subjection
Though something like a thousand times as large.

[1] *Air*: "The Interfering Parrot" (*Geisha*).

The corpuscle won the day
And in freedom went away
And became a cathode ray.
But his life was rather gay,
And he went at such a rate,
That he ran against a plate ;
When the aether saw his fate
Its pulse did palpitate.
And $d\gamma$ by dy less $d\beta$ by dz was equal $K . dX/dt$.

. . . .

While the curl of (X, Y, Z) was the minus d/dt of the vector (a, b, c).

A. A. R.

"$h\nu$." [1]

ALL black body radiations,
All the spectrum variations,
All atomic oscillations
    Vary as "$h\nu$."

Chorus.

Here's the right relation,
Governs radiation,
Here's the new,
And only true,
Electrodynamical equation ;
Never mind your d/dt^2,
Ve or half mv^2
(If you watch the factor "c^2")
's equal to "$h\nu$."

Ultraviolet vibrations,
X and gamma ray pulsations,
Ordinary light sensations
    All obey "$h\nu$."

Even in matters calorific,
Such things as the heat specific
Yield to treatment scientific
    If you use "$h\nu$."

In all questions energetic,
Whether static or kinetic,
Or electric, or magnetic,
    You must use "$h\nu$."

There would be a mighty clearance,
We should all be Planck's adherents,
Were it not that interference
    Still defies "$h\nu$."

---

[1] Reprinted from the Cavendish Physical Society's Post-Prandial Proceedings, by kind permission of the author, Dr. G. Shearer. (*Air* : "Men of Harlech.")

INTRODUCTION.

IN the early nineties, it was not infrequently maintained that the science of physics had put its house in complete order, and that any future advances could only be along the lines of precision measurement. Such pessimism has been utterly confounded by a sequence of discoveries since 1895, unparalleled in their fundamental nature and promise.

Even many not specially concerned have had their attention directed to the recent attempts at solving the riddle which has excited interest and taxed ingenuity since the beginning of civilisation—the problem of the ultimate structure of matter. The chemist and physicist have long built upon a theory of atoms and molecules ; though information as to the existence and behaviour of individual atoms was only based on speculation, however justifiable.

But within the last decade we have not only isolated the atom, but we have learnt a great deal about its internal structure. Radioactivity has, for example, introduced us to an electrically charged atom of helium (the α ray) with characteristics such that it can, in spite of its extreme smallness,[1] make individual appeal to our senses. The speed of α rays is so abnormally high,[2] that if, for instance, they are allowed to strike a fluorescent screen, as in the Spinthariscope of Sir Wm. Crookes, each atom possesses enough energy to record its arrival by a visible flash of light. This provided what was probably the first instance of the registering of a single individual atom. Rutherford and Geiger similarly turned to account the electric charge, and have

[1] Mass about 7×10^{-24} gramme ; diameter about 2×10^{-8} cm.
[2] About 12,000 miles or 2×10^9 cm. per sec.

actually recorded the arrival of single atoms by means of a delicate electrometer.

More recently, C. T. R. Wilson, by the aid of his most beautiful and ingenious experiments on fog condensation, has succeeded in rendering visible and photographing the paths, not only of single charged atoms, but of electrons and X rays as well.

The emission of such charged atoms from the radioactive elements proceeds entirely regardless of let or hindrance on our part : we have, however, the ability and means to create similar abnormal carriers for ourselves—they are, for instance, to be found in abundance in a rarefied gas through which an electric discharge is passed. Under these conditions, the gas molecules, which are ordinarily electrically inert, assume, in many cases, electrical charges and, in addition, may have their usual velocities [1] increased a thousand-fold, so that they acquire properties which single them out from their fellows.

These facts are sufficiently attractive in themselves, but they serve, if needs be, as an outstanding illustration of the value of "pure research." Even the severely practical cannot but agree that the close study which has been given to the phenomena of a discharge tube has already been more than repaid by the manifold industrial developments arising out of the discovery of electrons by J. J. Thomson and of the X rays by Röntgen.

The amazing properties of the X rays excited universal astonishment at the time of their discovery. An X-ray outfit is now indispensable to the surgeon and physician ; and the debt which the world of humanity owes the X rays, to take the late war alone, is a heavy and increasing one.

Through the efforts of a devoted band of workers, with an outlook on life not immediately utilitarian, the Röntgen rays have thrown a searchlight on many phases of atomic physics not susceptible to other methods of attack.

And, last of all, the X rays have come to the aid of the crystallographer and displayed in the hands of Laue, the Braggs, Debye, Hull and many others, the regular grouping

[1] About 20 miles per minute in the case of air molecules.

of the atoms peculiar to a crystal. The experiments, which have opened up an immense field of enquiry, have at the same time given the long-deferred answer to the problem of the nature of the unknown or " X " rays. In this connection the work of Moseley stands out pre-eminently. The early death of this brilliant young physicist, while serving as an officer in the Gallipoli campaign, was not the least of the tragedies of the late war.

We now know that the X rays are another manifestation of radiant energy and resemble light rays in almost every particular except that the X rays have wave-lengths several thousand times shorter.

There is little doubt that the X rays play a prominent part in Nature, for example, in atmospheric electricity. They are emitted continually by the radioactive elements, and recent speculations indicate that they are given out in abundance by the sun and stars.

The Geissler discharge tube [1]—the former beautiful plaything of the scientist—has proved the pioneer of some of the most wonderful discoveries and speculations that physical science of this or any generation has known. Truly, as Maxwell predicted in the early seventies, the vacuum tube has shed light upon the whole domain of electrical science, and even upon the constitution of matter itself.

Our present intent, that of the study of the X rays, is approached most naturally by way of a scrutiny of the general phenomena of a discharge tube and of electrons in particular. To these branches of the subject we accordingly first direct ourselves.

---

[1] Known at different times and in different countries as the Plücker, Hittorf, or Crookes tube.

ABBREVIATIONS OF REFERENCES TO JOURNALS.

A.d.P.	Annalen der Physik.
A.J.R.	American Journal of Roentgenology.
A.Rt.R.	Archives of the Röntgen Ray.*
C.R.	Comptes Rendus.
D.P.G.V.	Verhandlungen der Deutschen Physikalischen Gesellschaft.
J.d.P.	Journal de Physique.
J.Rt.S.	Journal of the Röntgen Society.
N.	Nature.
P.C.P.S.	Proceedings of the Cambridge Philosophical Society.
P.M.	Philosophical Magazine.
P.P.S.	Proceedings of the Physical Society.
P.R.	Physical Review.
P.R.S.	Proceedings of the Royal Society (Series A).
P.R.S.E.	Proceedings of the Royal Society of Edinburgh.
P.T.	Philosophical Transactions (Series A.).
P.Z.	Physikalische Zeitschrift.

* Now, Archives of Radiology and Electrotherapy.

CHAPTER I.

THE PHENOMENA OF A DISCHARGE TUBE.

WHEN a current of electricity from an induction coil or influence machine is sent between two metal electrodes fused into the ends of a glass tube (say 12 inches long) from which the air is gradually withdrawn by a pump, the tube presents a continuous succession of striking appearances.

At high pressures, air is a very bad conductor of electricity; and a large force is necessary to produce a visible discharge while the pressure remains in the region of atmospheric. But a reduction of pressure facilitates the passage of the spark, which after a time loses its noisy character and is replaced by a collection of sinuous and irregular pink streamers which later broaden and fill almost the whole of the tube with a pink diffuse glow known as the **positive column**. Simultaneously the alternative spark-gap of the coil diminishes to a small fraction of an inch—evidence that the rarefied air is now conducting well.

Meanwhile the cathode—the electrode by which the current leaves the tube [1]—assumes at its tip a luminous tuft —**the negative glow**—violet in colour, which later grows until it completely envelops the cathode. Between these two luminous glows comes a darker ill-defined region called the **Faraday dark-space**. These general appearances correspond to a pressure of some 8 to 10 millimetres of mercury.

As the pressure is further reduced, the alternative spark-gap begins to lengthen, the anode becomes tipped with a

[1] The electrode by which the current enters the tube is the anode.

vivid speck of glow, and the positive column proceeds, **if** the current density is suitable, to break up into thin fluctuating pink discs or striae, which subsequently thicken and diminish in number, intensity and extent. The Faraday dark-space enlarges, and in the meantime (at about 1 mm. pressure), the violet negative glow increases in brightness and volume,[1] and the glass walls of the tube are seen to fluoresce with an olive-green light which, as J. J. Thomson (*P.C.P.S.* 1910) has shown, is due to the action of extremely active ultra-violet light from the negative glow.[2]

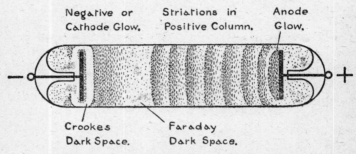

FIG. 3.—Discharge tube at low pressure, showing cathode dark-space and positive striations.

As the exhaustion proceeds, this fluorescence disappears, the negative glow detaches itself like a shell from the cathode, while a new violet film forms and spreads over the surface of the cathode. Thus the negative glow now consists of two parts : they are separated from each other by a narrow dark region called the Crookes or cathode dark-space, which has a sharply defined outline running parallel to that of the cathode. (See Fig. 3.)

With a reduction of pressure, the dark space increases in width, and pushes the outer negative glow before it. The dark space is often used as a rough indication of the pressure, though its width depends also on both the current

[1] The length of the glow on the cathode depends also on the current : the two are indeed roughly proportional (Hehl, 1903).

[2] This is especially marked in hydrogen. The fluorescence is bluishgreen with lead glass.

density and the metal of the cathode, and is not really a reliable guide to the degree of exhaustion.[1]

With higher rarefactions (say $\frac{1}{50}$ mm.) both positive and negative glows become less bright and definite in outline, and finally lose almost all traces of luminosity. Meanwhile the cathode dark space has grown at the expense of all else, until finally it becomes so large that its boundaries touch the glass walls of the tube. It is at this stage that the tube begins to shine, first in the region of the cathode, and then (as the dark space extends) over its whole surface, with the brilliant apple-green fluorescence[2] well known to those who are accustomed to "gas" X-ray tubes.

All this time the length of the alternative spark-gap has been steadily increasing. If the exhaustion is pressed still further, the fluorescence diminishes, and the resistance of the tube increases, until finally it becomes impossible for the discharge to pass at all. The pressure at which this comes about depends partly on the induction-coil and partly on the size of the discharge tube. A large tube always runs more easily than a small one at the same pressure.[3]

The above are the more salient features to be observed in a discharge tube. At atmospheric pressure the discharge consists mainly of positive column ; at low pressures it is the phenomena of the cathode dark-space which are most conspicuous and have attracted widespread attention.

[1] See Aston, *P.R.S.* 1912.

[2] This is quite different in appearance from, and much more brilliant than the olive-green fluorescence at higher pressures (see above). The yellow-green colour holds only for soda-glass tubes. Lead and lithium glasses yield a bluish fluorescence. In point of fact, Prof. H. Jackson (*N.* July 1915) has shown that a truly vitreous glass exhibits little if any fluorescence. The green fluorescence of X-ray tubes is associated with the presence of a small amount of manganese ; and manganese dioxide is, in fact, deliberately added so as to yield the colour of fluorescence by which the X-ray worker has grown accustomed to judge his tubes.

[3] When the gas pressure is not very low it may happen that both electrodes appear to function as cathode, due to the presence of "inverse" current. (See Chapter V.)

CHAPTER II.

CATHODE RAYS.

Historical.

The study of the green fluorescence on the glass was commenced by Plücker as long ago as 1859, and carried on vigorously by Hittorf (1869) and Goldstein (1876) in Germany, by Crookes (1879) in England, and by Puluj in Austria. It was soon ascertained that the fluorescence was produced by something coming from the region of the cathode ; for a suitably interposed obstacle cast a sharp shadow on the walls of the tube. This "something" was given the name cathode rays (*Kathodenstrahlen*) by Goldstein, who believed that the fluorescence was produced by waves in the ether for the propagation of which the gas in the tube was not necessary. The expression has been retained, and rightly, for although the word "ray" has come to be associated with a wave-motion in the ether, the connection is quite fortuitous ; indeed Newton used the term in his corpuscular theory of light.

The general properties of the cathode rays soon revealed themselves. Plücker had found that their path was bent by a magnet. Goldstein, by suitably contrived shadow experiments, confirmed Hittorf's observation that the rays travel in straight lines, and showed further that they start at right angles to the surface of the cathode. Crookes, by the use of cathodes shaped like a concave mirror, demonstrated that the rays concentrate near the centre of curvature, and there display in a marked degree heating properties and an ability to excite phosphorescence in

many substances. They tend also to push away any object
against which they strike, and cause, for example, paddle-
wheels of mica to rotate, although we now know that such
experiments depend for their success, not on the momentum
of the rays, but on heating effects such as prevail in a radiometer.[1] Most important of all, cathode rays, when they
strike matter, generate X rays, as Röntgen showed in 1895.

The Nature of the Cathode Rays.

For nearly thirty years the English and German schools
of physics disagreed as to the nature of the cathode rays.
German physicists, follow-
ing Goldstein's lead, held
that the rays were similar
to light—a wave motion
in the ether with which
matter had nothing to do.
This view received much
support from the experi-
ments of Hertz (1892), and

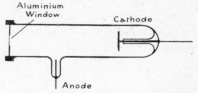

FIG. 4.—A Lenard tube for showing the passage of cathode rays through a thin aluminium
window.

his friend and colleague Lenard (*A.d.P.* 1894), who showed
that solid bodies were not absolutely opaque to the rays
which could pass, for example, through gold and aluminium
foil. Lenard's historic vacuum-tube was provided with a
small "window" of aluminium foil, 0·000265 cm. thick.
(See Fig. 4.) When the cathode rays were shot against
this window, he found that they passed through without
puncturing it, and were able to excite phosphorescence,
etc., a few millimetres away in air.[2] There was no difficulty in accounting for the transparency of thin solids on
the ether-wave theory, though it was apparent that the
relation to ordinary optical transparency was slight ; for
instance, gold leaf is more transparent than clear mica to

[1] A paddle-wheel made of a good thermal conductor such as aluminium
does not show the effect. In a radiometer the vanes are propelled by the
recoil of the gas molecules from the warmer face of each vane.

[2] The Lenard rays travel farther in attenuated air. We know now that
part, at any rate, of the phosphorescence which these "Lenard rays"
produced was due to X rays generated by the aluminium. X rays were
not discovered until the following year.

cathode rays. On the other hand, the normal emission of the rays from the cathode could scarcely have been anticipated on any wave theory : one would have inferred a general emission in all directions.

But the magnetic deflectibility of the cathode rays, and its unsatisfactory explanation on a wave theory, were regarded as crucial by English physicists, who were unanimous in the view that the rays consisted of particles of matter charged with negative electricity and projected with immense speeds from the cathode. Varley in 1870 seems to have been the first to suggest, though somewhat vaguely, the presence of such particles in the electric discharge ; and Sir Wm. Crookes, in a series of papers in the *Philosophical Transactions* (1879-1885), definitely adopted this standpoint to explain and coordinate the many striking results of his experiments.

In a flight of intuition, Crookes suggested that the matter constituting the cathode rays was neither gas nor liquid nor solid as ordinarily known, but in a fourth state transcending the gaseous condition—an extremely happy surmise, as events proved. It is interesting to recall that Faraday as long ago as 1816 speculated on the possibility of the existence of such a fourth state of matter.

Crookes supposed the cathode particles to have the dimensions of molecules, but this view became hard to reconcile with their penetrating power for metals found (as mentioned above) by Hertz and Lenard some years later. To meet the difficulty, the suggestion was put forward that the metal, under the bombardment of the cathode rays, acted as a pseudo-cathode, and itself emitted cathode rays. It was further pointed out that instances of the penetration of metals by molecules were not unknown ; to wit, the passage of hydrogen through hot palladium and platinum, the squeezing of water under hydraulic pressure through gold and other metals, and the gradual penetration of lead by gold when discs of the two are in close contact.[1] However, these explanations were not very satisfying, nor did

[1] The experiments of Roberts-Austen on the interdiffusion of metals were being conducted about this time (see *P.T.* 1896).

they prove to be necessary, for about this time new evidence began to accumulate in favour of the charged particle theory.

Sir J. J. Thomson came to the conclusion that the velocity of the cathode rays was appreciably less than that of light ; and the French physicist Perrin in 1895, by catching the rays in a Faraday cylinder, demonstrated that they carried a charge of negative electricity with them. But though Perrin's experiment carried conviction to the majority, it was not regarded as conclusive by the extreme ether-wave supporters, who looked on the electrification as merely

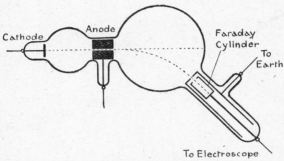

FIG. 5.—J. J. Thomson's modification of Perrin's apparatus for proving that cathode rays are negatively charged.

revealing the presence of electrified particles which were an accidental accompaniment of, and were not essentially connected with, the cathode waves.

But J. J. Thomson in 1897, by suitably modifying Perrin's apparatus, showed that when a magnet was used to deflect the cathode rays the negative electrification followed exactly the same course as the rays which produced the fluorescence on the glass (Fig. 5). He further succeeded in deflecting the cathode rays by an electric field : Hertz had tried this experiment fourteen years previously, and had failed because the pressure of his gas was too high, the gas conducting sufficiently well to mask the effect of the electric field.

After these results it could hardly be doubted that the cathode rays were negatively charged particles, and the objections to this view, on the score of their penetrating ability for solids, were finally set at rest by J. J. Thomson in 1897-1898. In a series of experiments, which for ingenuity and insight have rarely been equalled, Professor Thomson, by deflecting the cathode rays in magnetic and electric fields of known strength, was able to infer the size of the charged particles ; and later, to deduce their mass, velocity and electric charge. (See p. 14.) He showed that the cathode rays were neither atoms nor molecules, but something far smaller : the mass of each of the particles proved to be about $\frac{1}{1800}$th part of the smallest mass hitherto recognised by chemists—that of the atom of hydrogen. Their nature depends neither on the nature of the cathode nor on that of the residual gas in the discharge tube. The charge is invariable, and agrees with that carried by the hydrogen ion in liquid electrolysis : the velocity depends upon the electric force which is applied to the tube ; the speeds are found to be an appreciable fraction of the speed of light,[1] in some cases as much as one-third.

Thus the cathode rays proved to be neither ethereal waves nor ordinary material particles, but bodies of sub-atomic size moving with prodigious velocities, a state of things so nearly realising Newton's long-abandoned conception in his corpuscular theory of light that J. J. Thomson called the small particles which constitute the cathode rays, corpuscles. Johnstone Stoney had previously suggested the name electron for the electrolytic unit, or atom of electricity, and the suitability of the expression for the cathode rays was at once recognised : both terms have since come into common use.

It is perhaps difficult to realise the disproportion[2] between the size of an atom and the size of an electron : the two have been aptly compared to a fly in a cathedral, or a speck of dust in a room !

Wehnelt Cathode.

If the cathode is constructed of a strip of platinum which can be raised to a bright red heat,[3] and on which is mounted

---

[1] The velocity of light is 186,300 miles or 3×10^{10} cms. per sec.

[2] 1 : 100,000 in linear dimensions ; 1 : 10^{15} by volume.

[3] By means of an independent current.

a speck of lime [1] (see Fig. 6), all the ordinary phenomena of a discharge tube can be reproduced by means of quite small potentials—100 volts or less between the cathode and anode. The hot lime emits torrents of corpuscles and the pencil of cathode rays, owing to their low speed (see p. 12), produces vivid luminosity in the rarefied gas. The velocity of the rays is proportional to the square root of the potential applied : the velocities are of the order of $\frac{1}{10}$th of those in

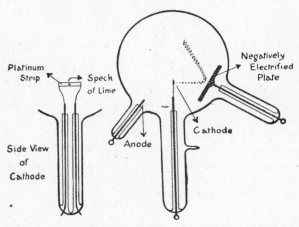

FIG. 6.—A discharge tube with a Wehnelt cathode, displaying the repulsion of the cathode rays by a negatively charged plate.

an ordinary discharge tube ; *e.g.* with 50 volts, the velocity $= 4\cdot2 \times 10^8$ cms. per sec. The magnetic and electrostatic deflection of these rays can be strikingly demonstrated owing to their relatively small velocity.

It is possible with the hot-lime cathodes to send very large currents through the discharge tube—currents of $\frac{1}{10}$ ampere and more are readily attained. With high cathode temperatures and voltages of 200 or 300 on the tube it requires precautions to prevent the discharge growing into an arc [2] with the consequent destruction of the cathode.

[1] Or any of the alkaline earths (a speck of sealing-wax, ignited *in situ*, is very convenient). See Wehnelt (*P.M.* July 1905).

[2] A water resistance in the potential circuit serves to prevent this.

Transmission and Absorption of Cathode Rays.

Lenard (*Wied. Ann.* 1895) showed that for fast-moving cathode rays, the extent of the absorption in different substances is roughly proportional to the density. The penetrating power of a cathode ray varies very greatly with its speed. The highest speed rays, which move at the rate of about 10^{10} cms. per sec., can only penetrate 2 or 3 mms. of air at ordinary temperature and pressure. The fastest β rays from radium are cathode rays which have no more than about three times this speed, and yet their range in air is nearly 100 times as great. The range is, of course, increased by lowering the pressure of the gas, as the molecules are not so closely packed, and the cathode rays suffer fewer encounters with the atoms.

During its journey, the cathode ray loses velocity both by ionising and by deflection. So long as its speed remains high, it pursues a fairly even course ; as it slows down, it becomes more and more liable to deflection by the encountered atoms, until finally it loses so much energy that it becomes undistinguishable as a cathode ray. Thus a fine pencil of cathode rays gradually becomes fuzzy and scattered.

Some of the cathode rays are actually swung completely round by the surface atoms, and so may be " reflected " with velocities up to the original velocity. The more obliquely incident the rays, the greater the number " reflected." In regard to the transmitted rays, Whiddington (*P.R.S.* 1912) has recently shown experimentally the truth of a relation deduced theoretically by Sir J. J. Thomson some years ago. He finds that the maximum velocity (V_d) with which a cathode ray may leave a material of thickness d is given by

$$V_0{}^4 - V_d{}^4 = ad,$$

where V_0 is the initial velocity of the cathode ray and a is a constant (2×10^{40} for air ; 732×10^{40} for Al ; 2540×10^{40} for gold ; all in cm.-sec. units). This fourth-power scattering law holds also for Ra β rays, except the very fastest. Whiddington was unable to trace any simple connection between the value of a and the atomic weight or density of the material.

Cathode rays lose their speed very quickly in passing through solids, and thin metal leaf has to be used in experimental work.[1] The maximum thickness of aluminium or glass which transmits high-speed cathode rays to any appreciable extent is about 0·0015 cm. (Cf. p. 49.)

Heating Effects produced by Cathode Rays.

The bulk of the energy of the cathode rays is dissipated as heat when the rays strike an obstacle. A simple calculation shows that if in a tube of moderate vacuum the current carried by the cathode rays is a milliampere (10^{-3} amp.), the energy given up by the rays per minute is of the order of 100 calories.[2] Now a milliampere is only a moderate current ; as will be seen later, currents up to 50 or 60 milliamperes and even more (with momentary discharges) obtain in practice. No target can withstand such currents for any length of time if the rays are concentrated by using a concave cathode. Platinum may be fused, diamonds converted into coke ; even tantalum and tungsten [3] with melting points in the neighbourhood of 3000° C. can be rendered molten. Owing also to the low pressure, most metals can be vaporised with ease.

The heating effects reach a maximum at a certain pressure, which is not very low, and are not so marked in very high vacua.

Ionisation produced by Cathode Rays.

A cathode ray has the property of ionising a gas, *i.e.* of rendering it electrically conducting. The ionising power is

[1] Al, Cu, Ag, Sn, Pt, and Au can be got in the form of thin leaf. (See Kaye and Laby's *Physical Constants*.)

[2] The energy $E = \frac{1}{2}i \cdot \frac{m}{e} \cdot v^2$, where i is the current, v is the velocity of the rays, m is the mass of and e the charge on each ray. If E is expressed in calories per min., i in milliamperes, and v in cms. per sec., then $E = 4 \cdot 10^{-18} i v^2$. This assumes that all the cathode ray energy is turned into heat.

[3] Von Wartenberg (1907) determined the melting point of tungsten by means of a cathode-ray vacuum furnace. He used a concave Wehnelt cathode (p. 8) for the purpose. See also Tiede (1913) for an account of a cathode-ray furnace with a water-cooled cathode.

especially conspicuous with the slower rays—the ionisation per centimetre of path was in fact found by Glasson (*P.M.* 1911) to vary approximately as 1/(velocity)². The faster rays have the greater energy, it is true, but they do not begin to ionise to any great extent until their velocity has dropped.[1] A cathode ray (like the a ray) ionises most towards the end of its path, until finally it loses so much energy that it can no longer ionise, and ceases to be distinguishable as a cathode ray.

The strong ionisation is responsible for the luminosity which cathode rays produce in the residual gas of a discharge tube—a luminosity which at higher pressures is displayed as the outer negative glow bounding the cathode dark-space (see p. 2), and at lower pressures lights up the path of the rays themselves (see p. 34). The luminosity of the track reaches a maximum at a certain pressure ; as the pressure is further reduced, the rays gradually become faster and less luminous, but simultaneously their power of exciting fluorescence in the glass walls of the tube increases, until finally the rays become quite invisible and are manifested solely by the fluorescence on the glass.

Fluorescence produced by Cathode Rays.

An ordinary X-ray tube affords abundant evidence of the fluorescing properties of glass subjected to cathode rays. Crookes found in 1879 that glass which had suffered prolonged bombardment by the rays fatigued and lost a good deal of its fluorescing ability. Most of the fatigue is only temporary, but a portion is very permanent. Crookes found, for instance, that complete recovery was not brought about even by fusion of the glass ; and Campbell-Swinton (*P.R.S.* 1908) refers to a tube in which the fatigue persisted for more than ten years. Swinton showed that the fatigue is purely a surface effect, and is removed by grinding away the surface of the glass. He found that the thickness which had to be removed for this purpose was always about ·015 mm.

---

[1] The *total* ionisation of the faster ray is, of course, greater than that of the slower.

There are many substances which afford striking and beautiful examples of the fluorescing ability of cathode rays. Among those which are useful in practice are barium platino-cyanide (a material of which fluorescent screens are usually made), the mineral willemite (a silicate of zinc), zinc blende (sulphide of zinc), calcium and cadmium tungstates, and kunzite (a lithium felspar).

The fluorescing power of a cathode ray increases with its velocity, and does not seem to be possessed by the very slowest rays. Rays as slow as those from a Wehnelt cathode are, however, capable of causing fluorescence.

Magnetic Deflection of Cathode Rays.

When a charged particle (mass m, charge e) is projected along a line of magnetic force, it continues to move along it ; but if it is projected (with velocity v) at an angle θ to the magnetic field (of strength H), the deflecting force acting upon it is $Hev \sin \theta$. Hence, if ρ is the radius of curvature of the resulting path,

$$Hev \sin \theta = mv^2/\rho$$

or

$$\rho = \frac{mv}{He \sin \theta},$$

which represents a helix. So that, in general, the effect of a magnetic field on the path of a moving corpuscle is to twist it into a helix wound on a cylinder with the lines of force as axis. With the slow cathode rays given out by a Wehnelt cathode (p. 8), the helix can be beautifully demonstrated : with strong fields, the helix becomes so long and attenuated that the rays appear to follow the lines of force.

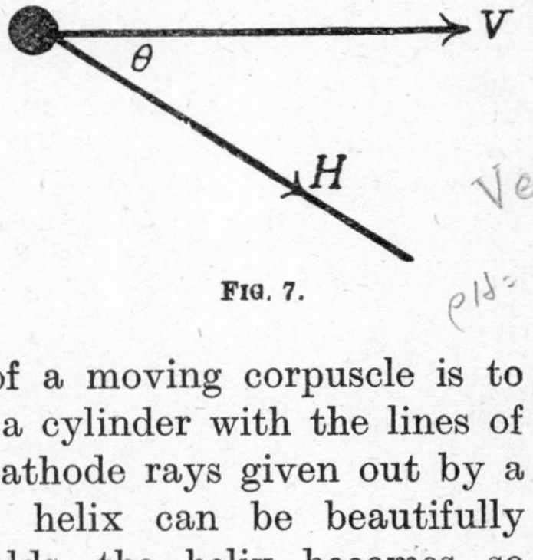

Fig. 7.

In the particular case when the cathode ray is projected at right angles to the magnetic lines of force, $\sin \theta = 1$, and

$$\rho = mv/He.$$

Thus in a uniform magnetic field, the path of the particle is a circle in a plane at right angles to the magnetic force, *i.e.* the particle is bent away in a direction at right angles

both to the field and to its former direction.[1] The extent
to which cathode rays are bent by a magnetic field thus
depends on the strength of the field, on the speed of the
particles, and on the quantity denoted by e/m. As to the
speed, that is related directly to the potential which is
applied to the tube ; the velocity is, indeed, roughly proportional to the square root of the potential or alternative
spark-length.

Electric Deflection of Cathode Rays.

If an electric field X is acting at right angles to the direction
of projection of the cathode ray, the force on it is Xe in the
direction of the field. Thus, as above, the radius of curvature is

$$\rho = \frac{mv^2}{Xe}.$$

The corresponding expression for the magnetic deflection
was

$$\rho = \frac{mv}{He}.$$

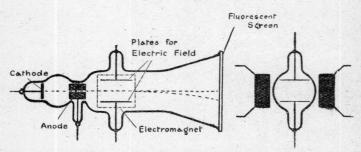

FIG. 8.—J. J. Thomson's apparatus for measuring e/m of cathode rays. An
electric and a magnetic field are contrived so that their effects on a beam of
cathode rays balance each other exactly, in which case the fluorescent spot
produced by the cathode rays remains undeviated.

If we contrive things so that the magnetic and electric
deflections are equal and opposite, we can, at once, from
a knowledge of the fields, derive both the velocity and e/m

---

[1] The following mnemonical rule is convenient for remembering in which
direction a cathode ray is deflected : If the magnetic field H (*i.e.* the
direction in which a N-seeking pole would move) is upwards towards
the Head, and the cathode Ray is moving horizontally towards the Right
hand, the mechanical Force on the ray is horizontally towards the Front.

for the cathode ray ; for $v = X/H$, and $e/m = X/(\rho H^2)$. It was in this way that J. J. Thomson first arrived at the nature of the cathode rays (p. 8).   (See Fig. 8.)

Cathode-Ray Oscillographs.

Cathode-ray oscillographs, which depend on the bending of cathode rays under magnetic or electric force, have come into use in electrical engineering for the purpose of studying the wave-form of rapidly changing alternating currents.   In the Braun tube, a narrow pencil of cathode rays is received on a fluorescent screen, and is subjected *en route* to both a magnetic and an electric field.   The two fields are at right angles, and are both actuated by the alternating current. The cathode rays, having practically no inertia, are able to follow the most rapid vagaries of the fields, and so trace out on the screen a pattern, from which the wave-form can be deduced.

Magnetic Spectrum of Cathode Rays.

Each interruption of the primary current in an induction coil produces a small train of strongly-damped oscillations in the discharge (p. 62).   Thus the potential on the tube is intermittent, and the result is a stream of cathode rays with a variety of speeds, each peaklet on the oscillatory potential curve producing a group of uniformly fast cathode rays, of which the speed diminishes with successive oscillations.

Accordingly, if the cathode rays are subjected to a magnetic field, the different groups are differently deviated—the greater the speed, the less the magnetic deviation.   Thus a slit of cathode rays, when allowed to fall on a fluorescent plate, produces in a magnetic field a number of bright lines or bands which go to make up a " magnetic spectrum "— an appearance first noticed by Birkeland (*C.R.*) in 1896. The brightness of each band is a measure of the number of rays moving with the same speed : the displacement of the band from the undeflected position is inversely proportional to the velocity, and directly proportional to e/m and the strength of the field.

If the gas pressure in the discharge tube is not very low, the bands may be numerous (30 or more), but if the pressure is lowered, the oscillations are more strongly damped, and so the lines become fewer, group themselves more closely, are less deviated as a whole (the cathode rays being faster), while the least deviated line becomes the brightest ; thus

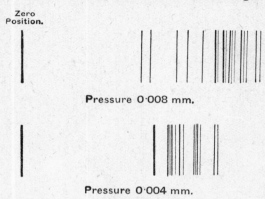

FIG. 9.—Examples of magnetic spectra of cathode rays.

most of the cathode rays now possess the maximum velocity. Fig. 9 shows two magnetic spectra obtained by Birkeland at different pressures.

Beatty (*P.R.S.* 1913) found that with a potential of about 60,000 volts on the tube, the main stream of cathode rays had a velocity corresponding to about two-thirds of the potential as given by a spark-gap.

A spectrum of rays can also be produced by an electric field, in which case the deviations are inversely proportional to the square of the velocity.

A tube driven by a Wimshurst machine or a battery of cells does not yield a magnetic spectrum, but only a single bright line, which is evidence of the fact that all the cathode particles have the same velocity.

Constants of Cathode Rays.

Measurements of the speed of cathode rays have been made by various experimenters ; the rays in an ordinary discharge tube have velocities ranging from about 10^9 to rather more than 10^{10} cms. per sec., *i.e.* from one-thirtieth to one-third of the speed of light.

The latest determinations of e/m (see p. 14) for the slowest rays give a value of $1 \cdot 77 \times 10^7$ expressed in electro-magnetic units. Measurements of the ionic charge make $e = 1 \cdot 59 \times 10^{-20}$ E.M.U., so that, for small velocities, m is $9 \cdot 0 \times 10^{-28}$ gramme. Theory indicates that electrons owe all their mass to their velocity, and that for cathode rays moving, for example, with one-third the speed of light m would have a value about 6% greater than the above.

Now, according to the best authorities, the mass of the hydrogen atom is $1 \cdot 66 \times 10^{-24}$ gramme, so that the number of electrons equal in mass to the hydrogen atom is about 1850.

Further constants will be found on p. **xv**.

The Ubiquity of Electrons.

Since their discovery in so artificial a source as a vacuum tube, electrons have been found literally to pervade the universe. Relatively low-speed electrons are emitted in many chemical reactions and by metals when exposed to light, especially ultra-violet. High-speed electrons with velocities almost up to that of light constitute the β rays of radium and the radioactive substances : the alkaline metals (at any rate K and probably Rb) also emit corpuscles. They are ejected in abundance from hot bodies, markedly so from the alkaline earths (lime, baryta, etc.) with velocities and in amounts depending on the temperature. Without doubt they play a part in cosmical physics : the most recent explanations of the aurora or northern lights regard them as due to enormously fast electrons ejected by the sun, which are collected and guided in long spirals (see p. 13) to the polar latitudes by the earth's magnetic lines of force.[1] They there ionise and cause luminosity in the

[1] Aurora occur most abundantly not at the poles, but at about latitude 68°. This requires for the electrons a velocity closely approaching that of light—a velocity even greater than that possessed by the fastest known β particles from radium.

upper attenuated regions of the earth's atmosphere, just as they do in a vacuum tube.

But whatever their origin, electrons have always been found to maintain their invariable and indivisible character : they carry the unit of electricity, and can indeed be regarded as the ult'mate fundamental carrier of negative electrification.

The Electron Theory of Matter.

Rutherford's theory of the constitution of matter, which is a development of that of J. J. Thomson, regards an atom as built up of a minute nucleus positively charged [1] (about 10^{-12} cm. in diameter) surrounded by a cluster of negatively charged electrons which are grouped in rings. The total negative charge of the electrons is equal to the positive charge of the nucleus. Present theory indicates that the number of electrons in an atom is equal to the atomic number N of the element, *i.e.* the number of the element in the periodic table (see p. 242). It would appear that the atom owes most of its mass to its positive nucleus, which is capable of deflecting both a and β particles out of their paths.

The nucleus of the atom is regarded as built up of hydrogen nuclei cemented together by electrons, the former being in excess to just such an extent that the nucleus as a whole contains N positive charges. The various elements differ only one from another in that they have different nuclear charges, the nucleus determining the mass and radioactive properties, while the number and grouping of the electrons in the rings control the chemical and spectroscopic properties.

In other words, all atoms, of whatever kind, are regarded as built up solely of two kinds of " bricks "—(a) negatively charged electrons, and (b) hydrogen nuclei, each 1800 times as heavy as an electron, and carrying a charge equal to that on the electron, but positive in sign.

[1] Rutherford (*P.M.* 1911). See also Bohr (*P.M.* July, Sept. and Nov. 1913, Sept. 1915), and J. J. Thomson, *Engineering*, March 21, 1913.

In the case of solids, there are supposed to exist un-attached and wandering electrons interspersed between the molecules. These can be ejected by ultra-violet light or heat : they are the important agents in thermo-electricity, and in the conduction of electricity and heat ; a good conductor, for example, is one which contains many of these free electrons. The electron theory has, among other things, led to important deductions concerning the specific heats of metals at low temperatures—a subject to which Nernst and others have lately given attention.

For an account of the electron theory see Lorentz, *Theory of Electrons*; Richardson, *The Electron Theory*; and N. R. Campbell, *Modern Electrical Theory*.

POSITIVE RAYS.

Though the ordinary cathode rays are the most conspicuous of the rays existing in a discharge tube, there are others also present. As long ago as 1886, Goldstein, by perforating the cathode of a discharge tube, observed that a stream of rays travelled through the tube in the reverse direction to the cathode rays. To these rays he gave the general name of Canal-rays (*Kanalstrahlen*). Wien showed that the Canal rays were deflected in the opposite direction to cathode rays when subjected to a magnetic force, and he came to the conclusion that they must consist of positively charged particles. The deflection detected in this case, however, was small compared with that obtained with cathode rays,[1] but the deflection in the electric field was of the same order of magnitude for both positive and negative particles. This pointed to the fact that the positive particle had greater mass than the cathode or negative particle ; Wien, in fact, found that the mass of the positive particle was of the same order of magnitude as that of a hydrogen molecule.

The existence of the two kinds of rays in a discharge tube can very easily be shown by the different colours they produce in lithium chloride. This substance fluoresces blue

---

[1] Positive rays require, roughly speaking, magnetic fields of 1000 gauss or more, *i.e.* at least forty times as strong as are needed to deflect cathode rays.

under the action of cathode rays, and red under the action of positive rays, so that a small glass bead coated with lithium chloride and placed in a suitable position between the electrodes in the tube will appear red on the side towards the anode, and blue on the side facing the cathode. This bead can be utilised to explore the region between the electrodes in order to determine in what part of the tube the positive rays have their origin. Starting with the bead at the anode, we should find that it does not appear red on the side facing the anode until we arrive at the boundary between the negative glow and the Crookes dark-space (p. 2); it continues to fluoresce red throughout the Crookes dark-space. The amount of fluorescence in various parts of the dark-space, however, shows that most of the rays start from the boundary of the dark-space.

The positive rays have strong ionising, fluorescing, and photographic actions. They cause soda glass to fluoresce a dull green; willemite, a bright green : in both cases, the effects are much inferior to those produced by cathode rays. The positive rays show strong pulverising properties, and roughen or disintegrate any surface against which they strike.

During the last few years the whole question of the electric discharge from the point of view of positive electricity has been taken up by Sir J. J. Thomson. He has shown that there exist in the tube high-speed atoms and molecules of the gases present, some positively charged, some negatively, and some uncharged. In no case has a positive ray been detected whose mass is smaller than that of the hydrogen atom ; a positive electron, if such exists, has hitherto eluded search. The velocities of these positive particles are in the neighbourhood of 10^8 cms. per second (the fastest have a speed of about 2×10^8 cms. per second) ; this is of the order of 1000 times the ordinary velocity of molecules as calculated from the kinetic theory of gases (p. 77).

It is found that there are many more of these high-speed charged particles (or ions) moving towards the cathode than from it.[1] If a hole is made in the cathode, the positive

[1] These latter " retrograde rays " travel with and among the cathode rays, but can be detected when the cathode rays are removed by a magnet.

rays stream through it and form the Canal rays of Goldstein ; and in this region, where they are separated from the cathode rays, they can be independently investigated.

Professor Thomson received a very fine pencil of these rays on a photographic plate, and *en route* subjected them simultaneously to the action of magnetic and electric fields, the magnetic field deflecting the rays at right angles to

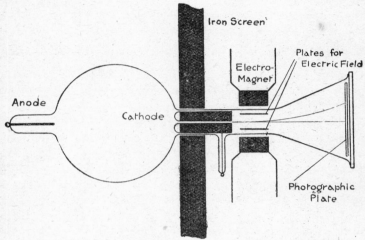

FIG. 10.—J. J. Thomson's apparatus for measuring *e/m* of positive rays (*Kanalstrahlen*).

the deflection caused by the electric field (see Fig. 10).[1] It is found that only a small portion of the beam is deflected, —the main part goes on unaffected by the deflecting forces.

If x and y are the deflections of a particle due to the action of the electric and magnetic fields respectively, and e, m, and v the charge, mass, and velocity of the particle, then we have

$$x = A \cdot \frac{e}{mv^2},$$

$$y = B \cdot \frac{e}{mv},$$

where A and B are constants depending upon the strengths

[1] In the corresponding cathode-ray experiment (p. 14) the magnetic force and electric force were parallel.

of the electric and magnetic forces, and the distances the rays have to travel from the time they enter the field of force until they reach the photographic plate.

The equation to the trace on the photographic plate becomes

$$\frac{y^2}{x} = \frac{B^2}{A} \cdot \frac{e}{m}.$$

This is the equation of a parabola, so that we have on the plate a series of parabolas representing the loci of particles

which have a constant value of e/m.[1] (See Fig. 11.) Different particles register different loci on the plate, and for each locus m has a definite value, so that the method affords a means of determining accurately the atomic weights of substances which are present in the tube. The system of curves obtained on the screen depends, of course, upon the nature of the gas in the tube. Most positive rays carry only one ionic charge (equal to that carried by the cathode rays), though with some elements multiply-charged rays have been found. (See J. J. Thomson, *Positive Rays* (Longmans).)

FIG. 11.—Photograph obtained by J. J. Thomson of parabolic loci of positive particles subjected to magnetic and electric fields at right angles to each other. The different traces represent different substances. In the figure, the magnetic deflections are vertical. The magnetic field was reversed half-way through the exposure, so that both halves of each parabola are recorded.

More recently, Aston (*P.M.* 1920) has modified Sir J. J. Thomson's method, and so obtained "mass-spectra," which throw striking light on the question of the isotopes (p. 244) of a considerable number of elements. He has shown that while some elements (*e.g.* H, He, C, N, O, F, P, S, As) are "simple" and consist of only one isotope, others consist of mixtures of isotopes whose several atomic weights closely approximate to whole numbers. This explains why the

[1] e/m for the hydrogen molecule carrying a single charge is 10^4 electromagnetic units.

atomic weight of an element, as determined by the chemist, is not a whole number in most instances.[1]

The positive rays are important from the point of view of the X-ray worker, in that by their bombardment of the cathode, they liberate the cathode rays. Furthermore, the positive rays are responsible for the positive electrification which the inner surface of the walls of a " gas " X-ray bulb always assumes (p. 32), and which serves to heighten the fluorescence of the glass by attracting the secondary cathode rays from the anticathode. Further, many of the positive rays strike and disintegrate the glass walls round the cathode.

The positive rays doubtless also play a prominent part in the action of valve-tubes (p. 70).

The " Ionics " of a " Gas " X-ray Tube.

Before leaving the subject of positive and cathode rays it is convenient to anticipate matters slightly and set forth simply the "ionics" of an ordinary X-ray bulb. The evacuation of a " gas " X-ray tube is deliberately never completed, but an appreciable amount of gas is always left, the pressure ranging from say 0·001 to 0·010 mm. of mercury. The number of ions (see p. 92) present in this residual gas is normally very small. But when a high potential is applied to the terminals of the tube, the effect is to accelerate the motion of these ions and cause them to produce many more ions by collision with the gas molecules. The electric field also serves to direct the positive ions towards the cathode which they bombard and cause to emit cathode rays. The electric field further impels these cathode rays towards the anticathode upon colliding with which their velocity is suddenly changed and X rays are generated.

[1] See Aston, *Isotopes* (Arnold).

CHAPTER III.

X RAYS.

The Discovery of X Rays.[1]

We have dealt above in some detail with many of the features which cathode rays possess ; we have, however, made no more than mention of their most striking property of all—that of generating X rays. In the autumn of 1895 Professor Wilhelm Konrad Röntgen of Würzburg, Bavaria, discovered, it may be said almost accidentally, the rays which now bear his name. During the course of a search for invisible light rays, he turned on a low-pressure discharge tube, which for the purpose was completely enclosed in stout black paper, and to his surprise noticed that a fluorescent screen lying on a table some 3 metres or so distant shone out brightly. The light-tight cover precluded any possibility of the effect being due to ordinary ultra-violet light ; there was evidently some curious radiation coming from the tube. If obstacles were interposed, Röntgen found that they cast shadows on the screen ; and in this way he traced back the unknown or " X " rays to their source, which proved to be the region of impact of the cathode rays on the glass walls of the tube.

Further investigation revealed the fundamental fact that Röntgen or X rays are produced whenever and wherever cathode rays encounter matter. It was imagined by many that X rays were present in the original cathode ray beam, and were obtained by mere subtraction. But this was disproved by the discovery that when the cathode rays were magnetically deflected, the source of the X rays also moved. The experiment also put out of court the notion that X rays were due to the impact of particles of metal from the cathode.

[1] See also p. 273.

But the fascinating feature of the new rays was their extraordinary ability to penetrate many substances quite opaque to light. The degree of penetration was found to depend on the density ; for example, bone is more absorbent than flesh, and if the hand is placed in the path of the rays, the bones stand out dark against the flesh in the shadow cast on a fluorescent screen. Röntgen at once appreciated the immense significance of his discovery to the surgical profession, and communicated his results to the Physico-Medical Society of Würzburg in November 1895.[1]

It was soon ascertained that X rays affected a photographic plate,[2] could not apparently be refracted or reflected (see p. 168), and, unlike cathode rays, were not bent by a magnetic or electric field,[3] a result which shows that the X rays do not carry a free electric charge. In 1896, J. J. Thomson, Hurmuzescu, Benoist, Dufour, and others found that Röntgen rays shared with cathode rays (and ultra-violet light) the property of ionising or imparting temporary electrical conductivity to a gas, which ordinarily is a nearly perfect insulator.

Before considering in any detail the advances that have been made in the various branches of the subject, it will probably be useful first to recount briefly the essential particulars of the working of a simple X-ray equipment.

A Brief Account of the Production of X Rays.

A "Gas" X-ray Bulb.

When a current of electricity from a Ruhmkorff induction coil is sent through an X-ray tube, a pencil of cathode rays from the concave cathode is focussed on the target or anti-

---

[1] See also L'Éclair Élect. 6. 241. 1896. For an account of Röntgen's later work, see Berl. Ber. 1897, and Ann. Phy. Chem. 1898. Röntgen's three memoirs are translated in the Electrician (Jan. 24, 1896 and April 24, 1897) and A.Rt.R. (Feb. 1899).

[2] The inexplicable fogging of unopened packets of photographic plates in the neighbourhood of a Crookes tube was engaging the attention of more than one English physicist at the time of the discovery of the X rays.

[3] Walter (A.d.P. 1904) used magnetic fields up to 19,000 gauss. Paschen (P.Z. 1904) similarly exposed Ra γ rays to fields of 30,000 gauss.

cathode, the surface of which is inclined at 45° to the rays, and is usually made of a metal of high atomic weight, such as tungsten or platinum (Fig. 12). An anode is usually provided, but is not indispensable. The anode and cathode are generally of aluminium. From the point of impact of the cathode rays on the anticathode, X rays are given out in all directions. The anticathode tends with continued use to become very hot, and is often either made massive

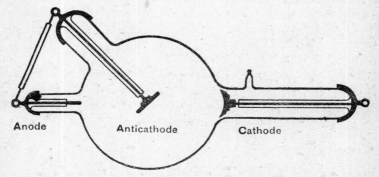

Anode   Anticathode   Cathode

FIG. 12.—A simple type of focus bulb showing the various electrodes.

or cooled in some fashion. The pressure of the gas in a "gas" X-ray tube becomes lower with use, and a device for "softening" the tube (*i.e.* raising the pressure) is therefore usually provided.

The higher the pressure, the less the potential required to drive the tube and the less penetrating the X rays ; both the X rays and the tube are often termed "soft" if the pressure is high. The lower the pressure, the "harder" are the rays. In the X rays from any particular tube there are many qualities present ; this is shown by the fact that rays which have traversed one thickness of material are more penetrating to a second.

X rays are invisible and do not make glass fluoresce ; the pale green hemisphere of fluorescence on the bulb is due to "reflected" cathode rays from the anticathode striking the glass walls. That this is so is shown by the distorting action of a magnet on the boundary of the fluorescence.

An Induction Coil.

An induction coil is merely a device for transforming a low-potential current, such as is yielded by a battery of a few cells, into a high-potential current of the kind suitable for driving an X-ray bulb.   An induction coil consists essentially of a cylindrical iron core round which is wound a coil of stout insulated wire ; this coil, which is known as the primary, consists of relatively few turns.   Outside this is the secondary coil consisting of many thousands of turns of finer wire carefully insulated.   Fig. 13 shows diagram-

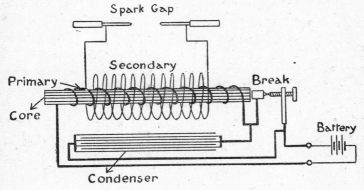

FIG. 13.—Diagrammatic representation of an induction coil.

matically the various parts of a small coil.   A hammer-break interrupter is shown in the primary circuit, and a condenser, usually mounted in the base of the coil, offers an alternative path to the break.   The primary circuit is joined to a suitable battery ; and the object of the interrupter is to make and break the current in rapid succession.   The consequence of this is at every " make " to induce in the secondary coil a momentary current, and at every " break " an equal momentary current in the opposite direction.

But in X-ray work it is important that the current through the X-ray tube should be all in one direction, and herein lies the chief function of the condenser.   When the circuit is made, the condenser takes and stores the first rush of current, which therefore grows relatively slowly and magnetises the core ; at break, however, the condenser discharges its electricity through the primary circuit with great rapidity and demagnetises the core. The induced potentials in the secondary are accordingly much feebler at make than at break ; the currents resulting from the former are known as " reverse " or " inverse " currents, and in a good coil are nearly suppressed. Thus the sparks which pass between the terminals of the secondary circuit are due chiefly to the break and only pass one way. The power of a coil is often designated by the length of its longest spark, *e.g.* a 6-inch coil.

The iron core serves to increase the number of lines of force through the coils. The condenser is made of alternate layers of tinfoil and paraffined paper. The hammer-break consists essentially of a steel strip on which is mounted a piece of soft iron ; this is attracted by the core when the current passes, and so breaks circuit between two platinum studs in the primary circuit. The spring is thus caused to vibrate backwards and forwards like the hammer of an electric bell, and so alternately makes and breaks the primary current.[1]

An extended account of the induction coil is given on p. 53 *et seq.*

[1] In a modern X-ray coil the hammer-break is rarely fitted, but terminals are provided for connecting up to an independent mercury or other type of break.

CHAPTER IV.

AN X-RAY BULB.

Early X-ray Tubes.

The vacuum tube with which Röntgen made his famous discovery in 1895 was pear-shaped, with a flat disc for cathode mounted in the body of the bulb at its narrow

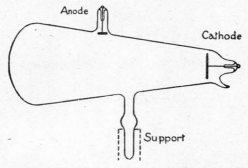

FIG. 14.—Type of tube with which Röntgen discovered X rays. The cathode rays impinged on the broad end of the tube.

end ; the anode was in a small side tube (Fig. 14).[1] The cathode rays impinged on the large end of the bulb, producing vivid fluorescence. This pattern of tube was widely copied, but it was soon found that it did not survive many of the prolonged exposures which were necessary to secure radiographs of any value. Moreover, owing to the large area of emission of the rays, the photographs were always blurred and somewhat indistinct. Experimenters set about

[1] In another early form of X-ray bulb used by Röntgen, the anode consisted of a large ring in the body of the bulb.

to find ways and means of prolonging the life of the tube, of shortening the exposure, and of improving the definition. Under the impression, then prevailing, that active fluorescence was essential for the genesis of the X rays,[1] various workers, about 1897, constructed tubes of fluorescent glass (*e.g.* uranium and didymium glasses) with the idea of enhancing the output of the tube; it was, however, found later that the fluorescence was quite immaterial.

Campbell-Swinton in 1896 modified Röntgen's design of tube by inserting a sheet of platinum obliquely in the path of the cathode rays. The improvement was considerable, though the radiographs were still lacking in sharpness, and the exposures unduly protracted.

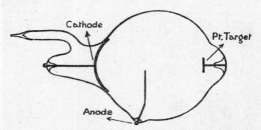

FIG. 15.—Tube used by Crookes to display the heating effects of focussed cathode rays.

The same year Professor H. Jackson of King's College, London, turned to account a former discovery of Sir Wm. Crookes, and replaced the flat cathode by a concave one. Crookes had shown in 1874 that a hollowed-out cathode brought the cathode rays to a focus, and five years later actually constructed a tube with a plate of platinum at the focus to display the heating effects of the rays (Fig. 15). The tube must have given out X rays in abundance, but they remained unnoticed. Professor Jackson mounted the platinum target at 45° to the rays (Fig. 16); in essential respects his tube agreed with that of Crookes. The new

---

[1] It may be recalled that the late Henri Becquerel, at the suggestion of M. Poincaré, was led to investigate whether X rays were an invariable accompaniment of phosphorescence in general. Among the substances he tried were uranium salts: the result was the discovery of radioactivity in 1896, two months after the discovery of X rays.

focus tube was a vast improvement on its predecessors ;
the exposures were shortened enormously, and, owing to
the small area of emission, the resulting photographs showed
wonderful sharpness and detail.

It is remarkable how slight the subsequent changes have
been ; many thousands of X-ray tubes have been made,
but in the case of most " gas " tubes the design agrees
essentially with that of fifteen years ago. It may be said
that the X-ray bulb has scarcely kept pace with the very
extensive improvements that have been made in the rest
of the X-ray equipment. There is no gainsaying the fact

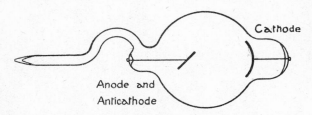

FIG. 16.—Jackson's first focus tube, employing focussed cathode rays.

that even now gas tubes are prone to be fickle, and it is
scarcely possible to guarantee their behaviour. A bulb will
be perfectly satisfactory one day, and yet refuse to work
reliably the next ; [1] and of two bulbs apparently precisely
similar, one may work well for months, the other may break
down within a few days. Many X-ray workers take the
precaution of resting a favourite bulb occasionally ; a bulb
is often improved by being allowed to lie idle for a few weeks.

In general, a large bulb is better than a small for passing
a heavy current (see p. 72). Some makers have accordingly
constructed monster bulbs, which have, however, little to
commend them. Indeed, if certain difficulties could be sur-
mounted, quite small bulbs would possess many advantages.

In all the earliest tubes, the cathode was mounted in the
body of the bulb, but by the end of 1896 it was withdrawn
just within the neck of a side tube—a design typical of all
later makes, and one which conduces to greater steadiness

[1] Due probably to variations in the gas-pressure.

and hardness [1] (see p. 73).   In Jackson's bulb and its predecessors the target served also as anode; we find an
auxiliary anode introduced in a tube by Gundelach in
1896.

Present-day X-ray bulbs are of two main types: (1)
"gas tubes," in which the residual gas plays a fundamental
part; (2) "hot-cathode tubes," in which the electrons are
generated by a heated cathode (p. 43), and in which the
pressure of the gas is so low that it plays no active part.

The Electrodes of an X-ray Bulb.

The electrodes are fixed to stout wires or rods which, for
ease of manufacture and repair, are invariably mounted in
side tubes projecting from the main bulb.   It was found
as early as 1896, that the discharge is materially steadied
by sheathing the supporting wires with glass tubes.   This
also serves to check the " sputtering " which is pronounced
with wires and points.   In the case of a gas tube the glass
walls become highly charged, negatively in the region of the
cathode (p. 74) and positively in the main body of the tube
(p. 23): these charges, particularly with a blackened tube,
may cause the focal-point to wander and lead to sparking
along the glass.   In the case of a hot-cathode tube, the
walls become negatively charged.

The discharge often tends to pass along the glass walls
both outside and inside the tube.   Alippi found in 1906
that if a large jet of steam were allowed to play on the
bulb, the X-ray output and general fluorescence greatly
increased.   The effect is probably due to the removal of
dust and the surface alkali in the glass with a consequent
diminution of conductivity.   Local surface electrification
is probably responsible for the green wisp-like discharges
which can often be seen on the inner surface of a bulb.
This is quite distinct from the flickering due to insufficient
voltage on the tube.

---

[1] J. J. Thomson (*P.M.* 1912) finds that this position of the cathode is
also the most favourable for the production of the positive "canal" rays.

The part that electrostatic effects and surface electrification play and the control they possess over the hardness and steadiness of a discharge are not generally appreciated by X-ray workers.

THE ANODE.

As remarked above, a "gas" bulb is almost always provided with an additional anode of aluminium which is joined externally to the anticathode (Fig. 12). The precise benefit of the anode is a little doubtful, though in some cases the result of disconnecting it from the anticathode is to soften the tube. C. E. S. Phillips (*A.Rt.R.* 1902) concluded that the auxiliary anode was helpful, probably by electrostatic action, in steadying the discharge. He remarks that the most advantageous position for the anode is behind the anticathode. The auxiliary anode is also probably beneficial during the passage of the inverse current which exists with all coil discharges : in these circumstances, the aluminium anode, rather than the platinum anticathode, tends to act as a temporary cathode, and as aluminium exhibits much less cathodic sputtering (p. 82) than platinum, the walls of the tube are not blackened to the same extent.

It is usually stated that the discharge is independent of the position of the anode. This is only true if the anode is outside the cathode dark-space : if the anode is within the dark-space, the discharge passes with greater difficulty. Now, in an X-ray tube, working under ordinary conditions, the cathode dark-space is big enough to enclose the anticathode within its boundaries, and the presence of the anode, which is invariably inserted within a confined side tube, may therefore be advantageous in the case of a gas tube.

There is this, too, to be remembered : the easiest direction for a discharge to cross an unsymmetrical tube is that which makes the less restricted electrode the cathode—in other words, that direction which offers the cathode dark-space least obstruction ; the tube runs harder if the dark-space touches the walls. If the design of an X-ray bulb is borne in mind, it will be realised that this property (which is made use of in the various valve-tubes, p. 70) would, in the absence of the confined anode, result in facilitating rather than in retarding the passage of the inverse current. Most workers have experienced this tendency of gas bulbs to act as rectifiers, and their refusal, on occasion, to let through the " break" current at all.

The Cathode.

In the case of " gas " bulbs, the cathode is always made of aluminium (see p. 82), and is mounted just within the neck of a side tube to the bulb. In a focus tube, the cathode is concave. Now, while the normal ejection of cathode rays holds for plane surfaces, it is not the case for concave cathodes except when the pressure is not very low. As the exhaustion proceeds, the focus of the rays recedes farther and farther from the cathode, and may reach a distance of something like four or five times the radius of curvature of the cathode : ordinarily the distance between the cathode and anticathode is some two or three times the radius of curvature. The size of the focal spot may vary somewhat capriciously in practice owing to variations in the gas-pressure. The harder the tube the smaller the spot (p. 32).

The correct disposition of anticathode and cathode is a matter of some nicety for the maker, who has to be guided mainly by his experience and the hardness at which the tube is to be run. The anticathode is usually mounted a shade out of focus to avoid its premature destruction by fusion, though for radiographic purposes this entails some loss in definition. Some of the earlier X-ray tubes were provided with devices for moving the anticathode to suit the conditions of use.

Campbell-Swinton (*P.R.S.* 1897) found that, at moderate pressures, the cathode rays do not form a solid cone of rays, but are condensed into a hollow conical shell. At low pressures, however, the rays are chiefly concentrated along the axis of the cathode. Owing to the ionising effect on the residual gas, this bundle of rays is displayed as a luminous pencil which stretches from cathode to anticathode. The origin of the pencil of rays, which usually is readily discernible in a soft X-ray bulb, is due to the repulsive effect of the electricity on the walls of the tube adjacent to the cathode. The same effect obtains also with plane cathodes (see p. 74). With a cathode made of a metal tube, a concentrated pencil of rays emerges from each end along the axis ; such cathodes are sometimes convenient in experimental bulbs.

It would appear from the work of some experimenters that to keep the cathode cool is of service in controlling the tendency of the bulb to harden with use. In the Gaiffe-Barret tube the cathode is cooled by an air blast : in the Müller " boiling tube," by water.

One may mention here that cathodes made of the electropositive metals conduce to smooth running of the discharge ; for example, a calcium cathode permits a tube to be run with safety much harder than one with an aluminium cathode. Coolidge describes a gas tube with a cathode of tungsten as being exceptionally " cranky," so long as the cathode was cool. The nature and condition of the cathode materially affects the " crankiness " of a tube.

THE ANTICATHODE.

The desiderata in an anticathode intended for modern radiography are :

(1) A high atomic weight or atomic number—to secure a large output of rays.

(2) A high melting point—to permit sharp focussing of the cathode rays without fusing the target.

(3) A high thermal conductivity and thermal capacity—to diminish local heating.

(4) A low vapour pressure at high temperatures—to avoid volatilisation on the walls (see p. 85).

The Atomic Weight of the Anticathode.

It was known almost from the first that the heavier metals, or rather those of high atomic weight, make the most efficient anticathodes. Röntgen himself found in 1896 that the rays from platinum were more intense than those from aluminium. Campbell-Swinton, Kaufmann, Roiti, Sir Oliver Lodge, S. P. Thompson, and Langer, all about 1897, did work connecting atomic weight and intensity of radiation.

These earlier workers used photographic or fluorescence methods of measuring intensities, and consequently most of their observations are of qualitative rather than quantitative interest.

In some experiments made by Kaye in 1908 [1] the metals used as anticathodes, some twenty in number, were mounted on a trolley inside the discharge tube (see Fig. 17). By

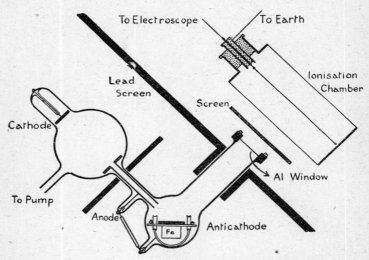

FIG. 17.—Apparatus for generating and measuring the X rays from different anticathode metals.

means of a magnetic control, the trolley could be moved and any metal desired brought under the beam of cathode rays. The tube was provided with an aluminium window 0·0065 cm. thick, and the emergent rays, which thus suffered but slight absorption, were measured by an ionisation method. The discharge was maintained by an induction coil.

The experiments showed that there are, in general, at least two classes of X rays given out by an anticathode [2]—

[1] *Phil. Trans. Roy. Soc.* A, 209, p. 123.

[2] The X rays from an anticathode will ordinarily be supplemented by at least two types of soft X rays—one produced by the X rays in passing through the glass walls ; the other from the impact of " reflected " cathode rays against the glass and the residual gas molecules.

a heterogeneous spectrum of "general" X rays, and homogeneous X rays characteristic of the metal.

The quality and amount of the latter rays are controlled by the nature of the anticathode and the potential on the tube; if the exciting voltage is correct the X rays

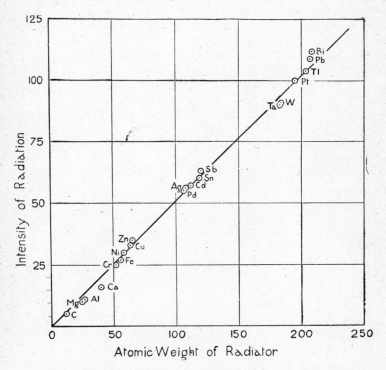

FIG. 18.—Graph connecting atomic weight of anticathode with intensity of "independent" X rays. (Pt = 100.)

are very largely characteristic (see p. 126). In some cases, such rays are too soft to penetrate the glass walls of an ordinary tube—for example, the characteristic (K) radiation of the chromium-zinc group.[1] However, the aluminium window enabled their presence to be readily detected. Their intensities did not follow any simple atomic weight order.

[1] Cr, Mn, Fe, Ni, Co, Cu, Zn.

To remove the characteristic rays, an aluminium screen 2 or more mms. thick was used, and it was then found that the intensity of the remaining harder " independent " rays increased with the atomic weight of the anticathode ; the two are indeed roughly proportional.[1] Fig. 18 shows the relation for a potential of about 25,000 volts on the tube. Very little change was produced in the relative intensities by increasing the thickness of the aluminium screen—the rays from all the metals were, under these conditions, very fairly homogeneous and of the same quality. Thick screens of other metals yielded much the same sort of curve, modified a little here and there. When the potential on the tube was raised the heavy-atomed anticathodes became slightly more efficient ; with a diminished potential the lighter elements somewhat increased their relative intensity values.

Suitable Anticathode Metals.

The list in Table I. gives the atomic weights, the radiation values, the melting points, and thermal conductivities (where known) of those elements which by reason of their refractoriness may be regarded as suitable for the anticathode of a focus bulb. The radiation values are for hard rays and are taken from Kaye's experiments (p. 36) ; in some cases the numbers have been obtained by interpolation. The thermal conductivities quoted are at room temperatures ; most metals diminish in conductivity as the temperature rises. The remaining constants are from Kaye and Laby's *Physical Constants*. The properties of some of the metals are not convenient, and to others the scarcity and price are at present an insurmountable objection.

Among the metals which have been commonly employed as anticathodes in radiography are osmium, iridium, tungsten, tantalum, molybdenum, and platinum. Platinum, which until recently was always used, has a melting point none too high for the purpose, sputters badly, and its high price was instrumental in directing attention to the properties of tungsten, a metal whose chemistry has become familiar

---

[1] Duane and Shimizu (*P.R.* 1919) have shown that atomic number rather than atomic weight is the main factor.

through its extensive employment in electric lamps. It does not sputter so badly as platinum,[1] it has a very much higher melting point, and but a slightly inferior radiation value, together with a superior thermal conductivity, thus permitting sharper focussing of the cathode rays. It is only within the last few years that the work of Coolidge has made it possible to obtain pure, dense, and malleable tungsten suitable for the purpose. Tungsten anticathodes are now usual for both hot-cathode and gas tubes, though platinum is still used for the latter type.

TABLE I.

Metal.	At. No.	Atomic Weight.	Density.	Intensity of Radiation.	Melting Point.	Thermal Conductivity.
		(O = 16)	grms./c.c.	(Pt = 100)	° C.	c.g.s.
Uranium -	92	238·5	c. 18·7	c. 125	—	—
Thorium -	90	232·0	11·3	c. 120	—	—
Gold -	79	197·2	19·3	101	1064	0·70
Platinum -	78	195·2	21·5	**100**	1750	0·17
Iridium -	77	193·1	22·4	98	2290	0·17
Osmium -	76	190·9	22·5	97	2700	0·17
Tungsten -	74	184·0	19·3	91	3200	0·35
Tantalum -	73	181·0	16·6	90	2900	0·12
Palladium -	46	106·7	11·4	55	1550	0·17
Rhodium -	45	102·9	12·4	54	c. 1900	—
Ruthenium -	44	101·7	12·3	53	1950 ?	—
Molybdenum	42	96·0	8·6	50	2500	—
Niobium -	41	93·1	12·7	49	2200 ?	—
Zirconium -	40	90·6	4·1	47	c. 1300	—
Yttrium -	39	89·0	3·8 ?	46	—	—
Copper -	29	63·6	8·9	33	1084	0·92
Cobalt -	27	59·0	8·6	30	1480	—
Nickel -	28	58·7	8·9	30	1450	0·14
Iron - -	26	55·9	7·9	27	1530	0·15
Manganese	25	54·9	7·4	26	1260	—
Chromium	24	52·0	6·5	25	1520	—
Vanadium	23	51·1	5·5	24	1720	—
Titanium -	22	48·1	3·5	22	1800	—

Iridium is even more expensive than platinum, but appears to behave satisfactorily if there is no oxygen in the X-ray

[1] It is important in the case of tungsten to get rid of water vapour, oxygen, or nitrogen in the tube, if excessive deposition is to be avoided.

tube. Osmium, which was employed in the early days of
X rays by the late Sir James Mackenzie Davidson, while
excellent as an anticathode, is very scarce and expensive.
Rhodium would seem to have much to recommend it as a
material for anticathodes; it has a high atomic weight
and low volatility. Bragg has, moreover, shown that the
rhodium radiation is remarkably homogeneous under the
right conditions (see also pp. 126 and 230).

Platinised Nickel Anticathodes.

It should be remarked that almost all the cheaper " gas "
tubes are fitted with nickel anticathodes faced with very

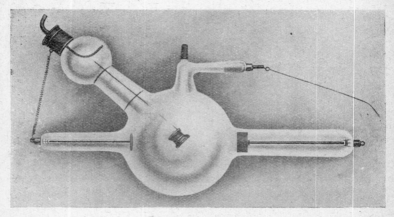

FIG. 19.—A gas X-ray bulb, showing water-cooled anticathode and automatic softening device.

thin platinum sheet (about $\frac{1}{100}$ mm. thick). The high price
of platinum was responsible for the introduction (in 1897)
of these composite anticathodes of which nowadays large
numbers are turned out. There is no objection to the plan
if the tube is intended only for moderate output; but care
should be taken that the platinum facing is not fused, as
nickel is a greatly inferior radiator.

Design of the Anticathode.

Some makers of gas bulbs mount the anticathode in
a glass sleeve or a porcelain ring. Both devices prevent

the incidence of cathode rays on the sides of the anticathode and the consequent generation of X rays which would interfere materially with sharp definition in photographic work. In some cases, the anticathode is made trough-shaped or is surrounded by a hollow aluminium cylinder to do away with the X rays produced by the reflected cathode rays striking the glass walls : the definition is described as. being improved. In certain makes of bulb the anticathode is provided with a "focussing ring" consisting of a stout ring of copper mounted in front of the anticathode (Fig. 25)

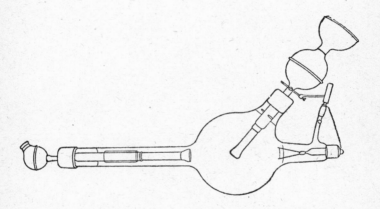

FIG. 20.—Müller deep-therapy tube with anticathode kept at constant temperature by water which is allowed to boil.

with which it is in metallic contact. The object is to prevent the wandering of the focal spot (p. 32).

Cooling the Anticathode.

The heating of the anticathode is overcome in many tubes by cooling the back surface by water (Fig. 19) or a stream of air. In the Müller "boiling tube" the water is allowed to boil (Fig. 20). In some makes of tube, no attempt at cooling is made, the anticathode being designed for continuous use at a red heat. With other designs of target, the temperature is kept down by increasing the massiveness of the anticathode (Fig. 21);

this is done by backing up the platinum or tungsten plate with copper, nickel, or iron. In some cases, the support extends to the outside of the tube, and is there provided with fin radiators (Fig. 22).

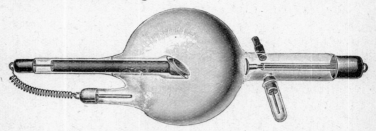

FIG. 21.—A gas bulb, showing massive anticathode and osmosis softening device.

Andrews is responsible for a method of cooling the anticathode by means of tongs. A thin copper tube is closed at one end to which is fastened the platinum target: the other end of the tube is fused to the glass through the

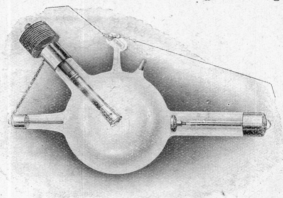

FIG. 22.—An Andrews gas bulb with automatic softening device and fin radiator for cooling anticathode.

intermediary of a platinum belt, and thus the inside of the copper tube is open to the air. Into the aperture can be introduced a pair of metal tongs, by means of which the massiveness of the anticathode can be greatly increased.

The point of impact of the cathode rays is generally not more than 1 or 2 mms. across, and with a heavy discharge the heating is so intensely restricted and rapid that the anti-cathode may be melted locally without damage to the rest of the plate. In the case of tubes designed for treatment purposes, the focus is broad, and such tubes permit greater energy-input than is possible with the finer focussed radiographic tubes. Fig. 23 is a photomicrograph of the focus spot of a tantalum anticathode subjected to a momentary heavy discharge. The metal was liquefied, and

Fig. 23.—Photomicrograph of fused focus-spot in a tantalum anticathode.

the pool of molten metal was blown away from the cathode.

Coolidge X-ray Tube.

In 1913 Dr. W. D. Coolidge [1] (*P.R.* Dec. 1913) designed a new X-ray bulb which marked an important step in the progress of the subject. The chief novelty is the fact that the gas pressure is so low that the residual gas plays little or no part in the ' ionics ' of the bulb. The source of the electrons

[1] Of the General Electric Co.'s Research Laboratory, Schenectady, New York.

is an incandescent cathode. This consists of a small flat spiral of tungsten wire, surrounding which is a molybdenum tube, the two being electrically connected. The tungsten spiral is heated by a subsidiary electric current (as with a Wehnelt cathode, p. 8), and so becomes a source of electrons (or cathode rays) to an extent which increases rapidly with the temperature. The molybdenum tube serves to focus the stream of electrons (see p. 75) on the anticathode, which is of tungsten and unusually heavy. There is no additional anode.

The vacuum within the tube is extremely high—about 20 times that of an ordinary X-ray tube—with the result that unless the cathode is heated, it is impossible to send

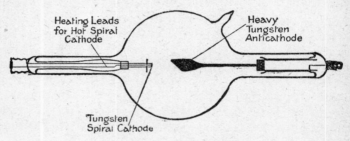

FIG. 24.—Coolidge X-ray tube.

a discharge through the tube. Furthermore, the greatest care is taken in freeing the electrodes and the glass walls from gas, before sealing off, during exhaustion.

By reason of the care taken in exhausting the tube, there are only slight changes in the vacuum, and, therefore, in the intensity of X rays, even after a run of many hours. The focal spot does not wander or vary in size.

The intensity of the X rays is precisely and readily controlled by adjusting the temperature of the cathode. A sensitive control over the cathode temperature is essential. At high temperatures (2300° C. or so) an enormous output of X rays is possible. With heavy continuous discharges the walls of the tube may well be kept cool by a blast of air.

The penetrating power of the rays depends, as with

a gas tube, solely on the potential difference between the electrodes. The X rays are heterogeneous (see p. 130). The anticathode becomes white hot after heavy or long discharges.

Owing to the low pressure, positive rays do not play an appreciable rôle, and there is in consequence no evidence of cathodic sputtering. There are slight traces of blackening due to vaporisation of the tungsten.

The starting and running voltages are the same, and the tube is remarkable in showing no fluorescence of the glass as in the ordinary X-ray tube, so that its appearance affords little notion of the output or indeed of any activity at all. The walls of the tube become negatively charged, and so differ from those of a gas-filled bulb (p. 32).

There is a considerable emission of X rays from all over the anticathode. A test with a pin-hole camera showed that the integrated value of these stray rays may amount to $\frac{1}{6}$ of the intensity from the focal spot. This disturbing factor, which is produced by secondary cathode rays, may be reduced by the use of a suitably perforated cap on the front of the target. The simplest cure in practice, however, is to " stop down " the rays as much as possible.

In the latest " radiator " type of tube, a tungsten target is embedded in a heavy copper anticathode which extends outside the tube where cooling fins are provided. Such a tube acts as its own rectifier, and can be excited by alternating current. In a still later " portable " model the tube is small in size and has walls of lead glass $\frac{1}{4}$ inch thick with a soda-glass window. A 200,000 volt model nearly a yard long has also been put on the market.

Coolidge (*American Journal of Röntgenology*, Dec. 1915) has also experimented with anticathodes cooled by a current of water. Such tubes permit enormous X-ray outputs. One tube ran continuously for 68 hours at 100 milliamperes and 70,000 volts. Others have been run continuously at 200 milliamperes, the power input being 14 kilowatts. It is anticipated that 50 kilowatt tubes may be possible.

Rutherford, Barnes and Richardson (*P.M.* Sept. 1915) found that with a cold cathode the perfection of the vacuum in a Coolidge tube under experiment was such that it withstood 175,000 volts without breaking down. When the cathode was heated, they could not detect (by an ionisation method) any radiation with a voltage less than 10,000 on the tube. As the voltage was increased the penetrating power of the radiation increased rapidly and regularly.

At constant voltage the composition of the X-ray beam and hence the shape of the absorption curves were found to be independent of either the current sent through the X-ray tube or of the temperature of the cathode. The tube was excited in turn by a Wimshurst machine and an induction coil : the absorption curves for the same voltage proved to be practically identical.

The hardest X rays obtained by Rutherford with a Coolidge tube had a penetrating power about half that of the hardest γ rays from RaC. Even with the highest voltages employed (175,000 volts) it was found that the intensity observable through 3 mm. of lead was less than $\frac{1}{10,000}$ of the initial value ; and this thickness of lead may be regarded as affording fairly adequate protection for the worker against the X rays from a Coolidge tube, at any rate for voltages under 200,000. For further data concerning the Coolidge tube, see p. 129.

Snook Hydrogen Tube.

In the hydrogen tube introduced by H. C. Snook, the residual gas is pure hydrogen. One of the features of the tube is the method of regulating the gas-pressure, in which an ingenious application of the osmosis method (p. 78) is employed. This method of regulating the vacuum depends on the fact that hydrogen will pass through red-hot platinum or palladium from a region of higher to one of lower hydrogen pressure. This diffusion takes place quite irrespective of the presence of other gases on either side of the metal boundary. In the Snook tube two osmosis tubes are sealed into the bulb. Either may be heated (to a bright red heat) by causing a discharge to pass from the tip of the tube to an adjacent metal electrode, the control obtained being rapid and convenient.

The one regulating tube, which is usually of palladium, is exposed to the atmosphere. Now the amount of hydrogen in the air is negligible, and consequently when this tube is heated, hydrogen passes from the interior of the bulb and the vacuum is raised.

The other regulating tube (usually of platinum) is surrounded by a small auxiliary bulb containing pure hydrogen at about atmospheric pressure, and the result of heating this tube is that hydrogen diffuses into the X-ray bulb and the vacuum is lowered. When necessary the auxiliary bulb can be replenished with hydrogen.

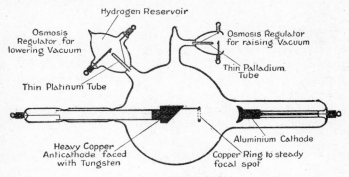

FIG. 25.—Snook hydrogen tube.

Fig. 25 shows the Snook bulb and the two osmosis tubes. The anticathode is of tungsten. There is very little "sputtering" of tungsten (see p. 80) in pure hydrogen, and, in passing, we may note that a tube filled with hydrogen runs harder for the same spark-gap than one containing air.

Metal X-ray Bulbs.

Sir Oliver Lodge designed an aluminium X-ray bulb in 1897, but the idea was not pursued. Zehnder (*Elect. Zeit.* Feb. 1915), Coolidge (*A.J.R.* 1915), and Siegbahn (*P.M.* 1919) have described all-metal X-ray tubes with porcelain-insulated electrodes. Siegbahn's tube was provided with a silver window which acted also as anticathode (see p. 143).

Lilienfeld Tube.

In the Lilienfeld tube, brought out in 1913 and since extensively modified, the cathode rays which are generated in an annexe by a hot-cathode pass through a perforated electrode, and are then subjected to the main exciting potential before they strike the target. Delicacy of control and approximate homogeneity of the rays are claimed for the tube.

Obliquity of the Anticathode.

The design of tube, in which the cathode rays are focussed on an anticathode inclined at 45° to the beam of cathode rays, has become universal for general practice. It has two disadvantages: (1) The obliquity of the anticathode increases the area of emission of the X rays; (2) if "inverse" current passes the cathode rays proceeding from the anticathode impinge on the glass walls, with the consequent risk of piercing the tube. Both objections could be met by mounting the anticathode parallel to the cathode or more nearly so. Such tubes are often used in X-ray spectrometry (p. 227).

The writer showed (*P.R.S.* 1909), in some preliminary experiments, that the output of a tube was almost independent of the obliquity of the anticathode. The fluorescence of the bulb, which is due to the " reflected " cathode rays from the anticathode, increased very markedly as the angle of incidence (to the normal) of the cathode rays increased, but the X rays did not show any corresponding variation either in quality or quantity.

Depth of Origin of X Rays in an Anticathode.

Various observers have found that the mean depth at which Röntgen rays originate in an anticathode is directly proportional to the potential employed. Ham (*P.R.* 1910) found that with a potential of 21,500 volts the mean depth was $5 \cdot 9 \times 10^{-5}$ cm. in the case of a lead anticathode. Davey (*P.R.* 1914) using a platinum target found the mean depth to be $0 \cdot 00004$B cm., where B is the Benoist hardness number (see p. 108).

The writer showed (*P.C.P.S.* 1909) that with spark-gaps of from 1 mm. to 1 cm. a thickness of from 1×10^{-5} to

4×10^{-5} cm. of gold, copper, or aluminium, was more than sufficient to generate X rays.

These distances may be compared with the minimum thicknesses which have been found essential for complete "reflection" of cathode rays of various velocities. These are as follows :

TABLE II.

Potential.	Thickness of Metal.		Authority.
11,000 volts	$5 \cdot 3 \times 10^{-5}$ cm.	Al	Warburg 1905
16,500 ,,	19·0 ,,	Al	,,
21,800 ,,	24·4 ,,	Al	,,
27,800 ,,	< 6·6 ,,	Cu	,,
90,000 ,,	0·25 ,,	Pb	Ham 1910

Distribution of the X Rays.

The distribution of the X rays from a bulb of the ordinary type is not quite uniform. Ham (*P.R.* 1908), Bordier (1908), and Gardiner (*J.Rt.S.* 1910) agree that in a plane determined

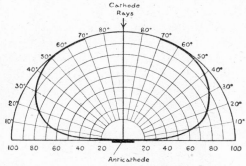

FIG. 26.—Graph showing distribution of X rays, the cathode rays being incident normally on anticathode.

by the beam of cathode rays and the normal to the anticathode, the intensity reaches a maximum in a direction at about 60° from the normal. (Cf. p. 117.) A distribution curve obtained by the writer (*P.R.S.* 1909) for normally incident cathode rays is given in Fig. 26, in which the length of the radius vector in any direction is proportional to the intensity. It should be noted that X rays are given off in all directions, but owing to absorption those from the back of the anticathode will naturally be weaker than those from the front.

Thin Anticathodes.

Some information on this point is afforded by the writer's experiments (*P.C.P.S.* 1909) on the emission of X rays in both backward and forward directions from anticathodes consisting of aluminium, copper, gold, or platinum leaf. The apparatus is shown in Fig. 27. The results indicate that

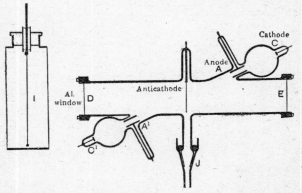

Fig. 27.—Apparatus for measuring X rays emitted from each side of a **very** thin anticathode.

the forward or " emergence " X rays exceed the backward or " incidence " rays both in intensity and hardness. In other words, the X rays tend to proceed in the same direction as the cathode rays which produce them. This is most pronounced in the case of aluminium, where with leaf about 0·00001 cm. thick, and a spark-gap of 1 to 2 cms., the emergence rays were two or three times as intense as the incidence. Stark (*P.Z.* 1909), using a photographic method, has obtained similar results for a carbon anticathode.

It would be of interest to test the homogeneity of the X rays from thin anticathodes. In many cases the proportion of characteristic radiation might be expected to be unusually large.

CHAPTER V.

HIGH-POTENTIAL GENERATORS.

THE voltages used to excite X-ray bulbs are of the order of up to 100,000 volts for radiography and superficial therapy; and up to 200,000 or more for deep therapy and radio-metallography. The high potential generators may be conveniently grouped into :—

(1) Influence machines.
(2) Induction coils or open-cored step-up transformers.
(3) Step-up transformers of the closed-core type.

INFLUENCE MACHINES.

Influence machines, which are nowadays almost always of the Wimshurst type, have been largely used in France, Germany, and the States for the production of X rays, but, probably owing to climatic reasons, have found little favour in this country. Very few influence machines, sold as such, are really suitable for the purpose ; nearly all of them need redesigning both from a mechanical and an electrical point of view. If glass is chosen for the material of the revolving plates, it should be free from excess of alkali, which in damp weather makes the surface conducting : ordinary window glass is quite unsuitable. Alkali-free glass is now procurable ; it is, for example, used in the Moscicki condenser. Such glass should not be coated with shellac varnish according to the usual custom ; shellac is slightly hygroscopic, and, although it is a better insulator than bad glass, it is not so good as the best glass. Care should be taken to avoid undue fingering of the plates.

Ebonite plates have advantages over glass (see p. 279), certainly on the score of safety for high-speed machines.

With continued exposure, however, to the stray brush-discharges, the ebonite tends to deteriorate, probably owing to the ozone, which is always generated in abundance, and which many workers find objectionable.

For leads, massive or india-rubber sheathed wires free from points and sharp bends, and as short as possible, should be used, otherwise the leakage by brush-discharge, always considerable, will prove excessive. When an X-ray bulb is run by a machine, either two short spark-gaps or two Leyden jars should be put in series with the bulb, one on each side of it : this will prevent undue frittering away of the electricity.

With a multiple-plate machine in good working order, a beautifully steady X-ray discharge can be obtained which is very efficient for radiography. The current is, moreover, unidirectional, and is found to be not so destructive to the anticathode as pulsating or alternating current.

The voltage from a Wimshurst machine is proportional to the speed of the plates : there is no theoretical limit to the potential obtainable, except such as is imposed by leakage or disruptive discharge. A Wimshurst machine is peculiar in that the current obtained is almost entirely independent of the voltage. The current output can be raised by increasing the number of plates. The voltage is readily controlled by altering the tilt of the rod supporting the brushes : a needle-point spark-gap is useful in regulating minor variations of the potential.

But, as has already been remarked, the idiosyncrasies and unreliability of influence machines have caused most workers to fight shy of them, at any rate for X-ray work. For instance, some machines refuse to work at all inside the glass cases provided for them ; yet, in their absence, the machines attract all the dust within reach and require continual cleaning. It is a habit with nearly all machines to reverse their electrification if stopped and restarted : in at least one type, a device is provided to counteract this.

It may be noted that although a Wimshurst machine generates homogeneous cathode rays, the resulting X rays are not homogeneous.

As an example of the successful large design of machine, one may mention that of Hulst in America. The plates, fifty in number and small in diameter, are constructed of compressed mica, and are motor-driven at a very high speed about a vertical axis. Such a machine will send a current of some 15 to 20 milliamperes [1] through an X-ray tube, and yield rays of an intensity such as would require double the current from a coil. The machine is, however, excessively noisy. It is sunk in a pit to lessen the danger attendant on the high speed of the whirling plates.

Villard and Abraham (*C.R.* 1911) describe a somewhat smaller 20-plate Wimshurst machine, whose construction allowed speeds of from 1200 to 1400 revolutions per minute. The plates were of ebonite 70 cms. across. The maximum current obtained was 3 milliamperes, the highest voltage about 320,000 volts, and the longest spark-gap 55 cms.

Some workers have been successful with Wimshursts, which work in air-tight cases into which air or carbonic acid is pumped under pressure. The idea is to kill the losses due to brush discharge; but the working difficulties are so great that the latest designs of Wimshursts have reverted to the simple unenclosed pattern.

INDUCTION COILS.

By an induction coil is meant an open-cored step-up transformer which depends for its action on the interruptions of the primary current by an independent interrupter. Precision measurements of coil phenomena are difficult if not impossible, and, as a consequence, coil design rests at present largely on arbitrary standards which have been evolved empirically from practical experience. Standardising of proportions proceeds, and any differences of design among the different coil makers depend more on individual predilections than on theoretical grounds.

It is not generally realised that the same coil cannot be equally efficient for all purposes; it cannot, for example,

[1] A milliampere $=\frac{1}{1000}$ ampere.

prove equally satisfactory for hard and soft bulbs, or for all speeds of interrupters.

While all the ambitious efforts of the early coil maker were directed towards phenomenally long sparks, nowadays, for X-ray work, he is content (except for deep therapy) with a 10 to 16 inch spark (between points), provided it is "fat." A fat spark means heavy current and intense X rays, and that satisfies the radiographer, who requires short exposures for much of his work, and finds that very long sparks mean rays too penetrating for his purpose.[1] Some of the later coils will pass through an X-ray tube sustained secondary currents up to 60 milliamperes with relatively small primary currents and but little inverse current. It will not be unprofitable to consider in some detail the various parts of a modern coil, a brief account of which was given on p. 27.

Core.

The aim of the coil-maker is to magnetise the core slowly (at make) and demagnetise it rapidly (at break). The spark-length depends on how quickly the core can be demagnetised. On the other hand, the output or power of the coil depends largely on the degree of magnetisation. With modern high-frequency interrupters the core is never either fully magnetised or demagnetised.

The ideal size of core depends on the size of the primary and the current in it, on the frequency and character of the break, and on the output required : the heavy discharge coil is allowed about 15 lbs. of iron per kilovolt-ampere : the core-length is some five to ten times the diameter.

The chief objects kept in mind in core design are (1) to diminish the inverse current, and (2) to reduce the losses due to eddy-currents and hysteresis in the iron. The inverse current is lessened by packing as much iron as possible into the space available for the core. The hysteresis loss is diminished by using stalloy or soft iron. The eddy-currents are reduced by using, instead of a solid iron core, closely packed wires or plates varnished to

---

[1] *À propos* of long-spark coils, Carpentier showed in 1910 at Paris a monster coil capable of a 50-inch spark.

diminish the electrical contact between them. Laminated plates have a better " space factor " than wire in a cylindrical core—in other words, there is less space unoccupied by iron—and accordingly plates are used for nearly all large coils. Iron with very high resistivity is now available, and so fairly thick plates can be employed.

Primary.

The primary is usually wound in three or more layers, as a simple or adjustable winding, covering almost the whole length of the core. There are in common use three different methods of winding primary coils which permit adjustment. In one, the connections are arranged so that each of the three layers can be put in series or parallel with its fellows ; in a second, a number of " tapping-off " wires permit connection to different parts of the primary circuit ; in a third, the primary is wound with several wires " abreast," so that these multiple windings can be put either in parallel or series at will.

A heavy-discharge coil has a primary stout enough to permit direct coupling to the electric light supply of 100 or 200 volts. Great care has to be paid to the insulation of the primary, owing to the induced E.M.F. from the secondary, of which all observers are well aware by reason of the shock which can be obtained from the primary of even a small coil in action. Nowadays, if a fault develops in a coil, it is often in the primary rather than in the secondary ; the defect is probably due to nitric acid formed by brush-discharges induced by the secondary.

Condenser.

It was Fizeau, nearly a century ago, who, by the addition of a condenser, revolutionised the induction coil and obtained sparks of lengths hitherto unheard of. But Lord Rayleigh demonstrated some years ago that if the primary current is interrupted with sufficient rapidity—e.g. by severing a wire with a rifle bullet—it is possible to dispense altogether with the condenser without impairing the length of the spark from the coil. Owing to the increasing use of Wehnelt and high-frequency mercury breaks, the condenser, once paramount in importance, has become in such cases unessential. With the older patterns of breaks the condenser is, of course, still important. Its functions are three in number : it performs each of them with incomplete success.[1]

(1) To increase the suddenness of the " break " and the slowness of the " make," and so to reduce the inverse current.

(2) To suppress undue sparking and arcing at the interrupter.

(3) To retard the formation of induced currents in the primary.

It is important that the capacity of the condenser should be as nearly as possible adapted for the particular value of the inductance of the primary as well as for the magnitude and frequency of the primary current. If the capacity is too large or too small, the secondary wave of potential will be neither so large nor so sudden.[2] The capacity required depends also very considerably on the type of break—for instance, less capacity is required with a gas break than with an oil break—and accordingly an adjustable condenser should be used if a coil is required for a variety of purposes. But for X-ray work alone the invariable condenser with a capacity no bigger than will prevent undue sparking at the interrupter is the simplest and best.

Condensers have improved out of all recognition during the last few years. With condensers of tin-foil and waxed-paper, this is chiefly due to a better knowledge of the hygroscopic properties of paper and paraffin wax and of the advantages of machine over hand manipulation.

Primary Tube.

Between the primary and secondary coils comes the primary tube made of ebonite, paxolin, micanite, or, less

[1] See W. H. Wilson, *P.R.S.* March 1912.
[2] See Taylor Jones' " Theory of the Induction Coil " (Pitman, 1921). In one instance, by reducing the capacity to one-fourth its value, the maximum potential was increased two and a half times.

commonly, porcelain. Ebonite has the advantage of being readily machined and worked, but micanite, on account of its greater electric strength, is generally used in large coils, though it is inconvenient mechanically.

Secondary.

The coil-maker estimates to get about 4000 volts from every 1000 turns in the secondary. He employs transformation ratios between about 75 and 500.

Simple winding is never used, partly because of the dangerous strain on the insulation owing to contiguous

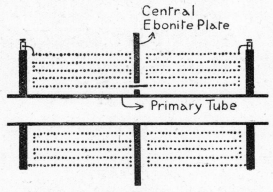

FIG. 28.—Diagrammatic representation of a bisectional winding of the secondary of an induction coil.

layers being at very different potentials, and partly because one end of the wire finishes up at the innermost layer. An obvious way to avoid this, is to divide the secondary into two sections, wind each of them simply, mount them side by side, and connect the two innermost ends of the wires together at the adjacent faces (Fig. 28). This plan has several advantages. The electric strain on the primary tube is slight ; the tube may accordingly be very thin, so that the primary and secondary windings are close together, with a consequent gain in the efficiency and a diminution in the size and weight of the coil. The method is accordingly of special value for smaller and portable coils. Owing to the electric stress between the outermost points of the adjacent faces of the two sections, the intermediate ebonite plate has to be made thick and protruding from the body of the coil (Fig. 29).

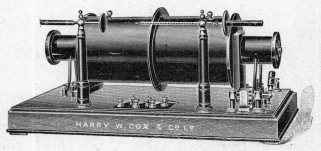

FIG. 29.—A Cox coil wound on the bisectional principle.

For large coils (such as Fig. 30), some form of sectional winding is used, in which a large number of circular flat

FIG. 30.—A Watson coil wound on a multisectional principle.

sections, one or more wires thick, are threaded side by side on the primary tube and separated by partitions of waxed or varnished paper. In some cases, these sections are connected up in series by joining the innermost wire of the first section to the innermost of the second, the outermost wire of the second section to the outermost of the third, and so on (Fig. 31), as in the bisectional method ; in others, by joining the innermost wire of one section to the outermost of the next, and so on. Much ingenuity has been exercised in devising methods of winding.[1] It may be noted that the method of sectional winding requires a thick primary tube.

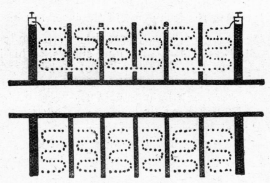

FIG. 31.—Diagrammatic representation of a method of multisectional winding of the secondary of an induction coil.

Whatever the method of winding, the secondary coil, when complete, is immersed in hot paraffin wax *in vacuo*. It is highly important to exclude air bubbles from the wax, and the method of vacuum-exhaustion is well nigh essential, if a break-down in the secondary is to be avoided.

Some Points in Coil Design.

The chief objection to induction coils for X-ray work is the inverse current which all coils generate, chiefly at " make," but also to some extent at " break." The inverse current may be lessened

(1) by making the number of turns in the primary as large as possible,

[1] See Codd's " Induction Coil Design " (Spon), 1920.

(2) by reducing the magnetic leakage between the primary and secondary : this means paying attention to the core.

The inverse current is augmented by irregular interruption, and care should therefore be taken to keep the break in good order. The inverse current also tends to increase if the X-ray bulb is softened.

Sparking at the interrupter, with its attendant waste of energy, may be reduced

(a) by increasing the self-induction of the primary,

(b) by lowering the frequency of the interruptions.

(1) and (a) are consonant, but they both imply a large secondary if the coil is to give long sparks. This is objectionable from the coil maker's point of view who, to obtain a heavy discharge, is very desirous of keeping down the resistance and the self-induction in the secondary. It is, however, possible to obtain long sparks with a secondary of reasonable size, by increasing the rate of interruption. (b), however, requires a low-frequency break ; and, moreover, eddy-current losses become considerable with very high frequencies.

If a heavy output is required from a coil, and the voltage available for the primary is only low, the self-induction of the primary should be kept down. This is inconsistent with but more important than (a). In such cases the output can often be materially improved by taking care that the leads from the battery to the coil are kept as short and straight as possible, the object being to diminish the self-induction in the circuit.

The efficiency of even the best induction coils, considered as transformers, is not high—in the region of 30 to 50 per cent. It could, of course, be increased by using a completely closed (ring) core instead of a straight one, and so diminishing the magnetic leakage. But the difficulty hitherto has been that, with a closed core, demagnetisation does not occur with the intermittent current which obtains in a coil discharge. The objection does not apply to true alternating current, in which there is a complete reversal.

A recent development in induction coil design is the so-called symmetrical coil, consisting of two separate coils, the primaries and secondaries each being connected in series. The coils are mounted vertically side by side, and the apparatus which is intended for deep therapy will operate a bulb for many hours at 200,000 volts and 2 to 3 milliamperes.

The Wave-form of the Primary and Secondary Currents.

The oscillograph [1] has been employed by a number of workers to investigate the shape of the waves of current

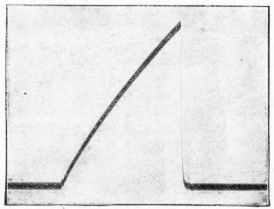

FIG. 32.—Oscillograph record of a make and break of the primary current of an induction coil.

and potential generated by a coil at each make and break of the interrupter. Fig. 32 shows a typical record (due to Salomonson, *J.Rt.S.* 1911) of a single make and break of the primary current in the case of a 13-inch coil giving a 10-inch spark : a mercury-oil break was used. As soon as the circuit is completed, the current starts from zero and rapidly grows in strength until the moment at which the circuit is broken. The current then falls to zero in about 1/1000 sec. In some cases, the curvature of the rising part of the curve is more marked than in Fig. 32. A close

---

[1] The oscillograph referred to is essentially a low-resistance, moving-coil galvanometer of few turns and with a very short time of swing.

inspection will show that superposed on the main current are extremely rapid oscillations : these are produced by the condenser. W. H. Wilson (*P.R.S.* 1912) noted that much longer sparks could be obtained from a coil when these high-frequency oscillations were pronounced in the primary current. Fig. 33 illustrates them very well. The frequency of these rapid oscillations may reach many thousands a second.

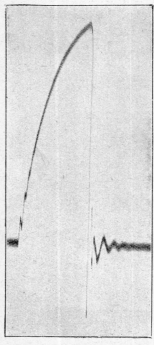

FIG. 33.—Oscillograph record of a primary current showing superposed high-frequency oscillations.

In regard to the secondary circuit, Duddell (*J.Rt.S.* 1908) found that the discharge consisted of isolated groups of strongly-damped impulses very abrupt and short-lived. The interval between successive groups of waves was relatively long compared with the actual duration of each group, which latter was of the order of 1/1000 sec. Fig. 34 gives a general notion of the state of things that obtains with a medium vacuum in the X-ray bulb.[1] The upper graph shows the current, the lower the potential. In the latter curve, the upper peak is the potential tending to send the current in the right direction through the tube : the smaller and broader inverted peak is due to the inverse potential, which in this case is conspicuous. The maximum direct potential is about 60,000 volts, the maximum inverse potential about 33,000 volts. The current curve is very similar to the potential curve : a small inverse current is detectable.

In Fig. 35 a rectifying spark-gap is inserted in the circuit : its ability to suppress the obnoxious inverse pulses is well

[1] A graph showing greater detail is a good deal more complicated.

displayed.   The maximum direct potential now supplied to
the bulb is 39,000 volts.   Thus some 21,000 volts have been

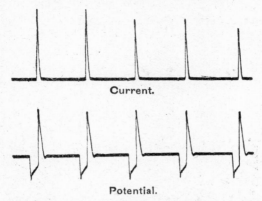

FIG. 34.—Oscillograph record of groups of impulses in the secondary circuit
of an induction coil.

used up in the spark-gap ; and the illustration serves to
point out the loss of energy that occurs in a spark-gap, and

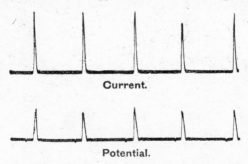

FIG. 35.—Conditions as in Fig. 34, but with rectifying spark-gap inserted.

the desirability of avoiding its use by not generating the
inverse current at all, if that were possible.

CLOSED-CORE STEP-UP TRANSFORMERS.

About 1908 the first high-tension transformer for X-ray
work was introduced by Snook.   Transformers are now
being more and more used in X-ray work.   They consist

essentially of a dry or oil-immersed step-up transformer, which is supplied with alternating current from an alternator. A rotating pole-changing switch rectifies the high potential alternating current from the secondary of the transformer. To secure the perfect synchronism which is essential for rectification, the commutator is mounted on

FIG. 36.—Present design of Snook high-tension transformer.

the same shaft as the alternator. The resulting current is, of course, not uniform, but pulsating as in *B* (Fig. 37); its amount can be varied at will.

The efficiency of the closed-core transformer is about 90 per cent.—roughly, twice that of an induction coil. They are capable of enormous output and precise control, and they have the advantage that no interrupter is needed. On the other hand, the initial cost is, roughly, twice that of

an induction coil of corresponding power, and repairs are
ordinarily more costly.

There has been much controversy as to the relative
merits of the sinusoidal potential curve of the closed-core

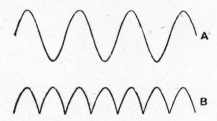

Fig. 37.—*A*. Alternating current of sine form. *B*. Pulsating current produced by rectification of *A*.

transformer and the long steep peak of an induction coil
(see p. 63). Most workers would probably prefer to use
a transformer outfit with a Coolidge tube, and to excite
a gas tube by a coil outfit. The former combination is
often selected by the radiographer, the latter by the
radiotherapist.

The oscillograph and X-ray spectrometer have thrown
a good deal of light on the subject.[1]

In one direction it would appear that simplification is
possible in the use of step-up transformers for X-ray
work. Instead of sending into the primary of the transformer a sinusoidal current, use an alternator specially
designed to give a very unsymmetrical wave form consisting of an abrupt high peak on one side and an
almost suppressed loop[2] on the other. The necessity for
the commutator thus disappears. Boas described such an
arrangement in 1911, and found it to work well in
practice, though the plan has not come into practice.

[1] See Kaye, *Practical Applications of X Rays* (Chapman & Hall).

[2] Merely sufficient, in fact, to demagnetise the core after each reversal
(see p. 60).

BREAKS AND INTERRUPTERS.

The interrupter is of paramount importance in the correct functioning of a coil. Rapidity of interruption and adjustability of period are essential if the interrupter is to give satisfaction. Mechanically, the interrupter should be robust and of generous proportions.

The Hammer Break.

The hammer break (see p. 28), the accompaniment of most of the earlier coils, has been greatly improved recently. Attention has been paid to its period and its mechanical stoutness. The frequency of a hammer break may vary between about 200 (per sec.) and (with a large coil) 25 to 30. The hammer break cannot carry a heavy current without excessive sparking and disintegration of the platinum. Accordingly a variety of other breaks have been introduced from time to time. These include the electrolytic interrupters, and the various kinds of motor-driven breaks which employ mercury.

The Wehnelt Electrolytic Interrupter.

Wehnelt in 1899, turning to account an earlier observation of Violle in 1892, devised his interrupter, which still enjoys considerable popularity. It consists of two electrodes immersed in dilute sulphuric acid.[1] The cathode is a large lead plate; the anode consists of one or more platinum points. The amount of the anode exposed to the liquid can be adjusted by means of a porcelain sleeve round each of the platinum points (Fig. 38).

For efficient interruption, the current must lie between certain

FIG. 38.—Wehnelt interrupter with single platinum anode (Siemens).

---

[1] A density of 1·2 is suitable. Some workers add a little $CuSO_4$.

limits ; if it is too small (below about 10 amperes) mere ordinary electrolysis occurs, if too great (say 40 amperes or more) the polarisation increases to such an extent that the current almost ceases and the anode becomes white-hot, and hisses and disintegrates in the liquid. With a suitable current the anode is normally surrounded by a violet light, and the interruptions are of an explosive and almost deafening character—a very unpleasant feature of the break.[1] Electrolytic breaks will not work with voltages exceeding 80 to 120 volts ; they are capable of a larger output than any type of break, but the reverse current is considerable and the X-ray tubes suffer in consequence.

Opinions are still very much divided as to the mode of action of the break : the usual explanation is that the interruptions are brought about by the periodic sealing and unsealing of the anode by liberated bubbles of gas ; but this does not meet all the circumstances. There are many factors to take into account—the size of the anode point, the current, the concentration and temperature of the acid, the inductance and capacity in the circuit : all these affect the interruptions. Compton (*P.R.* 1910) showed that just as with the ordinary hammer break, the " break " is more sudden than the " make."

The Wehnelt break usually requires a little humouring, and works rather better when the acid is warm, a state of things which soon results in practice ; indeed, for prolonged use, it is necessary for regular interruption to cool the acid, *e.g.* by means of a water-cooled worm of lead tubing. The interruptions are extremely rapid—as high as 1500 to 2000 per sec. when a very small anode point is used : even with very large currents the frequency may reach 200. The frequency is increased (1) by diminishing the size of the anode point, (2) by raising the temperature of the acid, (3) by diminishing the self-induction in circuit. Some self-induction is, however, essential or there will be no interruptions. A condenser across an electrolytic break is not beneficial, and is, in fact, generally detrimental to the working of the break, which itself functions as a condenser.

[1] Many makers now fit silencers to the break.

The energy required is diminished by raising the temperature and (slightly) by using stronger acid.   It is found that

to get the same spark-length, a more powerful coil is required with the Wehnelt than with any other break.   An electrolytic break does not, in fact, conduce to the highest efficiency in the working of a coil.

In another form of electrolytic break, both electrodes are of lead (Fig. 39), but one is surrounded by a porcelain cylinder pierced with a number of small holes, at which the bubbles of gas are formed.   This type permits no control over the current,[1] but the reverse current is said to be smaller.   This latter break is also

FIG. 39.—Wehnelt interrupter with perforated tube round lead anode (Schall).

suitable for alternating current, in which case it may be noted that the frequency is always equal to the frequency of the supply current, and is not affected by any of the controllable features of the break.

Mercury Breaks.

There are many ingenious forms of mercury breaks on the market.

They are invariably motor-driven either from above or below. The early (obsolete) forms depended on the rapid dipping of a plunger into a trough of mercury ; in some of the later types a jet of mercury is pumped against a series of rapidly revolving metal vanes.   To these and other types of breaks, the

FIG. 40. —Sanax mercury-paraffin break.

various makers' catalogues do full justice.   Two varieties of mercury break are illustrated in Figs. 40 and 41.

[1] In the Caldwell-Swinton pattern, the cylinder is pierced with only one hole, the size of which can be regulated and the current thus varied.

In the earlier forms the revolving system was immersed in paraffin oil or methylated spirit. With either liquid, but especially with the oil, the mercury emulsifies in most breaks, and the cleaning required is frequent and wasteful.

Coal gas or hydrogen at 1 or 2 atmospheres is generally used nowadays in mercury breaks : the break needs less cleaning, and is usually more reliable and economical than with a liquid dielectric. Salomonson has shown (*J.Rt.S.* 1911), by means of the oscillograph, that stronger and more abrupt quenching of the spark is obtained with a gaseous dielectric than with a liquid in which a conducting charred

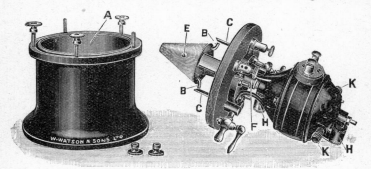

FIG. 41.—Mercury-gas turbine interrupter. (See also Fig. 93.)

track persists after each spark. Less condenser capacity is required for a gas break than for an oil or spirit break.

With most coils, these motor-driven breaks permit a heavier discharge current at the higher speeds. The mercury break is designed so that the current is " off " rather longer than " on " ; in this respect it is superior to the Wehnelt, in which the " on " period is equal to the " off," to the detriment of the demagnetisation of the core. When a high-speed break is employed it is beneficial for the bulb to receive periodic " rests." This can be brought about by inserting an additional break, but of low speed, in series with the high-speed break in the primary.

Doubtless most workers would prefer a mercury break to any other kind for general use ; though for heavy instantaneous work an electrolytic break is probably unequalled.

A mercury break permits greater control, however, and the good types are not subject to current and voltage limits of working, such as obtain with an electrolytic break.

RECTIFIERS AND VALVE-TUBES.

The chief defect of the induction coil from the point of view of the X-ray worker is that it does not give unidirectional currents : the reverse current at " make " has a disastrous effect on the X-ray tube, and requires to be suppressed.

For this purpose we may introduce into the circuit the simple point and plane spark-gap, which depends on the fact that the spark passes more readily when the point is positively charged than when it is negatively charged. The device is an old one, and is not always particularly efficient, more especially if the current is considerable. The greater the current which passes, the longer is the spark-gap required for rectification. For a current of about a milliampere, a spark-length of 1 cm. or more is suitable. Duddell (*J.Rt.S.* 1908) showed that with a point anode and a given spark-length, a cup-shaped cathode will rectify a larger current than a plane, and a plane a larger current than a sphere. Duddell has accordingly designed a rectifying spark-gap, in which the point electrode is surrounded by a hollow sphere, through which the point enters by means of a glass tube in a cork (Fig. 42). Correctly disposed, one rectifier in series with the X-ray tube and a second (reversed) in parallel with the tube, the arrangement is described as extremely efficient.

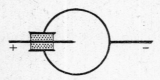

FIG. 42.—The Duddell spark-gap.

For most purposes, especially when electrolytic breaks are used, the various valve-tubes are more efficient than spark-gaps. These consist of a large aluminium cathode, often spiral in form, mounted in an exhausted bulb : the anode is small, and is contained in a restricted side tube (see p. 33). The design is due to Villard : in Sir Oliver Lodge's modification (Fig. 43), the anode (of iron wire) is surrounded with a copper sheath, partly to prevent sputtering on the glass walls, and partly to increase the resistance of the tube

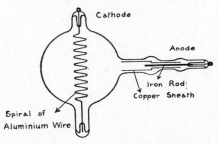

FIG. 43.—Section of a Lodge valve-tube

for the reverse current (see p. 73). Owing to the use of a phosphorus method of completing the exhaustion, the Lodge valve is red in colour (see p. 278). The Lodge tube is said not to harden with use, but other types of valves should be fitted with some softening device, as they harden considerably with use and do not rectify well if the pressure becomes very low. A valve-tube is only efficient over a limited range of pressures.

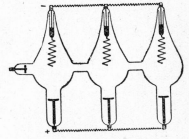

FIG. 44.—A multiple valve-tube.

For heavy work, multiple valve-tubes (Fig. 44) are advisable, in series and parallel with the X-ray bulb.

The hot-cathode valve (*e.g.* Kenetron) is a later development. Such a tube will rectify alternating or coil discharges up to 100,000 volts. The Morton rectifier is a four-point "sparking" commutator mounted on an extension of and rotating with the spindle of the interrupter. Its object is to cut out the inverse current from the coil. Miller's mica-disc valve is a somewhat similar device.

It may be noted that as many of these valve-tubes give out X rays during operation, the necessary protection should be provided for the operator.

CHAPTER VI.

THE HARDNESS OF A GAS X-RAY BULB.

Factors controlling the Hardness of a Gas X-ray Bulb.

The hardness of the X rays produced by a bulb is solely dependent on the potential difference between the electrodes of the bulb. There are a number of ways of controlling this potential difference in the case of a gas tube.

(1) The most generally recognised method is by varying the degree of exhaustion of the bulb. The lower the pressure, the higher the voltage required and the harder the X rays. The range of effective pressures for producing X rays is very wide. It is, however, possible to make use of other methods which do not involve any change in the gas pressure.

(2) By inserting a spark-gap or valve-tube (p. 70) in series with the bulb, the tube is hardened. With very soft bulbs, Winkelmann (*A.d.P.* 1900) states that the spark-gap should be placed between the cathode and the coil. At lower pressures, the position of the spark-gap is immaterial.

(3) By employing Tesla or other currents of extremely high potential, the tube runs harder. Tesla currents are obtained by transforming up the secondary current from a coil by means of a special transformer immersed in oil.

(4) By bringing the electrodes nearer together, the tube may be hardened (see p. 33).

(5) By altering the nature of the gas in the tube. For the same pressure, a tube runs harder in hydrogen and still harder in carbon dioxide than in air. In other words, in order to generate X rays of equal hardness, a tube filled with air must run at a lower pressure than one containing hydrogen or carbon dioxide.

(6) By increasing the current density through the tube. This can be done :

(*a*) By increasing the current in the primary of the coil.

(*b*) By diminishing the size of the cathode. A tube with a fine wire cathode runs harder than one with a cathode of moderate size.

(*c*) By diminishing the size of the tube. Winkelmann in 1900 experimented with various sizes of tubes, and found that with a tube 5 mms. in diameter, he could get X rays at as high a

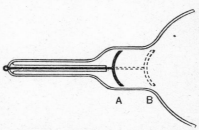

FIG. 45.—The discharge is hardened by withdrawing the cathode from *B* to *A*.

pressure as 10 mms. of mercury with air as the residual gas. In the case of hydrogen and a tube 10 mms. in diameter, he obtained X rays at the remarkably high pressure of 30 mms. of mercury. If the tube is made *too* narrow, the hardening effect is spoilt.

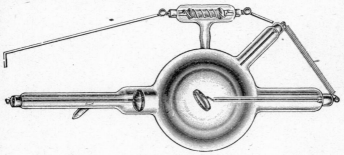

FIG. 46.—A Cossor bulb of lithium-glass with recessed cathode.   (See Fig. 45.)

(*d*) By diminishing the clearance between the cathode and the surrounding tube. It was pointed out on p. 31 that if the space round the cathode is restricted, the discharge passes with difficulty, so that if the cathode is withdrawn from the bulb into a side tube, the discharge hardens accordingly (Figs. 45 and 46). Precisely the same effect is obtained with a plane as with a concave cathode, and, indeed, with a tube in which the cathode is so inclosed the curvature of the cathode need only be very slight. A tube with a movable cathode employing this principle was described by Campbell-Swinton in 1897 (*Electrician*); the tube is in the Röntgen Society's collection of X-ray tubes in the South Kensington Museum. Swinton also employed an alternative device consisting of a glass sleeve, a part of which was narrowed to slide along the glass rod which supported the

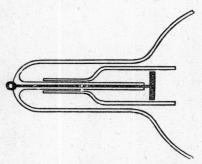

cathode (Fig. 47). The remaining portion was widened so as to form a sheath round the cathode and project a varying distance beyond it. Wehnelt (*D.P.G.V.* 1903) found that the arrangement allowed the alternative gap to be varied as much as eight times. Whiddington (*P.C.P.S.* 1913) observed that, within

FIG. 47.—Adjustable glass sleeve over the cathode for varying the hardness of the discharge.

limits, the distance the sheath projected beyond the cathode was proportional to the potential required to run the bulb.

The hardening effect, as Goldstein remarked (*D.P.G.V.* 1901), is due to the glass round the cathode becoming negatively charged owing to leakage from the cathode. The cathode rays accordingly retreat to the centre of the cathode, where they form a concentrated pencil. In this way, the current-density and effective resistance of the tube are increased, and the more markedly if the adjacent glass is coated with sputtered metal.

This charging up of the glass is responsible for a well-known effect produced by touching the tube near the cathode while the discharge is passing. The glass under the finger becomes vividly fluorescent, and a bundle of cathode rays is deviated towards the hand. Maltézos (*C.R.* 1897) showed that if the finger is replaced by the knob of a Leyden jar, the jar becomes positively charged, a clear indication of the negative electrification within that part of the tube (see

p. 32). It is possible to vary the hardness of a tube by putting patches of tin-foil on the outside in suitable places.

In the case of the hardening sleeve referred to above, Whiddington has shown that the tendency of the sleeve is to slide back into the side tube owing to electrostatic repulsion by the cathode ; and, further, that if part of the sleeve is cut away, the cathode rays are bent away from the portion which remains. It can readily be demonstrated that a metal tube, if slid over the cathode inside the glass, will harden the discharge just like a glass tube. In fact, the cathode may be removed altogether and the cylinder alone used in its place ; a sharply defined pencil of rays will still proceed out along the axis of the cylinder (see p. 35).

The Progressive Hardening of a Gas X-ray Bulb with Use.

With a new gas X-ray tube, the first effect of running the discharge is to cause an outburst of gas. The effect, which may persist for some time, is due largely to gas ejected from the cathode. Aluminium almost always contains large quantities of gas, chiefly carbon compounds. Such gas is more readily reabsorbed than air let into the tube. In an X-ray tube, the anticathode also gives out considerable amounts of gas : indeed, the method of bombardment by cathode rays is most effective for liberating the gas in a metal.

But, after some time, the gas-pressure becomes progressively lower with continued running of the discharge. The cause of this has been a problem ever since the days of Plücker (1858), and one to which a good deal of enquiry has been directed. The effect is undoubtedly not a simple one, and there appear to be several contributory causes. The responsibility for the hardening has been ascribed by Ratner (*P.M.* Jan. 1922) to the metal electrodes, not on the score of gaseous occlusion, but rather by reason of the presence of the gaseous surface-layer on the cathode which gradually arrests the electronic emission from the cathode.

But Hill (*P.P.S.* 1912) has shown that a marked absorption of gas occurs even with electrodeless discharges, and it would seem that some of the responsibility must be visited on the glass walls. Campbell-Swinton (*P.R.S.* 1907 and 1908) concluded from his experiments that the gas is actually driven into the glass by the discharge. He found that when the glass was subsequently fused, such gas (which proved to be chiefly hydrogen) segregated into small bubbles [1] whose depth below the surface did not exceed about 0·015 mm. This thickness of glass is, as Swinton points out, the greatest that will transmit cathode rays to any appreciable extent. *A propos* of this, it may be remarked that the effect appeared to be intimately associated with the fluorescence-fatigue which glass displays when subjected to prolonged bombardment by cathode rays (see p. 12). If the gas-permeated region of the glass is removed by grinding, the glass recovers its usual fluorescing ability. Hill (*loc. cit.*) found a similar absorption-fatigue ; and it would be interesting to test whether such removal of the fatigued surface promoted vigorous gas-absorption on further running of the discharge.

Hill agrees with Willows (*P.M.* 1901) in attributing the hardening of discharge tubes to chemical action between the gas and the glass. His experiments show that Jena glass gives the least absorption, lead glass coming next, while soda glass gives most of all. The greater stability of Jena glass is well known from its behaviour in other directions. Possibly fused silica [3] or alkali-free glass would prove to be superior even to Jena glass. It would be interesting to subject an ordinary soda glass bulb to steam or boiling-water treatment before exhaustion, to see if the removal of the alkali affected the rate of hardening.

Ramsay and Collie (*N.* 1912) discovered helium (and a trace of neon) along with hydrogen in the deeply stained glass of an old X-ray tube.[2] This is suggestive, for hydrogen

---

[1] The formation of bubbles in such circumstances was also noticed by Gouy (*C.R.* 1896) and Villard.

[2] Sir J. J. Thomson (*P.R.S.* 1913) finds, however, that nearly all substances when bombarded by cathode rays emit hydrogen and helium.

[3] See Willows and George, *P.P.S.* 1916.

and helium molecules have the highest speeds of all molecules. Under the electric discharge, these speeds may be increased a thousandfold, *e.g.* the average velocity of positive rays of hydrogen is 2×10^8 cms./sec. (see p. 20). Goldsmith (*P.R.* July 1913) found that such high-speed molecules of hydrogen and helium can penetrate, for example, mica sheet from 0·001 to 0·006 mm. thick, though the slower air, argon, or CO_2 molecules cannot. But molecules which could penetrate so great a distance as 0·015 mm. of glass would have to be considerably faster. How fast, we may infer from the fact that α particles (helium atoms) from RaC have a range of 0·04 mm. in glass. Such particles have an initial speed of about 2×10^9 cms./sec., *i.e.* ten times the above velocity. It has, of course, never been shown that sufficiently high instantaneous velocities are not possessed by individual hydrogen molecules in a discharge tube—one can only measure average velocities. But, in any case, it is obvious that any explanation such as this could only be a partial one ; it does not, for instance, explain the marked difference in the behaviour of different kinds of glass.

The absorption may be due in part to chemical activity excited in the gas by the discharge, such as has recently been found by Strutt to be the case with nitrogen. It may be, too, that the action is stimulated by a species of electrolysis of the glass produced by the high-tension discharge playing over its surface. It is well known that glass may be readily electrolysed by quite moderate potentials, if the temperature of the glass is raised, and it is a matter of experience that the discharge seems to have an ageing effect on the glass, to the detriment of subsequent working in the blowpipe. Such electrolysis might have a marked effect on the gas film which glass and other solids can condense on their surfaces. Possibly in such circumstances the gas film is capable of taking up abnormal amounts of the residual gas in the bulb.

The hardening of an X-ray tube is well known to be pronounced with tubes whose walls have become blackened by metal sputtered from the electrodes (see p. 80). The finely divided metal behaves like spongy platinum in its absorptive properties for gases.[1]   In many cases this is probably a main factor in the hardening.

To soften a Gas X-ray Tube.

It was early discovered that the resistance of a tube could be lowered by warming the bulb with a spirit lamp or gas burner, but the resulting benefit was only temporary, and various " softening " methods have been devised from time to time.   Many of these methods involve the heating of some substance which has been inserted in the tube, *e.g.* sealing-wax, carbon, and red phosphorus have each been employed by various experimenters in the past : Sir William Crookes used caustic potash for this purpose as long ago as 1879.

In many X-ray bulbs, this occlusion method is arranged to work automatically.   A small alternative discharge tube communicates with the main bulb (Fig. 22). When the resistance increases beyond a certain degree, the discharge chooses the alternative path, and in so doing heats up some absorbent material such as asbestos, sheets of mica, or glass-wool enclosed in the small tube (see Fig. 22).   The consequent liberation of gas (largely CO_2 and water vapour) lowers the resistance of the bulb, and the discharge resumes its proper path.   But, in time, such substances "fatigue," having yielded all their available gas ; and the only course is to open up the tube (see p. 198).

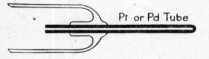

Pt or Pd Tube

FIG. 48.—Osmosis tube for admitting hydrogen into an X-ray bulb.

A plan often employed for softening gas X-ray bulbs is the " Osmosis " method, originated by Prof. Villard of Paris in 1898, and discovered independently by Profs. Winkelmann and Straubel of Jena in 1899.   A small platinum or palladium tube closed at one end is sealed into the bulb, the unclosed end being open to the bulb (Figs. 48 and 25).

[1] Soddy and Mackenzie (*P.R.S.* 1907) showed that helium was absorbed by aluminium scattered from the cathode of a discharge tube.   In such a case the gas may be mechanically trapped by a compact film of metal.

By applying a flame to the tube a small quantity of hydrogen diffuses through the hot metal, and the pressure of the bulb can be restored to the right amount. Palladium shows the effect so very markedly that care should be taken in the heating; otherwise the result will be a bulb too soft for use. Indeed, this method should never be employed except when the discharge is running.

The **Bauer valve** (*J.Rt.S.* Jan. 1907) is a more recent contrivance for letting minute quantities of air into gas X-ray bulbs. The valve (see Fig. 49) consists of a small unglazed porcelain disc, through the pores of which air can pass. Ordinarily the disc is sealed by mercury, but by means of a pneumatic piston the disc can be laid bare for a moment by pushing the mercury away (page 84).

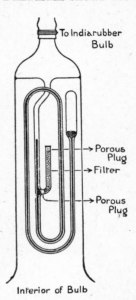

FIG. 49.—The Bauer valve for admitting air into an X-ray bulb. The filter is of gold leaf to absorb mercury vapour.

To harden an X-ray Bulb.

If by any mischance a bulb becomes too soft for use, the only thing possible, apart from drastic re-exhausting, is to try and harden it by prolonged running with as large a coil as can be got. Often it is beneficial to send this hardening discharge in the reverse direction, *i.e.* from cathode to anode, temporarily disconnecting the anticathode for the purpose. Care should be taken in carrying out this operation, and the discharge should only be passed intermittently, to avoid puncturing the tube by local over-heating of the glass walls.

An ingenious method of hardening a hydrogen tube is described on p. 47.

CHAPTER VII.

THE BLACKENING OF AN X-RAY BULB.

With continued use, an X-ray bulb becomes blackened on its inner surface. The blackening is mischievous from several points of view. Firstly, the deposit not only tends greatly to increase the resistance of the tube to the discharge, but accelerates the absorption of the residual gas; secondly, the discharge is wont to spark irregularly along the walls of the tube instead of through the gas; and thirdly, the film of metal arrests the softest X rays.

Two main causes are answerable for the blackening:

(1) The disintegration or " sputtering " of the anticathode while acting as cathode during the inverse current; and also of the cathode during the direct phase.

(2) The volatilisation of the anticathode due to its high temperature under reduced pressure.

CATHODIC SPUTTERING.

Workers with discharge tubes have long been aware that when a high-potential current is passed through a vacuum tube provided with platinum electrodes, the glass adjacent to the cathode generally becomes coated with a mirror of platinum (Fig. 50). The anode, on the contrary, shows little or no such effect. This property of cathodic sputtering is common in greater or less degree to all metals. The effect was noticed in the very early days of

vacuum tubes : both Geissler and Plücker (1858) remarked
on it.

Thus, quite apart from the cathode rays and positive
rays, there is a cathodic emission which consists of particles
of disintegrated metal from the cathode. These particles
appear to be projected normally (at any rate, very approximately) from the surface of the cathode, and to travel in
straight lines. The streams of metal are negatively charged,

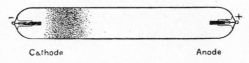

Cathode   Anode

Fig. 50.—Illustrating cathodic sputtering.

and it is found that they deposit more readily on surfaces
which are positive with respect to the cathode. The positive electrification which the inner surface of a gas X-ray
bulb usually possesses, is thus favourable to cathodic
deposition.

It does not appear that, in ordinary circumstances, the
disintegration of the cathode plays any appreciable part in
the passage of the current. Unlike the cathode rays, the
sputtered particles require strong magnetic fields (2000 gauss
and upwards) before any deviation of their path can be
detected. The inference would be, either that the particles
are very fast moving or that they are relatively large aggre-
gates of molecules ; the latter view is supported by other
evidence. The lower the pressure in the tube and the
higher the potential applied, the farther are the particles
hurled. There is no deposition within the cathode dark-
space. The sputtered metal does not appear to excite
fluorescence when it strikes the glass walls of the tube.

Cathodic disintegration is not a simple phenomenon, and
the exact mechanism of the production of the sputtered
particles is doubtful. It appears, however, to be connected
with the bombardment of the cathode by the positive
rays, the pulverising properties of which we have already
noticed (p. 20).

F

Experiment shows that the amount of metal shot from a cathode depends on

    (1) The nature of the metal of the cathode.
    (2) The temperature of the cathode.
    (3) The nature of the gas in the tube.
    (4) The current through the tube.
    (5) The fall of potential at the cathode.

(1) The Metal of the Cathode.

Sir William Crookes (*P.R.S.* 1891) was the first to investigate systematically the relative sputtering of a number of metals under like conditions of discharge. The residual gas was air; the pressure, that corresponding to a dark-space 6 mms. thick (say ·05 mm. Hg). A coil discharge was used, and in these circumstances the relative losses of weight at ordinary temperatures resulted as follows :

TABLE III.   CATHODIC SPUTTERING.
(Palladium = 100.)

Palladium - - -	100	Copper - - -	37
Gold - - - -	92	Cadmium - - -	31
Silver - - - -	76	Nickel - - -	10
Lead - - - -	69	Iridium - - -	10
Tin - - - -	52	Iron - - - -	5
Brass - - - -	47	Aluminium - -	0
Platinum - - -	40	Magnesium - -	0

The order of these metals must not be regarded as inviolable. It is affected to some extent by a change in the pressure of the gas (which may, for instance, put platinum above gold), the nature of the gas, or the temperature of the cathode. Nevertheless, the sequence is of value to users of discharge tubes in general and of X-ray tubes in particular. The reason for the invariable choice of aluminium [1] for the cathode is as readily apparent as the need for suppressing the inverse current through a tube and so preventing the platinum anticathode from officiating as cathode. It

---

[1] Geissler noticed that aluminium did not sputter appreciably.

is not right, however, to assume that it is impossible to make aluminium sputter appreciably,[1] as will be evident from a scrutiny of the cathode of an old X-ray bulb : a brown deposit may usually be found on the central area of the cathode as well as on the glass in the vicinity.[2]

Tantalum has also proved to be an excellent material for cathodes from the point of view of sputtering. I believe tungsten displays equally good properties.

(2) The Temperature of the Cathode.

Crookes showed that if the temperature of the cathode is raised appreciably, for instance by the passage of the discharge, the sputtering of many metals is markedly increased. The electrodes tend to get very hot if the tube is at all soft, as more current is then passed by the gas. The rise of temperature of the cathode is roughly proportional to the current. This effect is distinct from that dealt with on p. 85.

(3) The Nature of the Gas.

The nature of the residual gas has a very marked effect both on the degree of sputtering that a metal exhibits and on the appearance of the deposit. Hydrogen, nitrogen, and carbon dioxide do not in most cases favour the effect, while oxygen, the halogens, and the monatomic gases, mercury vapour, He, A, Ne, Kr, and Xe bring about pronounced disintegration of most metals. Helium shows the effect least of all these gases, but argon is particularly potent, and metals so varied as Al, Ag, Cd, Pt, and Au are all excited to a maximum activity in this gas. Aluminium shows only feeble sputtering in hydrogen or nitrogen, and but little more in oxygen. Iron sputters a little in hydrogen ; silver and lead sputter markedly in this gas.

Systematic work is needed to find the most suitable gas for an X-ray tube. Unless precautions to the contrary have been taken, the gas will probably consist largely of hydrogen and carbon dioxide liberated from the electrodes. Pt and especially Al (and Mg) emit large quantities of gas when used as cathodes. The point is also of importance in

[1] See Campbell, *P.M.* Sept. 1914.   [2] See Kaye, *P.P.S.* Ap. 1913.

connection with the various methods of controlling the
hardness of bulbs (p. 78). The automatic devices introduce
chiefly carbon dioxide, and, in some cases, a little water
vapour ; the osmosis valves, hydrogen ; the Bauer valve,
air. So far as sputtering goes, hydrogen and carbon dioxide
would appear to have advantages, though there is some
diversity of opinion on the point. On the other hand, it
may be remarked that a tube rendered unsteady by the
hardening effect of hydrogen may often be caused to run
smoothly by letting in a little air.

(4) The Current through the Tube.

The disintegration of a cathode increases with the current
through the tube, apparently either as the first power or
the square of the current.

(5) The Fall of Potential at the Cathode.

The volatilisation of the cathode is augmented by increasing the potential on the tube, and such control is

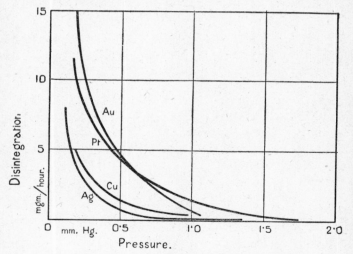

FIG. 51.—Relation between cathodic sputtering and pressure.

readily obtained by lowering the pressure of the gas. Sputtering is much more pronounced at low pressures than at

high, though at the very low pressures of an X-ray tube
the disintegration is not quite so marked as at rather higher
pressures, when the tube runs more easily.   Fig. 51 displays
the relation between the pressure and cathodic disintegration
of a number of metals.   It is due to Granquist (1898).

The potential that is applied to an X-ray tube is not
distributed evenly between the electrodes.   The greater part
is used up close to the cathode ; there is a gentle potential
gradient in the space between the electrodes, and the
remaining fall of potential occurs close to the anode.   The
amount of sputtering depends on the cathode-fall of
potential, and this increases as the pressure of the gas
is lowered.   It appears to be essential that the potential
fall at the cathode shall exceed a certain minimum value
before the metal becomes ionised and disintegrated to
any appreciable extent.   Holborn and Austin (1904) found
that this critical potential was about 500 volts for a number
of metals.

Volatilisation of the Anticathode.

The high temperatures which anticathodes may attain in
a focus tube are familiar enough, but the extent of the
sublimation which most metals exhibit at temperatures well
below their melting points may not have been brought home
to many observers.   A homely example of sublimation at
low pressure is provided by the blackening which is a not
uncommon feature of carbon and tungsten glow lamps.   The
subject has received attention at the hands of a number of
workers,[1] and it appears that the degree of volatilisation
is affected by :

    (1) The nature of the metal.
    (2) The temperature of the metal.
    (3) The nature of the surrounding gas.
    (4) The pressure of the gas.

The disintegration of metals increases rapidly as the temperature rises.   Of the platinum metals, platinum, rhodium,
and iridium all disintegrate less as the pressure is reduced,

[1] See Kaye, *Chemical World*, June 1913.

and there is evidence to show [1] that in these cases the volatilisation is not a simple process, but is brought about by the formation of endothermic oxides more volatile than the metals themselves. It would seem that in order to reduce the sublimation of these metals to a minimum, the important thing is to ensure the absence of oxygen in the surrounding gas [2]—a wise precaution, indeed, with most metals, as almost all observers agree. Hydrogen, nitrogen and argon do not in general favour disintegration.

With palladium and most other metals, a reduction of pressure is favourable to volatilisation—as would be anticipated in cases of true sublimation.

Table IV.[3] gives, for a number of metals, data concerning the effect of pressure on the boiling point, as well as the temperatures at which appreciable vaporisation has been detected (mostly at low pressures). The corresponding melting points are added for the sake of comparison.

TABLE IV.

Metal.	Boiling Point.		Volatilisation detectable at	Melting Point at 1 Atmos.
	At 1 Atmos.	In Vacuo.		
Cadmium - -	778° C.	450° C.	160° C.	321° C
Zinc - - -	918	550	180	419
Lead - - -	1525	1150	360	327
Silver - - -	1955	1400 ?	680	961
Copper - - -	2310	1600 ?	400	1084
Tin - - -	2270	1700 ?	360	232
Gold - - -	2530 ?	1800 ?	1370	1064
Iron - - -	2450	—	950	1530
Platinum - -	2500 ?	—	1200	1750
Osmium - -	—	—	2300	2200
Iridium - - -	2600 ?	—	1400	2290
Tungsten - -	3700 ?	—	1800	3200

The table gives a notion of the extent to which volatilisation occurs with metals, while still at temperatures well

[1] See Roberts, *P.M.* 1913.
[2] This is especially important in the case of iridium.
[3] See Kaye and Ewen, *P.R.S.* 1913.

below their melting points.   There is scope for a good deal of systematic work on the volatility of platinum, tungsten, iridium, etc., when heated at low pressures in different gases. The results would be of great practical value to the user of X-ray bulbs.   It is known that tungsten, for example, when heated, readily disintegrates and becomes brittle in the presence of oxygen or moisture.   Irving Langmuir[1] has recently traced this to the formation of oxides.

Coloration of the Glass of an X-ray Bulb with Use.

The cathode rays "reflected" from the anticathode are responsible either directly or indirectly for the violet colour which the glass assumes in well used X-ray tubes.   This coloration is most pronounced on the front side of the anticathode, and can be prevented by screening the glass with metal foil.   Radium rays affect glass and quartz in the same way, though to a greater depth ;   and cathode rays produce a similar colour in crystals of rocksalt or fluorspar.   Possibly, therefore, the action is of the same nature in all these cases ;   and may be the phenomenon is related to the violet permanganate coloration produced by ultra-violet light and sunlight in window glass.   The violet colour is in all cases destroyed by heating.

X-ray bulbs of lead glass become brown in colour rather than violet.   Elster and Geitel (1898) have suggested that the various colorations are due to ultra-microscopic particles of reduced metal in the salt.

[1] *Proc. Amer. Inst. Elect. Eng.* Oct. 1913.

CHAPTER VIII.

THE MEASUREMENT OF X RAYS.

The International Radium Standard.

The general desire to have a standard by which the output of an X-ray tube could be measured in a manner free from the defects of the usual methods, led the Röntgen Society in 1909 to appoint a Committee (with Dr. W. Deane Butcher as secretary) to consider the question. This Committee decided to initiate standards of radioactivity. These depended on the γ-ray activity of radium bromide and were prepared by Mr. C. E. S. Phillips. Largely owing to the efforts of Prof. Rutherford, the question was taken up by the Congress of Radiology at Brussels in September 1910. An International Committee was formed with Prof. Rutherford as President ; in March 1912 the Committee met at Paris and adopted as an International Radium Standard a specimen consisting of 21·99 milligrammes of pure radium chloride which had been prepared by Mme. Curie. The radium is contained in a thin-walled glass tube, and use is made of the γ-ray ionisation. The International Standard is preserved at the Bureau International at Sèvres near Paris. Secondary standards are obtainable by the various nations who require them.

The British Radium Standard.

The British Radium Standard, consisting of 21·10 milligrammes of pure radium chloride, has been certified in terms of the International Standard, and is now deposited at the National Physical Laboratory at Teddington. The radium salt is contained in a small glass tube, through which a platinum wire is inserted to dissipate accumulated electric charges (Fig. 52). The standard serves as a means of standardising radioactive preparations as well as the energy output of X-ray bulbs. In this connection it may be noted that Winawer and St. Sachs (*P.Z.* July 1915) have suggested that a beam of X rays should be regarded as having unit energy when, by its complete absorption in air, it produces the same number of ions as the γ rays from 1 gramme of radium (B $+$C) would produce under similar conditions.

FIG. 52.—The British Radium Standard at the National Physical Laboratory.

Standardisation of X-ray Bulbs.[1]

The difficulty of standardising the output of X-ray bulbs by means of such an ionisation standard is chiefly one of specifying and reproducing the working conditions of the bulbs. Possibly the various makers could be induced to work to standard dimensions, but few would assert that the design of an X-ray bulb has reached or even approached finality. Moreover, even if agreement in design were secured, the performance of a bulb is peculiarly susceptible to slight variations in the prevailing conditions (see p. 72), over some of which control is scarcely possible. The whole subject is receiving attention at the present time.

The output from an X-ray bulb must be specified with respect to (1) intensity, *i.e.* quantity per unit area, and (2) hardness or quality.

The X rays from a bulb consist of two main classes :

(1) the heterogeneous spectrum of " general " radiation with a range of quality which depends solely on the speeds of the parent cathode rays ;

(2) the homogeneous " characteristic " or " monochromatic " radiations which are characteristic of the metal of the anticathode (p. 117).

[1] For a full account of the various methods of measuring X rays (more especially for medical purposes), see Christen, *Messung und Dosierung der Röntgenstrahlen.*

The proportions of these two classes depend on the conditions of discharge, and on the metal of the anticathode. The general radiation is always present, and has a range of hardnesses which depends on the range of speeds of the cathode rays. The characteristic radiations only appear when the cathode rays are sufficiently fast ; their hardness depends only on the material of the anticathode.

METHODS OF MEASURING INTENSITY.

The intensity of the X rays at a particular point is defined as the energy falling on one square centimetre of a receiving surface passing through the point and placed at right angles to the rays. Röntgen showed, and the fact has been amply confirmed by later workers, that the intensity of a beam of X rays from a focus-bulb falls off as the inverse square of the distance from the anticathode.

General Remarks on Intensity Measurements.

It may be noted that almost all the methods of intensity-measurement, as ordinarily practised, are unduly favourable to the soft rays when regarded from an energy standpoint. The ideal method of test would afford an exact comparison of the energy of a hard X ray with that of a soft ray ; but what almost always happens is that the hard rays are not wholly arrested by the testing instrument, and hence show up relatively badly. In order to make a fair comparison between two bulbs, all the rays given out by both should be taken into account. The hard rays as well as the soft ones should be completely absorbed, in which case the measurements would give a fair estimate of the relative amounts of energy emitted from the bulbs.

(1) Current through the X-ray Tube.

A measure of the mean current passing through an X-ray tube may be obtained by the use of a milliammeter of approved type which may be relied upon to average up the fluctuating current. Kröncke (*A.d.P.* March 1914), Davey (*P.R.* Sept. 1914) and Rutherford, Barnes and

Richardson (*P.M.* Sept. 1915) all agree that for a given voltage the intensity of the "general" radiation is proportional to the current through the tube. Kröncke found that, except at low voltages, the following relation holds with sufficient accuracy for all practical purposes :

$$I = k . i \left(V^2 - V_0{}^2 \right)$$

where I is the intensity of the X rays, i the current, V the applied voltage, V_0 the breaking-down voltage, and k a constant for the tube. In the case of a Coolidge tube the expression becomes kiV^2 (see p. 112). This agrees with J. J. Thomson's formula (p. 134) that the energy of an X ray is proportional to the 4th power of the speed of the generating cathode ray.

As a practical fact, in the case of coil discharges, the proportionality between tube-current and X-ray intensity breaks down for heavy currents, the latter increasing but slightly as the current is raised.

It is difficult to estimate from the readings of a milliammeter the proportion of the fluctuating current, which is effective in producing rays of practical utility. As Salomonson (*J.Rt.S.* 1912) has shown, both the form and frequency of the interruptions must be controlled in exact measurements.

Alternatively the X-ray intensity is measured at some selected point in the beam by utilising one or other of the properties of the rays : heating, ionising, fluorescing, photographic, or chemical.

(2) **Thermal Methods of Measuring Intensity.**

The heat produced when X rays are completely absorbed by a metal was first measured by Dorn in 1897. Angerer (*A.d.P.* 1907) and Bumstead (*P.M.* 1908) have shown that the same amount of heat is generated by a stream of X rays, no matter what the absorbing metal. The heating effects are minute, and can only be detected by instruments as sensitive as the radiomicrometer, bolometer, or radiometer. It will be seen that the method is only fitted for the research laboratory, and does not enter into ordinary practice.

(3) **Ionisation Methods of Measuring Intensity.**

The exact mechanism of ionisation is even now not fully comprehended, but the outcome is the formation of positively

and negatively electrified particles—ions—the presence of
which imparts to the gas a conductivity that persists for
some little time. The extent of the ionisation depends on
the number of ions produced, and this is reflected in the
degree of excellence with which the gas conducts. The
generally accepted view of the formation of ions is that a
negative nucleus (the electron) is broken off from the atom,
leaving a positive nucleus ; each of these charged nuclei
gathers round itself a cluster of gas molecules—sometimes
in considerable numbers—and the resulting molecular aggre-
gates constitute the gaseous ions, both positive and negative.
At low pressures, the negative ion exists as the electron
unencumbered by any attached molecules.

An ionisation method of evaluating X rays thus resolves
itself into the measurement of an electric current—an operation which can be carried out with such delicacy and convenience that practically all recent workers have utilised
this property of the rays. The ionised gas is subjected to
an electric field which drives the two classes of ions—
positive and negative—in opposite directions with velocities
which depend on the strength of the field. The magnitude
of the current generated by the motion of these charged
particles depends to some extent on the potential difference
of the surfaces between which the field is applied ; with
small potentials, the two are roughly proportional, just as
in cases of metallic conduction ; but with higher potentials
the current responds less and less to the potential, and finally
reaches a constant value called the saturation current (see
Fig. 53). This is the current which should always be
measured in practice, and care should accordingly be exercised that the potential difference applied to the surfaces
is sufficient to give the saturation current. The electric
field necessary increases with the degree of ionisation, but
for most cases likely to arise in X-ray work, 100 volts per
cm. is adequate.

The shape of the first part of the current-potential curve
is explained by the liability of a charged particle to encounter
and coalesce with another of opposite sign before reaching
one of the bounding surfaces. But this tendency, which

militates, of course, against the growth of the current, will be lessened if the speed of the particles is increased by putting up the voltage between the surfaces. For the higher the speed, the shorter the time of passage, and the less likely are the chances of recombination. Finally, with the saturation voltage, all the ions reach the boundaries, and the number arriving exactly equals the number produced in the same time by the X rays passing through the gas. This

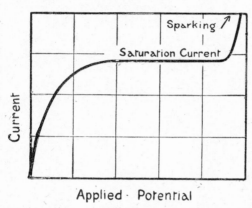

FIG. 53.—Diagrammatic representation of the relation between current and potential for an ionised gas.

is not the case with the lower voltages, and thus only from a knowledge of the saturation current can we infer the true degree of ionisation that the rays have produced.

With still higher potentials, the current rapidly increases until the sparking point is reached. On this steep part of the curve, both positive and negative ions acquire sufficient speed to produce fresh ions by colliding with the atoms of the gas. Thus, by working with potentials just insufficient to cause the passage of a spark, the original ionisation may be greatly increased—a hundredfold or so. The plan has been adopted for the measurement of very feeble ionisations.

Before adopting one or other of the various forms of ionisation chamber for any particular purpose, it is necessary to decide what we want. If it is the total energy of the rays that is desired, then we must arrange for the rays to be completely absorbed in the gas of the chamber, if necessary by contriving a suitably long path, or by increasing the pressure of the gas, or, again, by choosing a sufficiently dense gas [1] : the total ionisation, we have reason to believe, is a satisfactory measure of the total energy in the rays provided certain conditions are satisfied (see p. 155). If, on the other hand, we wish merely to ascertain the ionising power of a beam of rays at some particular point, then almost any form of ionisation chamber will suffice.

One convenient design is shown in Fig. 54. A circular thin aluminium sheet is mounted midway between two

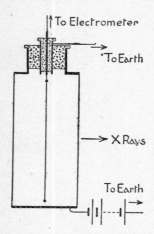

similar sheets which are raised to a potential of a few hundred volts by a battery of cells. The central sheet is carefully insulated and joined to an electrometer. It is easy to calculate the electric field with this shape of vessel, a statement that does not apply to the very common design made up of a cylinder provided with an insulated wire electrode along the axis.[2] In this latter form, the field, which is very strong near the wire, falls off a great deal towards the surface of the cylinder; the applied potential must be very considerable to ensure a saturating field throughout the chamber.

FIG. 54.—An ionisation chamber, showing earthed guard-tube in the insulation.

Ionisation currents produced by X rays are usually of the order of 10^{-10} to 10^{-15} ampere ; the exact amount varies a great deal according to the circumstances. For the larger currents, it is sometimes possible to use a sensitive galvanometer [3] ; but in general it is much more convenient to

---

[1] *E.g.* sulphur dioxide or methyl iodide are very useful for the purpose.

[2] See, for instance, the comparison ionisation chamber in Fig. 73.

[3] The most sensitive galvanometers yet introduced are the Paschen and the Einthoven. The former, with a low resistance and a short period, will readily indicate 10^{-10} ampere.

deduce the current from the change of potential as measured by means of a Dolezalek quadrant electrometer or some form of gold-leaf electroscope.   With an electrometer and a suitable condenser, currents from 10^{-8} to 10^{-14} ampere can be measured.   For smaller currents—down to 10^{-17} ampere—an electroscope is better.

Of the electroscopes, the C. T. R. Wilson tilted variety [1] is convenient and sensitive, and possesses a small capacity. Some observers use electroscopes provided with aluminium windows, the X rays being sent directly into the electroscope instead of into a separate chamber.   The leaf in this case is charged to a high potential, and its rate of leak to the outer case is measured.   There are on the market several direct reading X-ray quantimeters of this type, for example, the Szilard ionto-quantimeter, which is being increasingly used in deep radiotherapy.   All such instruments require to be calibrated, and their capacity (as well as that of the ionisation vessel) determined, before the currents can be deduced from the potential measurements.

The French workers largely employ the late Prof. Curie's piézo-électrique, in which the electricity generated by gradually relieving the tension on a stretched quartz lamina is balanced against the ionisation current to be measured. The method requires considerable manipulative skill.[2]

(4) Photographic and Fluorescence Methods of Measuring Intensity.

Practically all the earlier workers used photographic or fluorescence methods of measuring the intensity of their X rays, but nowadays these methods, at any rate for most purposes, have been displaced by ionisation methods.   An ordinary photographic plate records only about 1 per cent. of the energy of the X rays, and this figure is less for hard rays than for soft, so that the softer rays are given undue weight when a heterogeneous beam is tested.   We need, therefore, to exercise care in drawing conclusions from the density of the photographic image as to the intensity of the rays. Moreover, Barkla and Martyn (*P.M.* 1913) have shown that

---

[1] See, for example, the Camb. & Paul Inst. Co.'s list of electrometers.
[2] See Rutherford's *Radioactive Substances*.

if the X rays are just sufficiently hard to excite the radiations characteristic of silver or of bromine (the heaviest constituents of a photographic film), they are selectively absorbed and the photographic effect is greatly enhanced. X rays a little softer than this do not excite the characteristic rays, and are, therefore, recorded disadvantageously. Thus the photographic action may not be proportional to the absorption of the X rays by the sensitive film.[1]

As far as practical difficulties are concerned, it should be remarked that the emulsion on an ordinary plate may vary in thickness by as much as 10 per cent., through want of flatness of the glass backing. This can be reduced to the order of 5 per cent. by the use of patent plate glass and the exercise of special care in the coating. The slower fine grained plates are to be preferred for more precise work, and, of course, one should adhere to some standard developer and method of development.

To the worker with limited resources the photographic method of measuring intensity offers advantages because of its simplicity. Some form of opacity-meter for obtaining a measure of the density of the image is the chief requirement. The opacity meter measures the extent to which a standard beam of light is cut down by the photographic film whose density is required. If I_0 is the intensity of the testing light which is incident on the developed film, and I_t that of the transmitted light, then, if μx is the fraction of the energy which is absorbed by a very small thickness, x, of the film,

$$I_t = I_0 e^{-\mu d},$$

where d is the thickness of the film [2] (see p. 104). The film is assumed equally dense throughout its thickness.

For films of uniform thickness, d is constant, so that μ is proportional to $\log (I_0/I_t)$. μ is called the absorp-

---

[1] See Voltz (*P.Z.* Aug. 1915), who investigated the point and considers the photographic measurement of X rays should be discarded. Kröncke (*A.d.P.* March 1914) came to a similar conclusion. He obtained 50 per cent. discrepancy between ionisation and photographic methods.

[2] More precisely, this assumes monochromatic light. μ is different for different wave-lengths.

tion coefficient ; (I_0/I_t) is known as the opacity,[1] and equals the number of times the incident light is cut down. $\text{Log}\,(I_0/I_t)$ is termed the opacity-logarithm. Now, by definition, μ is proportional to the density of the image, *i.e.* to the amount of silver per unit area of film. Thus the ratio of two opacity-logarithms gives the ratio of the film densities, and therefore the ratio of the photographic energies in the two cases. The opacity meter is graduated to read directly in opacity-logarithms.

In fluorescence methods the luminosity is matched against some standard fluorescence excited by a steady source of radiation such as radium. The drawback to such methods is that the fluorescing salt becomes " tired " under the action of the rays. The sensitivity of a screen may also vary considerably from point to point, so that it is difficult to make a fair comparison. Barium platinocyanide is the material commonly used to sensitise a fluorescent screen. This salt, which has the formula $BaPt(CN)_4, 4H_2O$ exists in three different forms, of which the green crystalline variety is by far the most efficient for fluorescent purposes (Levy, *J.Rt.S.* 1916). Cadmium tungstate is also used. (p. 167).

(5) Methods of Measuring Intensity used in Medicine.

In the therapeutic use of X rays, various chemical reactions brought about by the rays have been suggested and employed from time to time as aids to " dosage " ; for example, the discolouring of various alkaline salts (Holzknecht, 1902) ; the liberation of iodine from a 2 per cent. solution of iodoform in chloroform [2] (Freund, 1904 ; Bordier and Galimard, 1906) ; the darkening of a photographic paper (Kienböck), see p. 96 ; the precipitation of calomel from a mixture of mercuric chloride and ammonium oxalate solutions [2] (Schwarz, 1907) ; and the change of colour of pastilles of compressed barium platinocyanide (Sabouraud-Noiré and Bordier). X rays resemble light in their property of lowering the electrical resistance of selenium ; this property, which is discounted by the fatiguing of the

---

[1] The transparency is the reciprocal of the opacity.

[2] X rays share this property with Ra rays and ultra-violet light.

selenium, is turned to account in the intensimeter of Fürstenau (*P.Z.* Aug. 1915). Most of these methods furnish only a rough notion of the intensity of a beam of X rays.

Of all the various intensity-measurers, the pastille finds most favour with medical men. The barium-platinocyanide discs are some 5 mms. in diameter, and their colour, initially a bright green, changes, when exposed to the rays, to a pale yellow, and finally to a deep orange. The pastille is placed at a specified distance from the anticathode of the bulb, and the colour is matched against one of a number of standard tints. The method is extremely easy in practice, and is fairly reliable as a guide for short exposures, but it is not very trustworthy for times exceeding ten minutes or so.[1] The pastille method is defective in that it attempts to measure rays of all qualities by a surface coloration. Other platinocyanides show similar colour changes when exposed to X rays. Levy has shown that the change of colour is due to a change from the crystalline to the amorphous condition. If the pastille is put aside, the reverse change slowly takes place, especially in the presence of light, so that the pastille should not be exposed to full daylight during the X-ray treatment. Ultra-violet light and radium rays cause similar browning in such pastilles.

The following table gives an idea of the relation between the different dosemeter scales :

5H units [2]	(Holzknecht ; alkaline salt)
= Tint B	(Sabouraud-Noiré ; pastille)
= Tint 1	(Bordier ; varnished pastille)
= 3 to 4I	(Bordier and Galimard ; iodine solution)
= 10X units	(Kienböck ; photographic plate)
= 3·5 Kaloms	(Schwarz ; mercury solution)
= Villard dose.	

[1] See, however, Owen and Bowes, *J.Rt.S.* July 1921.

[2] Unit 1H = one-third of the radiation necessary to set up the first signs of reaction in the healthy skin of the face.

METHODS OF MEASURING QUALITY OR HARDNESS.

The range of qualities of X rays is very wide, as would be inferred from the fact that, while some rays are unable to penetrate more than a millimetre or two of air at atmospheric pressure, others have been detected at distances of 100 metres or more.

It is now well established that no matter whether the exciting voltage is constant or pulsating, a spectrum of X rays is generated containing a wide range of qualities or wave-lengths. As pointed out on p. 246, this spectrum is terminated very sharply at the short-wave end at a point connected by Planck's quantum relation with the maximum voltage applied. The potential difference between the electrodes is thus the dominating factor, controlling as it does the speed of the cathode rays.

With fluctuating potential, the maximum potential difference is doubtless responsible for generating a large proportion of the X rays. There are several ways of measuring this maximum potential.

In the case of the characteristic radiations, the quality can be defined rigorously in terms of the atomic weight of the anticathode. A certain minimum voltage on the tube is required to excite a particular series of lines. There is thus a critical cathode-ray velocity for each characteristic X radiation : slower cathode rays can only excite " independent " rays ; faster cathode rays are, within limits, increasingly effective generators of the characteristic rays, but with very high-speed rays the " independent " radiation is once again generated. The subject is dealt with later (p. 133), but it may here be mentioned that the critical cathode-ray speed is proportional to the atomic weight, or rather the atomic number of the anticathode.

If E is the potential difference to which a cathode ray owes its velocity (v), then the two are connected by the energy equation

$$\tfrac{1}{2}m \cdot v^2 = E \cdot e,$$

where e and m are respectively the charge and the mass of the cathode ray.

Taking $e/m = 1.77 \times 10^7$, E in volts and v in cms./sec.,

$$E = 2.82v^2 \cdot 10^{-16}$$

or
$$v = 5.95\sqrt{E} \cdot 10^7.$$

It is thus possible by measuring v by means of the magnetic deflection in a known field to arrive at the value of E. A series of values of cathode-ray velocities and potentials up to 200,000 volts is tabulated on p. 286.

The Alternative Spark-Gap.

The maximum voltage applied to a tube may be measured by a high-potential electrostatic voltmeter or, more commonly, by means of the alternative spark-gap between points or spheres. Some experience is necessary with the spark-gap, especially in the case of a gas X-ray tube where the method tends to give too high values, especially with pulsating potentials. In the case of Coolidge radiator tubes, excited by unrectified alternating potential, the spark-gap will register the "inverse" voltage rather than the lower "effective" voltage.

The work of Peek and others has shown that a spark-gap between spherical electrodes of equal size is preferable to that between points. The spark between points is now generally discredited for high voltages on account of its inconsistent dependency on atmospheric humidity and frequency of discharge. By reason of its time-lag, its readings may be largely in error in the case of high-frequency steep impulses.

On the other hand, frequency and wave shape have no appreciable effect in the case of the sphere gap, and the effects of variation in the atmospheric conditions are well known and can be readily corrected for.

The size of the spheres is important. A good rule is not to use a gap bigger than the diameter of either of the balls, though some latitude may be permitted in this direction. The main point is to avoid the break-down discharge being preceded by brush-discharge or corona, otherwise a pulsating discharge will, in general, give gap readings much too high. With the above precaution a sphere gap is capable of measuring voltages from, say, 10,000 volts to 500,000 volts to an accuracy of about 2 per cent. It must be understood that the method yields peak voltages and not the usual root-mean-square voltage ($=$peak/1·4) of the electrical engineer.

The table below is based on Dr. A. Russell's formula and incorporates the latest results of the American Institute of Electrical Engineers (1918). The spheres are smooth polished metal balls of the same size. The table includes also, for convenience, a column of figures for a needle-point gap (No. 00 new sewing needles) which furnish a rough notion of the voltages for an instrument which is still much used. The A.I.E.E. recommend that for voltages above 70,000 (and preferably above 40,000) a sphere gap should always be employed.

The gap should not be exposed to any extraneous ionising influence, such as an arc or an adjacent spark, nor should the gap be enclosed. The first spark is the one for which the reading should be taken, but repeat observations should be made to avoid measuring adventitious surging. The use of a water resistance in series with the gap will prevent arcing and pitting of the sphere surfaces.

It may be added that a point-and-plane gap is longer than a point-and-point gap for the same voltage. For example, with a 6 cm. diameter plate the former is longer by about

50 per cent. at	50,000 volts.
25 ,, ,,	75,000 ,,
15 ,, ,,	100,000 ,,
10 ,, ,,	125,000 ,,

The plate should be made the negative electrode.

The figures below refer to an atmospheric pressure of 760 mm., a temp. of 25° C., and a humidity of 80 per cent. Where any gap is being used outside its recommended limits the figures are shown in brackets. The blank spaces indicate that the gap is no longer suitable. The gaps are given to three significant figures for interpolation purposes.

Table V. A (applicable only to sphere gaps) gives the relative air-density under different conditions. The figures are relative to dry air at 25° C. and 760 mm. pressure.

TABLE V. SPARK-GAP VOLTAGES.

Kilo Volts (Peak).	Diameter of Spheres.					
	Needle-points.		2·5 cm.	5 cm.	10 cm.	25 cm.	50 cm.
	cm. gap.	inches gap.	cm. gap.	cm. gap.	cm. gap.	cm. gap.	cm. gap.
5	(0·42)	(0·17)	(0·13)	(0·15)	(0·15)	(0·16)	(0·17)
10	(0·85)	(0·33)	0·27	0·29	0·30	0·32	0·33
15	1·30	0·51	0·42	0·44	0·46	0·48	0·50
20	1·75	0·69	0·58	0·60	0·62	0·64	0·67
25	2·20	0·87	0·76	0·77	0·78	0·81	0·84
30	2·69	1·06	0·95	0·94	0·95	0·98	1·01
35	3·20	1·26	1·17	1·12	1·12	1·15	1·18
40	3·81	1·50	1·41	1·30	1·29	1·32	1·35
45	4·49	1·77	1·68	1·50	1·47	1·49	1·52
50	5·20	2·05	2·00	1·71	1·65	1·66	1·69
60	6·81	2·68	2·82	2·17	2·02	2·01	2·04
70	8·81	3·47	(4·05)	2·68	2·42	2·37	2·39
80	(11·1)	(4·36)	—	3·26	2·84	2·74	2·75
90	(13·3)	(5·23)	—	3·94	3·28	3·11	3·10
100	(15·5)	(6·10)	—	4·77	3·75	3·49	3·46
110	(17·7)	(6·96)	—	5·79	4·25	3·88	3·83
120	(19·8)	(7·81)	—	(7·07)	4·78	4·28	4·20
130	(22·0)	(8·65)	—	—	5·35	4·69	4·57
140	(24·1)	(9·48)	—	—	5·97	5·10	4·94
150	(26·1)	(10·3)	—	—	6·64	5·52	5·32
160	(28·1)	(11·1)	—	—	7·37	5·95	5·70
170	(30·1)	(11·9)	—	—	8·16	6·39	6·09
180	(32·0)	(12·6)	—	—	9·03	6·84	6·48
190	(33·9)	(13·3)	—	—	10·0	7·30	6·88
200	(35·7)	(14·0)	—	—	11·1	7·76	7·28
210	(37·6)	(14·8)	—	—	(12·3)	8·24	7·68
220	(39·5)	(15·5)	—	—	(13·7)	8·73	8·09
230	(41·4)	(16·3)	—	—	(15·3)	9·24	8·50
240	(43·3)	(17·0)	—	—	—	9·76	8·92
250	(45·2)	(17·8)	—	—	—	10·3	9·34
300	(54·7)	(21·6)	—	—	—	13·3	11·5

TABLE V. A.

Temperature.	Pressure 720 mm.	Pressure 740 mm.	Pressure 760 mm.	Pressure 780 mm.
0° C.	1·04	1·06	1·09	1·12
10°	1·00	1·02	1·05	1·08
20°	0·96	0·99	1·02	1·04
30°	0·93	0·96	0·98	1·01

Within the limits of the above table, the correction factor for a sphere gap agrees substantially with the relative air-density. Thus for a given length of spark-gap the tabulated kilovoltage in Table V. must be multiplied by the appropriate correction factor in Table V.A. Alternatively, to calculate the gap which will just be sparked over by some specified voltage, the voltage must first be divided by the appropriate correction factor before Table V. is used. It will be seen that under normal conditions the correction is small or negligible.

If a spark-gap with unequal-sized balls is used, the smaller electrode controls the spark-gap for moderate lengths of spark : the larger ball should be made the negative electrode.

It may be added that Trowbridge (*P.M.* 1898) found a spark-length of 200 cms. with a potential of 3,000,000 volts.

(1) Wave-Length.

We have good reason now for believing that X rays and light are identical, and that the hardness or penetrating power of an X ray is precisely defined by its wave-length : the shorter the wave-length, the harder the ray. The subject is dealt with elsewhere (p. 209), but it has been shown by many observers that X rays may be diffracted by the invisible parallel planes of atoms in the interior of a crystal. From a knowledge of the distances separating the atoms, we can arrive at the wave-lengths of the X rays. W. L. Bragg (*P.R.S.* 1913) has calculated the atomic distances in the case of rock-salt (p. 237), and the wave-lengths of the X rays, so far examined by this method, are found to lie mainly between 10^{-7} cm. and 10^{-9} cm. (see p. 240).

(2) Absorption-Coefficients.

The customary way of specifying the character of X rays is to measure their absorption in a sheet of aluminium of definite thickness. Aluminium is not an ideal standard of reference, but it is chosen because it is readily procurable in convenient form, and, so far as we know, does not, in the majority of cases, complicate matters unduly by superposing a characteristic radiation.

Now it is found that if all the rays both entering and leaving a plate of material are homogeneous (that is, wholly of the same quality), then the rays are absorbed exponentially by the plate, i.e. if 1, 2, 3, ... similar sheets are successively introduced, each additional sheet absorbs the same fraction of what it receives. In other words, if there is no " scattering " or transformation of the X rays, and if μx is the fraction of the intensity which is absorbed when the rays pass normally through a very thin screen of thickness x (cm.), then for a plate of thickness d (cms.),

$$I = I_0 \cdot e^{-\mu d},$$

in which I_0 is the intensity of the beam when it enters, and I that of the beam when it leaves the screen. $e(=2 \cdot 72)$ is the base of the hyperbolic system of logarithms. μ is termed the linear absorption coefficient.[1]

It follows that $\mu = \dfrac{2 \cdot 3}{d} (\log I_0 - \log I)$; the logarithms are to base 10. If in a set of observations with homogeneous rays, $\log I$ is plotted as ordinate against d, the graph is a straight line and μ is $2 \cdot 3$ times the slope of the line.

With ordinary heterogeneous rays, μ is greater for thin screens than for thick, and so we can only deal with an average μ, which, however, varies more and more slowly as the screen becomes thicker.

The logarithmic curve of absorption for heterogeneous rays, such as are given out by an ordinary X-ray bulb, is not a straight line, but a curve which is steeper for thin screens

---

[1] The precise physical interpretation of an exponential law of absorption is not so simple as its compact and convenient mathematical expression would lead one to suppose.

than for thick. The general shape is rather steeper than the heavy curve in Fig. 64. For a method of finding analytically the absorption coefficients of the constituents of a complex beam of rays, see J. J. Thomson, *P.M.* Dec. 1915.

In the case of the characteristic radiations, an element exhibits a maximum transparency to radiations approximating to its characteristic. For slightly harder rays than these, the absorption rapidly increases, the rays characteristic of the screen are produced and superposed on the transmitted rays to an extent which diminishes as the incident rays are increasingly hardened. For incident rays softer than the critical type, no characteristic rays are produced. Thus, as the incident rays are gradually hardened, the transmitted rays reach a maximum intensity when the incident rays approximate in quality to each of the characteristic rays in turn.

A large value of μ corresponds to easily absorbed rays, and a small one to very penetrating rays. μ also varies with the nature of the absorbing screen, so that it is necessary to specify the material used. For medical purposes, it has recently been suggested that water should be chosen as the standard absorbing medium, since the absorptive power of water agrees closely with that of animal tissue.

Some workers prefer to think in terms of the thickness, D, which reduces the intensity to half value. D is connected with μ by the expression $D = 0 \cdot 69/\mu$. A notion of the order of values of μ may be got from the fact that for an X-ray beam of average hardness μ_{Al} lies between 4 and 8 cm.$^{-1}$; for hard rays between 2 and 4 cm.$^{-1}$. μ for fatty tissue varies from about $0 \cdot 4$ for hard rays to $0 \cdot 7$ for medium rays. 1 cm. of flesh absorbs from 30 to 90 per cent. of X rays. A table connecting I_0/I and μd is given on p. 285.

A more fundamentally important constant is obtained by dividing the absorption coefficient (μ) by the density (ρ) of the absorbing screen.[1] This quantity, μ/ρ—usually called the mass-absorption coefficient—gives a measure of the absorption per unit mass of the screen for a normally incident pencil of rays of unit cross section. Since it is mass alone that affects absorption, at any rate as determined by the usual

[1] For aluminium, $\rho = 2 \cdot 7$.

methods of measurement, it is more profitable to use mass-coefficients than linear-coefficients.

If, as was at one time supposed, the absorbing powers of different materials were truly proportional to their densities, then for the same rays μ/ρ would be a constant, no matter what the substance used as screen. In point of fact, dense substances are a good deal more absorptive, mass for mass, than light, and μ/ρ increases rapidly with the atomic weight of the screen.[1] The increase is more noticeable with hard rays than with soft (see also p. 140).

Benoist (*J.d.P.* 1901) was the first to examine systematically the absorption of a beam of ordinary heterogeneous X rays in various absorbing elements. For our purposes it is convenient to translate his results into quantities proportional to absorption coefficients ; and, when this is done, Fig. 55 is the result. It will be noticed that μ/ρ increases steadily with atomic weight both for hard and soft X rays. For example, with hard rays, lead is twenty-five, silver eighteen, and copper eight times as absorbent as an equal mass of aluminium. There would appear to be a region of abnormal absorption round and about silver.

The relationship between absorption coefficients and wave-lengths (λ) is dealt with on p. 253. As is there shown, when the effect of scattering is allowed for

$$\mu = k\ \lambda^n,$$

where k is a constant, and n lies between 5/2 and 3.

Absorption Coefficients of Heterogeneous Rays.

But it may be urged that although characteristic rays have a perfectly definite μ, the X rays from an ordinary bulb are so very far from being homogeneous that the absorption coefficients as above defined are not particularly useful in X-ray practice. However, considerable guidance can be obtained from a knowledge of even an average value of μ, calculated though it may be, on loose assumptions.

---

[1] A similar relation holds for the soft γ rays from radium. For hard γ rays, a density law holds, and μ/ρ is constant, except for the heaviest metals, which are a little more absorbent. In other words, these very penetrating rays almost entirely ignore atomic structure. For hard γ rays, $\mu/\rho = 0.04$ for all absorbing substances with an atomic weight less than 100.

And, moreover, while it is true that the X rays from a bulb are in general very heterogeneous, they become less so as the spark-gap is increased.[1] The rays from a bulb with a spark-gap of some centimetres, which are transmitted by

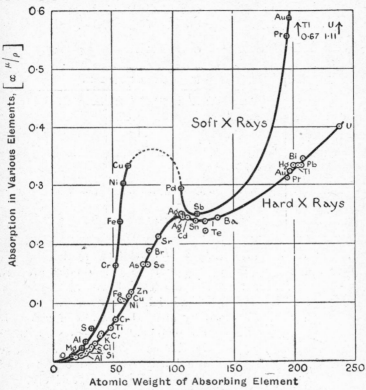

FIG. 55.—Graph (derived from Benoist's transparency curve) connecting absorption with atomic weight and displaying a region of selective absorption.

an aluminium screen 5 mms. or more thick, are very fairly though not strictly homogeneous.

Absorption Coefficients in Air.

On a density basis, the absorption by 1 cm. of air under

---

[1] The explanation of this is probably bound up with the simpler character of the magnetic spectrum of the cathode rays at low pressures (see p. 16).

ordinary conditions is equivalent to that by $\frac{1}{820}$ cm. of water.

Eve and Day (*P.M.* 1912) have measured at various ranges (up to 100 metres) the absorption coefficients in air of the rays from X-ray bulbs of different degrees of hardness. Table VI. contains some of their results.

TABLE VI. ABSORPTION COEFFICIENTS IN AIR.

Alternative Spark-gap.	Distances from X-ray Bulb.					
	4 to 10 metres.		20 to 40 metres.		40 to 60 metres.	
	μ	μ/ρ	μ	μ/ρ	μ	μ/ρ
1·5 to 5 cm. (soft bulb) -	$\begin{cases} 0\cdot0018 \\ \text{to} \\ 0\cdot0010 \end{cases}$	$\begin{cases} 1\cdot4 \\ \text{to} \\ 0\cdot8 \end{cases}$	—	—	—	—
11 cm. (medium bulb) -	0·00040	0·32	0·00040	0·32	0·00029	0·23
30 cm. (hard bulb) -	0·00029	0·23	0·00027	0·21	0·00014(?)	0·11(?)

Eve and Day note that $\mu = 0\cdot0004$ is a good value for radiographic work; but rays whose μ is 0·0003 are too penetrating for such a purpose. The above values may be compared with those of Chadwick (*P.P.S.* 1912) for the Ra γ rays when absorbed by air. His values of μ for air are 0·000062 and 0·000059 cm.$^{-1}$ in the case of rays which have previously traversed 3 mms. and 10 mms. of lead respectively.

The absorption coefficients for the various characteristic radiations are given on pp. 120 and 139.

(3) The Benoist Penetrometer.

Among medical men Benoist's radiochromometer or penetrometer enjoys extensive use as a measurer of hardness. It consists of a thin silver disc 0·11 mm. thick, surrounded by twelve numbered aluminium sectors from 1 to

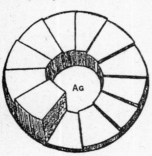

FIG. 56.—Benoist's penetrometer.

12 mms. thick (Fig. 56).   The X rays are sent through the instrument, and the observations consist merely in matching on a fluorescent screen or photographic plate the image cast by the silver disc against the images of the aluminium plates : the thickness of the matching sector increases with the hardness of the rays.[1]   "Benoist No. 4 to 5" is a good average hardness for curative work, while for general radiography No. 6 on Benoist's scale is useful.   A notion of the discharge potential across a tube may be got from the very rough relation that the peak voltage is from 5,000 to 10,000 times the Benoist reading of the X rays.

Table VII. gives very approximately the relation between Benoist numbers and absorption coefficients in aluminium.

TABLE VII.

Benoist No.	Mean μ/ρ_{Al}.
2	20
3	8
4	4
6	2
8	1·5
10	1
12	0·5

(4) **Other Penetrometers.**

Walter Penetrometer.   This consists of a number of holes in a lead disc, which are covered by a sequence of platinum discs of gradually increasing thickness.

The *Wehnelt Penetrometer* agrees in principle with that of Benoist.   An aluminium wedge is used instead of a series of stepped sectors.

Röntgen in his third memoir described an instrument essentially similar to Benoist's, with the exception that the comparison metal was platinum instead of silver.

[1] Benoist (*C.R.* 1902) based the theory of his instrument on the curves displayed in Fig. 55, which go to show that while the transparency of aluminium alters a good deal with the quality of the X rays, silver is almost equally transparent to both hard and soft rays.   As Table XI. shows, the assumption of a constant transparency for silver is by no means correct.

Christen's Half-value Penetrometer. Christen adopts as a definition of quality the thickness of a layer of water (or, in actual practice, bakelite), which will reduce the intensity of a beam of rays to half its original value.

The rays are sent through a stepped wedge of bakelite, alongside which is a perforated metal plate. This provides a standard of reference on a fluorescent screen, the two images being side by side. The holes in the plate are so designed that the area of the metal removed equals that which remains, so that the plate by this means reduces the intensity of a beam of rays to half-value. The holes are small enough to produce uniform illumination on a screen placed a short distance behind the plate.

Bauer Qualimeter. This is a species of uni-polar electrostatic voltmeter, which serves to measure the potential difference between the electrodes of a tube.   (See p. 197.)

The *Klingelfuss Qualimeter* consists of an auxiliary search coil and electrostatic voltmeter. The instrument works somewhat similarly to the Bauer.

The hardness-numbers of the various penetrometers are all much the same as Benoist's, except those of Wehnelt, which are 50 per cent. bigger for the same quality of rays.

The " Energetics " of an X-ray Bulb.

When a stream of cathode rays strikes an anticathode, the different rays suffer a variety of fates. By far the greater number merely fritter away their energy until it becomes too small to render them distinguishable : the heat generated at the anticathode is ample proof that the energy of the cathode rays is mostly dissipated into heat.

A large proportion of the cathode rays, in some cases as much as 75 per cent., are " reflected " by the anticathode in all directions against the glass walls of the tube with velocities which may be anything up to the original speed of the cathode rays. There is good evidence for believing that a cathode ray can pass through many atoms without being in any way deflected or transformed. The fate of the cathode ray is to some extent dependent on the material

of the anticathode.   The heavier the atom the more capable
it is of swinging round a cathode ray which endeavours to
pass it.

Only a small proportion of the cathode rays are effective in
producing X rays.   The chances that a cathode ray will
ultimately come into suitable conflict with some atom and
so generate an X ray are slight.   In fact, the efficiency of
the present methods of generation of X rays is very low :
the X ray is merely a small bye-product in the energy
transformations of a Röntgen tube.

Wien, Angerer, and Carter (*A.d.P.* 1905 and 1906) have
worked independently at the subject.   They agree that the
ratio of the energy of the X rays to that of the exciting
(heterogeneous) cathode rays is of the order of $\frac{1}{1000}$; Carter
found that the efficiency increases with the hardness (is, in
fact, proportional to the voltage on the tube), is independent
of the current, but increases with the atomic weight of the
anticathode.   This value of the efficiency is not inconsistent
with the estimate of Eve and Day (*P.M.* 1912), who remark
that, of the energy supplied to an ordinary X-ray bulb, not
more than about 1 in 20,000 is contained in the X rays as
measured by their ionising ability.

The efficiency of a soft bulb is probably even less than
this, for more energy is converted into heat with low-speed
cathode rays.   The energy of general X radiation is proportional to the 4th power of the velocity of the exciting
cathode rays (see p. 134).

Winawer (*P.Z.* Nov. 1915) claims from his experiments that
to work an X-ray bulb to greatest advantage, the exciting
current should for a given load :

(1) be made up of short duration impulses as widely
separated as possible,

(2) produce the greatest heating of the anticathode.

Beatty's Experiments.

Beatty (*P.R.S.* Nov. 1913) carefully evaluated the energy
of X rays in terms of the velocity of the parent cathode rays
and of the atomic weight of the anticathode.   Homogeneous
rays of known velocity were sifted from a cathode stream

by a magnetic-spectrum method, and fell upon one of a number of anticathodes affixed to a sliding tray. The X rays so produced passed through a sheet of Al foil 0·0002 cm. thick, and were *completely* absorbed in an ionisation chamber consisting of a cylinder over a metre long filled with the vapour of methyl iodide. The resulting total ionisation was taken as measuring the energy of the X rays. The ionisation current was balanced against a fraction taken from the primary cathode-ray current by a variable shunt, so that a null deflection was obtained in the electroscope (see p. 135). Thus reliable readings could be obtained even when the cathode-ray current was very irregular.

The ionisation which the cathode rays would have produced in methyl iodide vapour was deduced from the work of Glasson (p. 12) and Whiddington (p. 10) on the passage of cathode rays in air.

The result finally established by Beatty was

$$\frac{E_X}{E_C} = 0·51 \times 10^{-4} A\beta^2,[1]$$

where E_X = energy of the X rays,
              E_C = energy of the parent cathode rays,
              A = atomic weight of anticathode,
              β = velocity of the cathode rays expressed as a fraction of the velocity of light (*i.e.* 3×10^{10} cms./sec.).

Thus, for an anticathode of platinum (with an atomic weight of 195) and a bulb of medium hardness, with cathode rays of speed, say $9·5 \times 10^9$ cms./sec., $\frac{1}{1000}$ of the cathode-ray energy reappears as X rays. With slower cathode rays, or an anticathode of lower atomic weight, the fraction would be smaller.

These results refer only to the " independent " or primary X rays (p. 134). When characteristic rays are excited, their effects have to be added to those given by the above formula. The efficiency of an X-ray bulb is much greater when a characteristic radiation is strongly excited. A formula comprising both classes of radiation has not yet been obtained.

[1] See p. 91 ; also Rutherford and Barnes, *P.M.* Sept. 1915.

CHAPTER IX.

SCATTERED, CHARACTERISTIC AND SECONDARY CORPUSCULAR RAYS.

WHEN a beam of X rays strikes a substance there are two things that may happen. Part of the beam may be absorbed, which means that it is transformed into radiations characteristic of the material, the process always being accompanied by the liberation of electrons or corpuscular rays. The rest of the beam is scattered or dispersed which, in effect, is equivalent to stating that while the rays are unaltered in quality a considerable proportion of them have their direction altered. Scattering finds a close parallel in the dispersion of light by a fog.

The proportions of the two classes depend both on the substance and on the quality of the primary rays. With materials of low atomic weight, by far the greater proportion of the X rays, if of a penetrating type, is merely scattered. With a medium weight or heavy atom, the proportion of scattered radiation depends upon the wave-length and may be small.

SCATTERED X RAYS.

All substances, when exposed to a beam of X rays, themselves give out X rays, some of which are identical with the primary rays in quality, and can, in fact, be conveniently regarded as so many unchanged primary rays which have been merely "scattered" or deviated in direction by the substance. Such scattered radiation may be readily perceived experimentally by exposing a body of low density to X rays and viewing it with a fluorescent screen which is itself shielded from the direct action of the rays from the bulb.

Scattering produced by Different Elements.

Scattering occurs at all depths, and increases in amount with the thickness traversed by the rays.

The elements of low atomic weight (up to sulphur) scatter very much the same, mass for mass; but the heavier elements scatter proportionally more than the light elements, though, owing to the greater absorbing power of the denser elements, it may happen that less of the scattered radiation actually escapes. With elements of quite low atomic weight, such as carbon, a considerable proportion of the emerging rays is merely scattered radiation, more especially if the primary rays are of a penetrating type. The scattered radiation from aluminium is a good deal less in amount than that from vegetable or animal matter, in which cases it may amount to 90 per cent. or more.

With the copper group of elements, the scattered radiation is so small in amount (sometimes less than $\frac{1}{200}$ of the total radiation) that it is, for most purposes, negligible.

Barkla has introduced a coefficient of scattering, σ, which is defined similarly to the absorption coefficient μ (p. 104). For an absorbing screen of low atomic weight, Barkla and Dunlop (*P.M.* March 1916) find that σ is roughly proportional to the density, ρ, of the scattering substance; and the mass-scattering coefficient, σ/ρ, is approximately constant (0·2) no matter what the screen or the quality of the X rays. For elements of higher atomic weight, σ/ρ increases only slightly with atomic weight in the case of hard rays, but with soft rays, σ/ρ increases very considerably with atomic weight. Crowther (*P.R.S.* 1912) came to much the same conclusion.

In those instances where scattering accompanies absorption, for example, when hard rays are sent through light elements it is necessary to subtract the scattering term from the total absorption to obtain the true or transformation absorption. In other words :—

$$\frac{\mu}{\rho} = \frac{\tau}{\rho} + \frac{\sigma}{\rho},$$

i.e., $\left(\begin{smallmatrix}\text{Observed absorption}\\\text{coefficient.}\end{smallmatrix}\right) = \left(\begin{smallmatrix}\text{Transformation}\\\text{coefficient.}\end{smallmatrix}\right) + \left(\begin{smallmatrix}\text{Scattering}\\\text{coefficient.}\end{smallmatrix}\right)$

Distribution of Scattered X Rays.

The scattered X rays are distributed in all directions, though not uniformly ; more are to be found in the backward and forward directions of the original beam than at right angles.

Barkla and Ayres (*P.M.* 1911) and Owen (*P.C.P.S.* 1911) have experimentally verified, over a considerable angular range, the approximate truth of the distribution formula derived from Sir J. J. Thomson's theory of scattering :

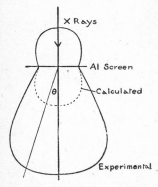

$$I_\theta = I_{\pi/2}(1+\cos^2\theta),$$

FIG. 57.—Distribution of scattered X rays from an aluminium screen.

where I_θ is the intensity of the scattered radiation along the direction angle θ to the primary beam. Thus the " fore and aft " intensity is roughly twice that at right angles. Experiment shows, however, that the expression is inadequate for small values of θ—the calculated values are too small— and that, moreover, the forward intensity always exceeds the backward. Fig. 57 shows the distribution obtained by Crowther (*P.R.S.* 1912) in the case of an aluminium plate.

It follows that the intensity of the rays received on a specified area at a depth within the interior of a body may be considerably augmented by scattered rays which originally were not directed at the area in question.

Polarisation of Scattered X Rays.

In 1905, Barkla (*P.T.*) found that the scattered X rays from a plate bombarded by primary X rays do not distribute themselves quite uniformly in a plane at right angles to the line of flight of the primary rays, but tend to congregate in one particular plane passing through the line of flight of the primary rays. This plane of maximum intensity is at right angles to the path of the cathode rays in the generating X-ray tube. The intensity of the scattered rays falls off on either side of this plane, and reaches a minimum in a perpendicular plane (see Fig. 58). Thus, if X rays were visible, an observer, looking along the beam of primary X rays at the plate, would notice that the scattered rays would be brighter in two opposite quadrants than in the intervening quadrants.

The distribution of the scattered rays thus reveals a peculiarity in the primary rays ; evidently they also predominate in one plane, and hence may be said to be polarised. If the scattered rays themselves are allowed to fall on a second radiator, the asymmetry or " polarisation " is more complete in the resulting twice-scattered rays.

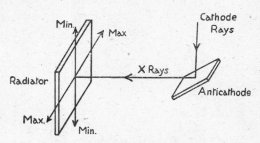

FIG. 58.—To explain polarisation of X rays.

Prof. Barkla measured his rays by an ionisation method. His results have been confirmed and extended by Haga (*A.d.P.* 1907), Bassler (*A.d.P.* 1909), Herweg (*A.d.P.* 1909), and Vegard (*P.R.S.* 1910), some of whom employed photographic methods.

In experimental work, it is convenient to use radiators which do not possess a marked characteristic radiation. The characteristic radiations from materials of very low or very high atomic weight are either very soft or absent altogether ; and so carbon, paraffin wax, aluminium, lead, and metals of the platinum group are ordinarily to be preferred to metals of the chromium-zinc group, which possess pronounced characteristic radiations. The characteristic radiations are not polarised, at least not to any appreciable extent, and their presence only serves to mask the results.

The polarisation in the case of carbon or wax amounts

to about 10 per cent., *i.e.* the maximum intensity is about $\frac{100}{90}$ times the minimum.   By filtering out the soft rays from the primary beam by the use of a suitable screen, the polarisation can be doubled.   Hardening the primary X-ray tube, however, apparently diminishes the effect.

Ham (*P.R.* 1910) has also proved that primary X rays are polarised, by direct measurement of the intensity in different directions from an X-ray bulb.   He found that the intensity reaches a maximum in a plane through the anticathode at right angles to the cathode stream.   The intensity decreases symmetrically on either side of the maximum.   Ham used a lead anticathode, and Miller (*P.R.* 1911) confirmed his results with a silver target.   (Cf. p. 49.)

CHARACTERISTIC OR "MONOCHROMATIC" X RAYS.

The discovery by Barkla and Sadler in 1908 (*P.M.*) of the various characteristic radiations ranks as of the first importance.   From an experimental point of view, the simplification brought about by the use of these radiations can hardly be overestimated.   An ordinary X-ray tube generates a mixture of rays of many qualities, and the interpretation of the results obtained with such heterogeneous rays is correspondingly difficult.   But by allowing X rays to fall on different metals—copper, silver, iron, platinum, etc.—characteristic X rays of uniform quality [1] are given off which comprise a wide range of qualities.   The quality of each of these radiations depends on the metal alone, and not at all on the exciting X rays.   The only proviso is that the exciting rays shall be harder than the characteristic radiation : if the primary rays are too soft, no characteristic radiation is generated.

When precautions are taken to eliminate the effects of the scattered and corpuscular rays, it is found that all the characteristic radiations are homogeneous and, unlike the scattered radiation, are uniformly distributed round the radiator.   The penetrating power of a characteristic radiation increases with the atomic weight of the element from

---

[1] In point of fact, not truly uniform (see p. 240).

which it is emitted, so that the characteristic radiation of any atom can excite the corresponding radiation of a lighter atom, but not that of a heavier atom.

K and L Series of Radiations.

Experiment has shown that elements give out at least two characteristic radiations under suitable conditions.

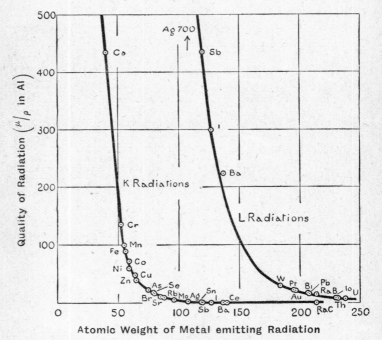

FIG. 59.—Relation between mass-absorption coefficient (in Al) of a characteristic radiation and atomic weight of metal emitting radiation. The characteristic γ rays are included (see p.123).

Barkla has called these two types, series *K* and series *L* fluorescent radiations. For each metal, the *K* radiation is something like 300 times more penetrating than the *L* radiation. Both radiations become harder as the atomic weight or number of the radiator increases.

As will be seen later, the *K* and *L* radiations are the most conspicuous of the several characteristic radiations which an element can emit. Just as in the case of light, the characteristic X-ray spectra can be sorted out into groups or series of associated lines, and the K and L radiations refer to two of these groups.

An M series is known in the case of some metals, and there is some evidence (which needs confirmation) that a J and an N series exist, the J being the hardest and the N the softest of the several characteristic radiations.

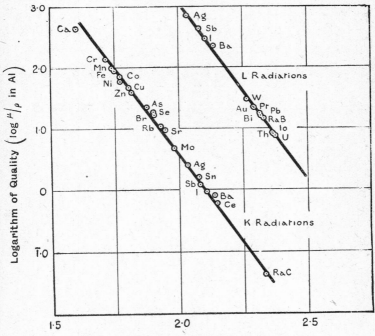

Fig. 60.—Relation between the log of the mass-absorption coefficient (in Al) of a characteristic radiation, and the log of the atomic weight of the element emitting the radiation. (Cf. Fig. 59.)

It may here be added that all the constituent spectrum lines of a group are simultaneously excited, and that while it is not possible, for example, to excite the K radiation of an element without the L radiation, the latter can be excited in the absence of the K radiation.

Relation between Quality of Characteristic Radiation and Atomic Weight of Emitting Metal.

In Table VIII. are given the qualities of the various characteristic radiations expressed as mass-absorption coefficients in aluminium, together with the thickness of aluminium required to halve their intensity. Fig. 59 displays graphically the relation between the quality of the radiation and the atomic weight of the emitting metal.

TABLE VIII. MASS-ABSORPTION COEFFICIENTS (μ/ρ) IN ALUMINIUM OF CHARACTERISTIC RADIATIONS.

μ is defined by $I = I_0 e^{-\mu d}$ (see p. 104) ; ρ is the density of aluminium (2·7); $d_{I/2}$ is the thickness of aluminium required to reduce the radiation by one-half, and is calculated from the formula $d = \dfrac{0 \cdot 2567}{\mu/\rho}$, which is derived from the above. The corresponding thickness of animal tissue (or of water) is about ten times that of Al. The values of μ/ρ are due chiefly to Barkla, Sadler, Nicol, and Chapman.

Element emitting characteristic Radiation.	μ/ρ in Al.		$d_{I/2}$		Element emitting characteristic Radiation.	μ/ρ in Al.		$d_{I/2}$	
	Series K.	Series L.	Series K.	Series L.		Series K.	Series L.	Series K.	Series L.
	cm. gm.	cm. gm.	cm.	cm.		cm. gm.	cm. gm.	cm.	cm.
C (12)					Rh (103)				
Na (23)					Pd (107)				
Mg (24)					Ag (108)	2·5	700	0·103	0·00037
Al (27)					Cd (112)				
Si (28)					Sn (119)	1·57		0·164	
P (31)					Sb (120)	1·21	435	0·212	0·00059
S (32)					I (127)	0·92	300	0·28	0·00086
Cl (35)					Te (128)				
K (39)					Ba (137)	0·8	224	0·32	0·00115
Ca (40)	435		0·00059		Ce (140)	0·6		0·43	
Ti (48)					Ta (181)				
V (51)					W (184)		30·0		0·0086
Cr (52)	136		0·0019		Os (191)				
Mn (55)	100		0·0026		Ir (193)				
Fe (56)	88·5		0·0029		Pt (195)		22·2		0·0116
Co (59)	71·6		0·0036		Au (197)		21·6		0·0119
Ni (59)	59·1		0·0043		Hg (200)				
Cu (64)	47·7		0·0054		Tl (204)				
Zn (65)	39·4		0·0065		Pb (207)		17·4		0·0148
As (75)	22·5		0·0114		Bi (208)		16·1		0·016
Se (79)	18·5		0·0139		RaB (214)[1]		14·7		0·0175
Br (80)	16·3		0·0157		RaC (214)[1]	0·042		6·1	
Rb (85)	10·9		0·0235		Io (230)[1]		8·35		0·031
Sr (88)	9·4		0·027		Th (232)		8·0		0·032
Zr (91)					U (238)		7·5		0·034
Mo (96)	4·8		0·053						
Ru (102)									

[1] γ rays (see p. 123).

The general resemblance between the K and L curves will be remarked. If the logarithms of both coordinates of Fig. 59 are plotted, the result is two straight lines (Fig. 60), the slope of which indicates that the penetrability is proportional to the 5th or 6th power of the atomic weight of the radiator. This result was first established by E. A. Owen (*P.R.S.* 1912)[1] from his experiments on the absorption of characteristic rays in light gases (see p. 143). If similar logarithmic curves are plotted for any other absorber than aluminium, the resulting straight lines are parallel to the aluminium lines, except in the regions of abnormal absorption (see p. 137).

As shown on p. 253, the above relation may be correlated with Moseley's famous atomic number law, and the expression connecting wave-length and the absorption coefficient.

Relation between K and L Series.

The characteristic radiations clearly correspond to the lines in an optical spectrum ; and the well-known series relations between the wave-lengths of associated spectral lines suggested the probability of some such relation between the hard (K) and soft (L) series of X radiations. Whiddington (*N.* 1911) was able to derive a simple empirical relation connecting the penetrating powers of the two radiations with the atomic weight. If an element of atomic weight A_L possesses a soft (L) radiation of a certain hardness, then the atomic weight (A_K) of the particular element whose K radiation is of the same hardness, is given by

$$A_K = \tfrac{1}{2}(A_L - 50).$$

Chapman (*P.R.S.* 1912), having investigated the L radiations from the metals of high atomic weight, derived the expression $A_K = \tfrac{1}{2}(A_L - 48),$

which fits in a little more closely with the observed results.

As an example of the application of this formula, bismuth with an atomic weight of 208 is found to have a soft radiation

---

[1] See also Kaufmann (*P.Z.* 1913).

which is of the same penetrating power as the hard radiation from bromine (with an atomic weight of $80[= \frac{1}{2}(208 - 48)]$).

Characteristic Radiations from the Heavy Elements.

With elements of high atomic weight, the scattered radiation may be so excessive as to mask or even swamp the characteristic radiation. Chapman (*P.R.S.* 1912), in an investigation of the characteristic rays of the heavy metals (from tungsten and platinum to uranium), attacked the difficulty by choosing an exceedingly penetrating beam of X rays, so that the scattered radiation was very much harder than the characteristic radiation. The heterogeneous mixture of characteristic radiation and the superposed scattered radiation was examined in the usual way by a series of aluminium absorption-screens of increasing thickness, the

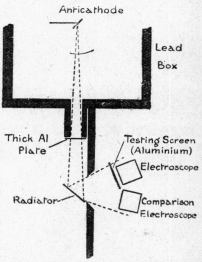

FIG. 61—Chapman's apparatus for investigating the characteristic radiations of the heavy metals.

result being gradually to remove the characteristic radiation. Ultimately, the residual rays consisted almost wholly of scattered radiation; its amount was thus revealed, and could be applied as a correction to the earlier observations with the thinner screens. In this way, the absorption curve of the characteristic radiation was ascertained; it revealed the homogeneity common to all such radiations.

Chapman (whose apparatus is shown in Fig. 61) worked with very thin radiators, and by so doing minimised the scattered radiation. For the homogeneous radiation, being soft, emerges only from a small depth: if this thickness is exceeded the result is merely to increase the proportion of scattered radiation which is able to emerge from deeper layers.

Radiations other than *K* and *L*.

We have so far dealt mainly with the *K* and *L* characteristic radiations, but, as already remarked, recent work has shown the existence of an *M* radiation, at any rate in the case of the elements of high atomic weight. This *M* radiation is very soft, *i.e.* of long wave-length. The existence of a very hard *J* radiation has also been claimed by Barkla and others, but the evidence is conflicting. There are some grounds for believing that it consists of a large number of isolated lines. The *L* and *M* radiations are of little practical interest to the radiologist, as they are almost, if not completely, absorbed by the walls of the X-ray bulb.

As already stated, each of the characteristic radiations— *K*, *L*, *M*—consists of a group of associated spectral lines. See p. 240.

Characteristic γ Radiations from Radioactive Elements.

Rutherford has brought forward evidence that the many and various groups of homogeneous γ rays which radium emits can be regarded as so many characteristic X radiations produced by the expulsion of β particles. Some of these groups correspond to the *K*, *L*, and *M* radiations, others are much harder, and are possibly members of a *J* series. For example, the γ rays from RaC are homogeneous and have a value of μ/ρ in Al $= 0.0424$, which finds a place among the *K* series corresponding to the atomic weight, 214, of RaC. Again, Rutherford and Richardson (*P.M.* 1913) have shown that among the various groups of γ rays from RaB are three which have values of $\mu/\rho_{Al} = 85$, 14.7, and 0.188, the second of which appears to be the *L* radiation for an atomic weight of 214. Further, Chadwick and Russell (*P.R.S.* 1913) found that among the γ rays from ionium (atomic weight 230) are homogeneous components having

$\mu/\rho_{Al} = 400$, 8·35, and 0·15 respectively. The second of these corresponds to the L series for a metal with an atomic weight of 230. See p. 288.

Gray observed (*P.R.S.* 1912) that the γ rays of RaE are capable of exciting the K radiations of silver, lead, and barium. Also Richardson (*P.R.S.* Aug. 1914) excited the K and L radiations of a number of metals by the β rays from RaB and RaC.

Very soft X Rays.

Ordinary X rays are usually produced by potentials of between say 10,000 to 100,000 volts or more, but it is possible to generate X rays with much lower voltages. Such X rays are soft and have only a short range in air.

Dember (*D.P.G.V.* July 1913) gradually increased, by means of an electric field, the speed of the photo-electrons liberated by ultra-violet light, and found that they were capable of exciting X rays from a platinum anticathode at as low a voltage as 18·7. Seitz (*P.Z.* 1912) got X rays from Pt with voltages ranging from 400 to 900 volts. Wehnelt and Trinkle (*Sitz. Phys. Med. Soc. Erlangen,* 37, 1905) generated soft X rays by the use of slow cathode rays from hot-lime cathodes (p. 8) excited by voltages of from 400 to 1000. J. J. Thomson (*P.P.S.* Dec. 1914) produced extremely soft X rays by the impact of positive rays or slow cathode rays on platinum. More recent workers using photoelectric methods have traced X-ray spectrum lines in the ultra-violet region. (See p. 245.)

Characteristic Light Rays.

When a variety of qualities of X rays is allowed to penetrate a substance, it is found that the absorption becomes abnormally large for the particular qualities of ray which are capable of exciting the characteristic radiations of the substance (see p. 137). Such abnormal absorption is accompanied by a large increase in the corpuscular emission. This effect corresponds somewhat to the selective photo-electric effect discovered by Pohl and Pringsheim (*D.P.G.V.* 1911 and 1912) in the case of ultra-violet light polarised in a plane parallel to the plane of incidence. They ascertained that the emission of electrons produced by the impact of ultra-violet light on metals reaches a maximum for a particular wave-length of the light : the wave-lengths for the alkali metals are approximately as follows :

Wave-length.
Li 2800 A.U.[1]
Na 3400
K 4400
Rb 4800

Thus these several ultra-violet radiations may be regarded as analogous to soft characteristic X rays.

It is worth while adding the remark here that Pohl and Pringsheim have succeeded in carrying the photoelectric effect well into the infra-red (10,000 A.U.).

Characteristic X Rays are independent of Chemical Combination.

Chapman and Guest (*P.C.P.S.* 1911) showed that the intensity of the characteristic X radiation from a metal was the same, no matter whether the metal was combined or not. For example, a given weight of tin continued to give the same quantity of characteristic tin rays after it was converted into the nitrate. Thus, in common with all X-ray phenomena, the effect is a purely atomic one.

Chapman (*P.M.* 1911) found that methyl iodide and ethyl bromide vapours gave out strong iodine and bromine characteristic radiations respectively when struck by hard X rays.

Glasson (*P.C.P.S.* 1910) noticed that the quality of the characteristic radiation from, say, iron was independent of whether the iron was free or combined ; in the latter case, neither the valency nor the position of the ion was material, *e.g.* $FeSO_4$, Fe_3O_4, Fe_2O_3, $K_4Fe(CN)_6$, all excited iron rays of the same quality.

All the available evidence goes to show that the absorption coefficients of the characteristic radiations are independent of either temperature or chemical association.

---

[1] One A.U. (Ångström Unit) is 10^{-8} cm.

The Direct Generation of Characteristic Rays.

By the ordinary " reflection " method, using a radiator at 45° to the primary beam of X rays,[1] the amount of energy which is transformed into characteristic radiation does not at the most reach 50 per cent. ; and of this, only a fraction, say $\frac{1}{10}$, manages to escape from the surface of the radiator. Thus the arrangement is very inefficient as a source of characteristic rays. The writer showed, however, in 1908 (*P.T.*) (see p. 36) that a large proportion of the radiation from the anticathode of an X-ray bulb may consist of the characteristic radiation of the metal of the anticathode, with a suitable exciting voltage. By the employment of screens of the same metal as the anticathode, the other radiations present are either absorbed or transformed into the characteristic radiation, the result being an intense and almost pure beam of characteristic rays. The potential on the tube should not be too high, otherwise the proportion of heterogeneous primary rays in the emitted beam will increase in amount.

Figs. 62 to 65, taken from the above paper, give the log-absorption curves for three such different metals as Al, Cu, and Pt. The homogeneity of much of the radiation, when screen and anticathode are alike, will be apparent. With all three metals, there is a superposed softer homogeneous radiation, which is removed by quite thin screens. In the case of copper, the K radiation shows up prominently.

Figs. 64 and 65 show the way in which the radiation from a platinum anticathode is absorbed by aluminium and platinum screens respectively. In the former case, the (thick) absorption curve betrays no apparent homogeneity in the rays. It is, however, possible to analyse the curve into three homogeneous components, having $\mu/\rho = 5\cdot6$, $23\cdot7$, and 70 respectively. These are represented both in amount and hardness by the three thin lines. The hardest is probably independent radiation, the second proves to be the characteristic L radiation of platinum. With the platinum screen, the independent radiation has disappeared, and the absorption curve shows that the X rays transmitted by a screen $0\cdot0005$ cm. thick are almost entirely homogeneous L rays.

[1] See, for example, Fig. 61.

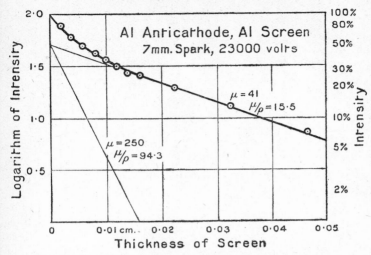

FIG. 62.—The heavy curve is the log-absorption curve, for an Al screen, of the X rays from an Al anticathode. The curve can be resolved into two homogeneous components (indicated in amount and absorbability by the two thin straight lines).

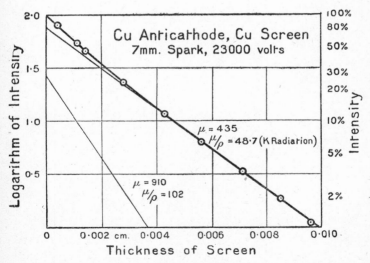

FIG. 63.—The heavy curve is the log-absorption curve, for a Cu screen, of the X rays from a Cu anticathode. The homogeneity of much of the radiation is apparent. The curve can be resolved into two homogeneous components (indicated in amount and absorbability by the two thin straight lines), one of which is the K radiation of Cu.

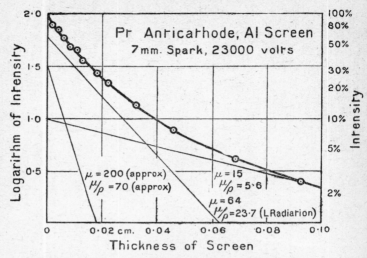

FIG. 64.—The heavy curve is the log-absorption curve, for an Al screen, of the X rays from a Pt anticathode. The curve can be resolved into three homogeneous components (indicated in amount and absorbability by the three thin straight lines), one of which is the L radiation of Pt.

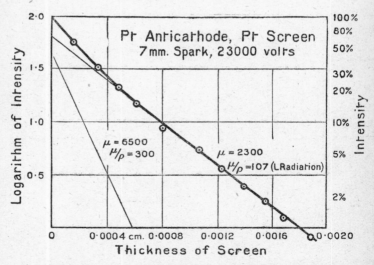

FIG. 65.—Conditions as in Fig. 64, except that the Pt X rays are absorbed by a Pt screen instead of Al. The homogeneous L radiation now predominates in the absorption curve, which is resolvable into the L radiation and a second softer component.

The proportion of the L radiation from a platinum anti-cathode varies with the voltage on the tube. At about 11,000 volts the L rays constitute about 35 per cent. of the whole radiation transmitted through an aluminium window 0·0065 cm. thick ; at 32,000 volts, 63 per cent. ; and at 50,000 volts, 40 per cent. If the rays have to traverse the glass walls of an ordinary X-ray tube, the proportion of the L radiation is small, except at low voltages. With the higher voltages the proportion of hard radiation is considerable. This " end radiation " increases both in hardness and amount with the voltage.

In the case of copper, nickel and iron radiations transmitted through an aluminium window as above, the proportion of K radiation amounts to between 80 and 90 per cent. at voltages between 20,000 and 30,000. In the case of all three metals the K radiation would be almost wholly absorbed by the glass walls of an X-ray bulb, which are usually between $\frac{1}{2}$ mm. and 1 mm. thick.

The relation between maximum hardness and voltage is of importance in connection with Planck's quantum theory (p. 268), from which we should anticipate that the maximum X-ray frequency would be reached with a voltage which diminishes with the atomic weight. On the experimental evidence available at present, we cannot say with certainty that there is a limit to the hardness of the X rays which may be generated by any particular anticathode. We know, however, that radiations much harder than the K radiations can be obtained from various metals. For example, the writer has obtained from aluminium, rays which have $\mu/\rho_{Al} = 1$; from iron, $\mu/\rho_{Al} = 13\cdot5$; from nickel, $\mu/\rho_{Al} = 10\cdot8$; from copper, $\mu/\rho_{Al} = 6\cdot6$.

Coolidge Tube.

Fig. 66, due to Rutherford, Barnes and Richardson ($P.M.$ Sept. 1915), shows a set of log-absorption curves dealing with the absorption in aluminium of the X rays from a Coolidge tube (see p. 44) run at a variety of voltages. Just as with an ordinary tube, the radiation in all cases diminishes more rapidly with thin screens than with thick, owing to the absorption of the softer components. It is not until the radiation is reduced to about $\frac{1}{500}$ of its initial value that the absorption curve becomes very nearly a straight line, at any rate with the higher voltages. This shows that the "end-radiation" is approximately homogeneous. At the lowest voltages the main radiation proved to be the L characteristic radiation of tungsten, that being the material of the anticathode. At high voltages the radiation is mainly of the independent type.

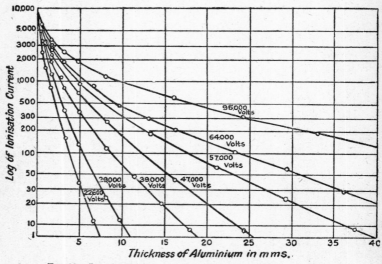

FIG. 66.—Log-absorption curves, for Al screens, of the X rays from a Coolidge tube with tungsten anticathode.

The highest voltage used by Rutherford (*P.M.* 1917) was 196,000 volts. The rays were filtered through 1 cm. of lead, the reduction in intensity being over a million fold. The end-rays had $\mu_{Al} = 0.23$ cm.$^{-1}$, $\mu_{Pb} = 9$ cm.$^{-1}$, and a wave-length of about 0·06 A.U.

Duane and Hunt (*P.R.* 1915) have shown that voltage and the hardest X ray are connected by Planck's relation, $Ve = h\nu$ (p. 268). Inserting Millikan's values of these constants (*P.M.* 1917) we have:

Wave-length in A.U. $= 12,400/$voltage.

—a relation turned to practical account (p. 247).

Quality of Characteristic Rays in terms of Parent Cathode Ray Velocity.

The writer in 1909 (see *J.Rt.S.* 1913) attempted to associate the hardness of the characteristic radiation emitted by an anticathode, with the speed of the cathode ray required to excite the radiation. The underlying notion was that unless the cathode rays possessed a velocity greater than a certain critical value, no characteristic rays would be generated. If this were so, the X rays could, so to speak, be labelled in terms of the speed of the exciting cathode rays.

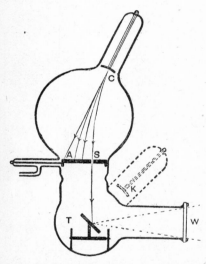

FIG. 67.—Apparatus for showing production of X rays with cathode rays of varying speed.

Obviously a first simplification was to work with cathode rays of uniform speed. This can be done by the use of either (1) an influence machine or (2) a magnetic-spectrum method applied to a coil discharge. In the latter plan, the cathode ray energy is, at suitable pressures, largely concentrated in the fastest cathode rays (see p. 16); and the method had other obvious advantages which led to its adoption.

The apparatus is indicated in Fig. 67. The cathode rays from *C* were spread by a magnetic field into a magnetic spectrum, plainly visible along the plate anode, *AS*, which was coated with willemite. By varying the strength of the field, any part of the spectrum could be brought over the slit, *S*. The pencil of cathode rays which passed through *S* impinged on the anticathode, *T*, below, and a bundle of X rays passed out through the thin aluminium window, *W*, and was measured by an ionisation method. Some half-dozen anticathodes were mounted on a trolley as described on p. 36. The additional cathode K was provided to bombard the anticathodes so as to liberate the occluded gas, which otherwise, by its continued emission, softens the tube during the actual measurements.

The experiments, which were arrested soon after their commencement, served, however, to show the extreme inefficiency of the slowest cathode rays as producers of X rays. As the different parts of the cathode spectrum were passed over the slit, and faster and faster cathode rays were brought into action, the rapid gain in the intensity of the X rays was very noticeable. The increase in intensity came in quite suddenly for some one speed of the cathode rays which did not appear to be the same for the different anticathodes employed.

Whiddington's Experiments.

In 1910 Whiddington continued the research on somewhat similar lines, and obtained quantitative measurements of

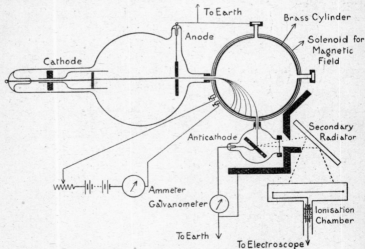

FIG. 68.—Whiddington's apparatus for connecting the speed of cathode rays with the quality of various characteristic radiations.

great importance (*P.R.S.* 1911) for the K radiations of a number of elements. His final apparatus is shown in Fig. 68. The cathode-ray spectrum was produced by a solenoid which yielded a uniform and calculable magnetic field. The anticathode was of silver, and the generated X rays struck a secondary radiator. The speed of the cathode rays was increased (by the hardening device described on p. 74) until the secondary radiator emitted its characteristic radiation, which of course was duly indicated in the ionisation chamber. Below this critical value of the velocity, there was little effect in the chamber ; above it, the ionisation current grew very rapidly. Thus the cathode ray in the X-ray tube must possess a minimum velocity if it is to excite an X ray of given quality. Different radiators were tried, and the critical velocity was found to be roughly proportional to the atomic weight of the radiator : in point of fact, the speed in cms. per sec. was 100 million (10^8) times the atomic weight. Beatty (see next page) has since shown that the same result is true if the metal is used, not as a secondary radiator, but as an anticathode.

Thus, to recapitulate, if V_K is the critical velocity of the cathode rays in cms. per sec., and A is the atomic weight of the anticathode, then in the case of the K series of radiations, the empirical relation

$$V_K = A \ . \ 10^8 *$$

is approximately satisfied for the elements Al to Se.

By combining this expression with Chapman's formula (p. 121), it follows that for the L series

$$V_L = \tfrac{1}{2}(A - 48)10^8. *$$

In Table IX., Whiddington's experimental values for the K radiations are given in heavy type in columns 3 and 5. The values for the other K radiations and the whole of the L radiations are calculated by the formulæ above. Some of these radiations have not yet been discovered.

---

* More recently Whiddington (*P. M.* June 1920) derived the expressions

$$V_K = 2(N - 2)10^8 ; \quad V_L = (N - 15)10^8$$

where N is the atomic number.

TABLE IX. MINIMUM SPEED OF CATHODE RAYS REQUIRED TO EXCITE CHARACTERISTIC RADIATIONS.

Radiator.	Atomic Weight (O=16).	Critical Velocity of Cathode Rays to excite		Requisite Potential to impart Critical Speed to Cathode Rays.[1]	
		K radiation.	L radiation:	K radn.	L radn.
		cm./sec.	cm./sec.	volts.	volts.
Hydrogen -	1·01	$1·0 \times 10^8$	—	3	—
Carbon -	12·0	$1·2 \times 10^9$	—	410	—
Aluminium	27·1	2·06 ,,	—	1200	—
Chromium -	52·0	5·09 ,,	$2·0 \times 10^8$	7320	11
Iron - -	55·8	5·83 ,,	3·9 ,,	9600	43
Nickel -	58·7	6·17 ,,	5·4 ,,	10,750	80
Copper -	63·6	6·26 ,,	7·8 ,,	11,080	170
Zinc - -	65·4	6·32 ,,	8·7 ,,	11,280	210
Selenium -	79·2	7·38 ,,	$1·56 \times 10^9$	15,400	690
Rhodium -	102·9	$1·03 \times 10^{10}$	2·7 ,,	29,900	2,100
Silver -	107·9	1·08 ,,	3·0 ,,	33,000	2,500
Tin - -	119·0	1·19 ,,	3·6 ,,	40,000	3,600
Tungsten -	184·0	1·84 ,,	6·8 ,,	95,000	13,000
Platinum -	195·0	1·95 ,,	7·4 ,,	108,000	15,000
Lead - -	207·1	2·07 ,,	8·0 ,,	120,000	18,000
Uranium -	238·5	2·38 ,,	9·5 ,,	160,000	26,000

Energy of an X Ray.

By slightly modifying the arrangement, and putting the ionisation chamber in place of the secondary radiator,[2] Whiddington was able to correlate the energy of the X rays with the velocity of the parent cathode rays, and so to establish the truth of a relation deduced theoretically by Sir J. J. Thomson in 1907, that the energy of an X ray is proportional to the fourth power of the velocity of the exciting cathode ray. Beatty (*P.R.S.* 1913) has recently proved that this relation is only true for "independent" X rays : if characteristic rays are generated, the expression no longer holds (see p. 112).

Beatty's Experiments.

Beatty (*P.R.S.* 1912) has shown that the bulk of the characteristic rays generated in Kaye's experiments (p. 126).

[1] See p. 100 for relation between cathode-ray speed and potential.
[2] See Fig. 68.

is due to a direct transformation of the cathode radiation into characteristic radiation ; and that only a small remainder owes its origin, as one would perhaps infer, to the indirect action of primary X rays in emerging from beneath the surface of the anticathode. Beatty obtained cathode rays of uniform speed by means of the magnetic-spectrum method, and was able to show that the direct and indirect effects occur simultaneously as soon as the speed of the cathode rays exceeds the critical value (see p. 133). Fig. 69 shows for the case of a copper anticathode, the relative amounts of characteristic copper radiation generated directly and indirectly by cathode rays of different velocities. Both effects disappear if the speed

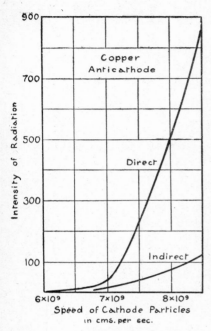

FIG. 69.—Showing relative amounts of characteristic X rays generated directly and indirectly from a copper anticathode by cathode rays of a variety of speeds.

falls below $6\cdot25 \times 10^9$ cm./sec., a value which agrees very closely with Whiddington's critical speed for copper.

To overcome the difficulties of measuring the X rays due to the vagaries of a coil discharge, an ingenious null method was devised which consisted in balancing the current in the ionisation chamber against part of that carried by the cathode-ray discharge. Fig. 70 shows the connections. The interior of the anticathode tube A was lined with aluminium and joined to the anticathode. The greater part of the cathode ray current passed to earth through the variable resistance P. A smaller fraction passed through the high resistance Q to the ionisation chamber. The resistance P was altered until the latter current just neutralised the leak in the ionisation chamber. Of the current leaving A, $P/(P+Q)$ goes to the chamber. Since

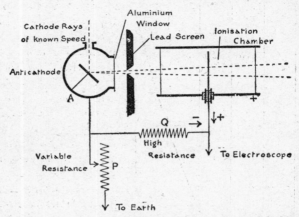

FIG. 70.—Beatty's apparatus for measuring the characteristic X rays generated directly and indirectly by cathode rays of various speeds (see Fig. 69).

Q was very large—of the order of 10^{12} ohms—we may write this, P/Q. Thus the relative intensity of the X rays is evaluated by determining P in each case.

ABSORPTION OF CHARACTERISTIC RADIATIONS.

Barkla and Sadler's Relation for Normal Absorption.

As Table XII. shows, a constant absorption-ratio exists for each absorber no matter what the hardness of the X ray outside a certain limited range. Some of the departures from proportionality with the harder types of rays, in what should be regions of normal absorption, are due to the fact that the coefficients for many of the elements given in Table XI. have not been corrected for scattering. If we make the proper scattering correction (p. 114), it is found that the ratio of the absorptions of a radiation in any two particular elements is approximately constant, and does not depend on the quality of the radiation, provided only that such radiation does not excite the characteristic radiations of either element.   This important relation was first pointed out by Barkla and Sadler.

To take an example, Barkla and Collier have shown that in the case of carbon, the absorption values relative to aluminium—which rise in Table XII. from 0·11 for soft rays to 0·41 for hard rays—become, when corrected for scattering, a steady value of 0·11 for all types of X ray.

Abnormal Absorption of Certain Qualities of Radiation by a Particular Element.

It is found that an element exhibits a maximum transparency for X rays of a quality approximating to that of either

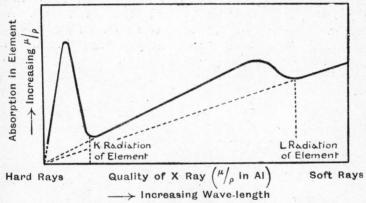

FIG. 71.—Diagrammatic representation of the absorption by a particular element of a range of qualities of X rays.   The absorption reaches a minimum for rays approximating in quality to either of the characteristic radiations ; for rays a little harder than these, the absorption increases rapidly and becomes permanently larger. Elsewhere the absorption is normal.

of its own characteristic radiations ; and, further, the absorption becomes abnormally large for X rays which have a penetrating power just greater than that of either of the characteristic radiations.   For example, if the absorption in copper is measured for a variety of homogeneous X radiations from, say, calcium rays to cerium rays, then if we start with the soft Ca rays and pass up the series, the absorption in copper steadily diminishes in normal fashion as the rays are hardened.   But as soon as the

stage is reached when the rays approximate in penetrability to the Cu radiation, the absorption slows up, and
reaches a minimum. With slightly harder rays the Cu (K)
radiation is excited, and the absorption then rapidly increases. As the incident rays are hardened still further,
the absorption, though now permanently higher, begins once
more to diminish, and eventually reassumes the normal type,
steadily lessening as the hardness increases, but now more
rapidly than was the case before the "loop."

These various phenomena are displayed in Fig. 71, which
shows, for a range of qualities of incident X rays, the two
loops in the absorption curve of an element which possesses
both K and L radiations. It must be emphasised that
Fig. 71 is purely diagrammatic and not at all to scale. As
yet, the complete absorption curve for any single element
has not been obtained. The corresponding curve for an
absorbing metal of lower atomic weight or number would
have the loops shifted to the right; for one of higher atomic
number, to the left.

TABLE X.   SHOWING RELATIVE TRANSMISSION OF VARIOUS
RADIATIONS.   (Al radiation = 100.)

Anticathode and Atomic Number.	Screeen of				
	Al	Fe	Ni	Cu	Pt
Aluminium (13) - -	100	100	100	100	100
Iron (26) - -	160	600	340	380	160
Nickel (28) - -	180	200	740	570	220
Copper (29) - -	210	210	810	740	270
Platinum (78) - -	530	450	480	480	670

The relative transmission of the various characteristic
radiations was well displayed in Kaye's experiments [1] on
the direct generation of characteristic rays from anticathodes
of X-ray bulbs. Table X. shows the effect of interposing
the same metal screen in turn in the path of the X rays
from various anticathodes. It will be noticed that, in most

[1] See p. 126, and *P.C.P.S.* May 1907.

TABLE XI. MASS-ABSORPTION COEFFICIENTS (μ/ρ) OF CHARACTERISTIC RADIATIONS IN VARIOUS ABSORBERS.

μ is defined by $I = I_0 e^{-\mu d}$ (see p. 104); ρ is the density of the absorbing element; μ/ρ is in cm.-gm. units.

Element emitting Characteristic Radiation and Atomic Number.	Series.	ABSORBING SUBSTANCE.											
		C (12)	Air* (14·4)	Mg (24)	Al (27)	Fe (56)	Ni (59)	Cu (64)	Zn (65)	Ag (108)	Sn (119)	Pt (195)	Au (197)
Cr (24)	K	15·3	—	126	136	104	129	143	170	580	714	517	>507
Fe (26)	K	10·1	15·6	80	88·5	66·1	83·8	95·1	112	381	472	340	367
Co (27)	K	7·96	12·7	63·5	71·6	67·2	67·2	75·3	91·5	314	392	281	306
Ni (28)	K	6·58	10·5	51·8	59·1	314	56·3	61·8	74·4	262	328	236	253
Cu (29)	K	5·22	8·43	41·4	47·7	268	62·7	53·0	60·9	214	272	194	210
Zn (30)	K	4·26	6·96	34·7	39·4	221	265	55·5	50·1	175	225	162	178
As (33)	K	2·49	4·10	19·3	22·5	134	166	176	203	105	131	106	106
Se (34)	K	2·04	3·40	15·7	18·5	116	141	150	175	87·5	112	92	102
Br (35)	K	1·9	3·02	—	16·3	—	—	128	—	75·4	—	181	135
Rb (37)	K	1·32	—	—	10·9	—	—	—	—	52·3	—	168	147
Sr (38)	K	1·16	1·78	—	9·4	—	—	83·4	—	48·8	—	180	160
Mo (42)	K	0·81	0·98	2·2	4·8	—	—	40·3	—	24·4	—	95·5	111
Ag (47)	K	0·46	0·59	—	2·5	17·4	22·7	24·3	27·1	13·3	16·5	56·5	61·4
Sn (50)	K	0·35	0·39	—	1·57	—	—	—	—	16·5	—	47·1	51·7
Sb (51)	K	0·31	—	—	1·21	—	—	—	—	56·1	—	—	—
I (53)	K	0·29	—	—	0·92	—	—	—	—	46	—	—	—
Ba (56)	K	0·26	—	—	0·8	—	—	—	—	35·4	—	—	—
Ce (58)	K	0·248	—	—	0·6	—	—	—	—	—	—	—	—
W (74)	L	—	—	—	30·0	—	—	127	—	140	—	133	—
Pt (78)	L	—	—	—	22·2	—	—	177	—	106	—	113	—
Pb (82)	L	—	—	—	17·4	—	—	139	—	77·5	—	128	—
Bi (83)	L	—	—	—	16·1	—	—	127	—	72·9	—	125	—
Th (90)	L	—	—	—	8·0	—	—	76·6	—	42·3	—	134	—
U (92)	L	—	—	—	7·5	—	—	70·2	—	40·3	—	132	—
Density (ρ) =		1·0†	0·00129*	1·74	2·70	7·86	8·9	8·93	7·1	10·5	7·29	21·5	19·3

* At 0° C. and 760 mm.   † For paper.

TABLE XII. RATIO OF μ/ρ OF CHARACTERISTIC RADIATIONS IN VARIOUS ABSORBERS TO μ/ρ IN ALUMINIUM.

Element emitting Characteristic Radiation and Atomic Number.	Series.	Ratio of μ/ρ in Substance to μ/ρ in Aluminium.										
		$\frac{C}{Al}$	$\frac{Air}{Al}$	$\frac{Mg}{Al}$	$\frac{Fe}{Al}$	$\frac{Ni}{Al}$	$\frac{Cu}{Al}$	$\frac{Zn}{Al}$	$\frac{Ag}{Al}$	$\frac{Sn}{Al}$	$\frac{Pt}{Al}$	$\frac{Au}{Al}$
Cr (24)	K	0·112	—	0·93	0·76	0·95	1·05	1·25	4·25	5·24	3·80	> 3·72
Fe (26)	K	0·114	0·176	0·90	0·75	0·95	1·07	1·27	4·30	5·33	3·84	4·15
Co (27)	K	0·111	0·179	0·89	0·94	0·94	1·05	1·27	4·39	5·46	3·92	4·28
Ni (28)	K	0·111	0·178	0·88	5·31	0·95	1·04	1·26	4·43	5·55	4·00	4·28
Cu (29)	K	0·109	0·177	0·87	5·62	1·31	1·11	1·27	4·50	5·71	4·07	4·40
Zn (30)	K	0·108	0·176	0·88	5·61	6·73	1·41	1·27	4·45	5·72	4·12	4·52
As (33)	K	0·110	0·182	0·86	5·96	7·39	7·84	9·0	4·67	5·83	4·72	4·72
Se (34)	K	0·110	0·184	0·85	6·27	7·64	8·1	9·5	4·72	6·06	4·96	5·52
Br (35)	K	0·116	0·185	—	—	—	7·9	—	4·62	—	11·1	8·3
Rb (37)	K	0·121	—	—	—	—	—	—	4·80	—	15·4	13·5
Sr (38)	K	0·124	0·190	—	—	—	8·9	—	5·19	—	19·2	17·0
Mo (42)	K	0·168	0·204	—	—	—	8·4	—	5·08	—	19·9	23·2
Ag (47)	K	0·184	0·236	0·88	6·96	9·1	9·7	10·8	5·32	6·60	22·6	24·6
Sn (50)	K	0·223	0·248	—	—	—	—	—	10·5	—	30·0	32·8
Sb (51)	K	0·256	—	—	—	—	—	—	46·4	—	—	—
I (53)	K	0·316	—	—	—	—	—	—	50·0	—	—	—
Ba (56)	K	0·326	—	—	—	—	—	—	44·2	—	—	—
Ce (58)	K	0·413	—	—	—	—	—	—	—	—	—	—
W (74)	L	—	—	—	—	—	4·23	—	4·66	—	4·43	—
Pt (78)	L	—	—	—	—	—	8·0	—	4·78	—	5·10	—
Pb (82)	L	—	—	—	—	—	8·0	—	4·45	—	7·36	—
Bi (83)	L	—	—	—	—	—	7·8	—	4·53	—	7·78	—
Th (90)	L	—	—	—	—	—	9·6	—	5·29	—	16·7	—
U (92)	L	—	—	—	—	—	9·4	—	5·37	—	17·6	—

cases, the intensity of the transmitted rays reaches a maximum when the anticathode is of the same material as the screen. To provide a basis of comparison for the results for each metal screen, the intensity of the transmitted radiation from the Al anticathode is called 100 in the table.

The various absorption phenomena illustrated in Fig. 71 are further revealed from a scrutiny of Table XI., or, better still, from Table XII. In Table XI. are put out the mass-absorption coefficients of a number of characteristic radiations in various absorbers, while in Table XII. the values are, in every case, relative to the absorption in aluminium. Table XII. is, of course, immediately derivable from Table XI. Barkla and Collier (*P.M.* 1912) have pointed out that the shape of either of the absorption loops, indicated roughly in Fig. 71 for some particular absorber, is not only similar to, but identical with, the corresponding loop for any other absorber, provided proper choice is made of the scales of coordinates for each absorption curve. This may be secured by arranging that the particular ordinate corresponding to the characteristic radiation of the absorber, both occupies the same position and has the same length in all the different curves. In other words, by arranging the scales of absorption and wave-length so that the absorption of Fe (K) radiation in Fe, of Cu (K) radiation in Cu, etc., are all represented by the one point (A) on the graph, the various absorption curves in the region of the K loop will coincide if superimposed. And similarly for the L loop.

Abnormal Absorption of a Particular Radiation by Certain Elements.

The kink in the curve of absorption of X rays (to which we have referred above), is perhaps better brought out by Fig. 72 (taken from Barkla and Collier's paper, *P.M.* 1912), which exhibits the way in which the absorption of Ni (K) radiation in a number of elements varies with the atomic number of the absorber.

It will be noticed that, if we start with the light elements, the absorption of the Ni rays increases steadily with the atomic number of the absorbing substance, so long as all the various characteristic radiations (K, L, . . .) of the absorber are excited. But as soon as the atomic number of the absorber becomes so high that its K characteristic ceases to be excited (though the others remain), then the absorption suddenly drops. With higher atomic numbers, the Ni radiation can only excite the L, M, . . . radiations, and so the absorption steadily increases until the stage when the Ni radiation no longer excites the L radiation, and the

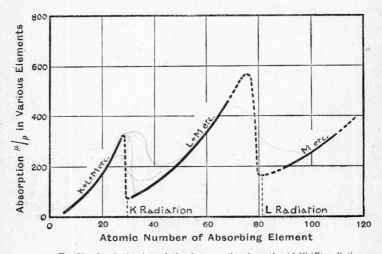

Fig. 72.—Graph showing relation between the absorption of Ni (K) radiation by various elements and the atomic number of the absorbing element. The absorption passes through a minimum for a screen of Ni and also for one of atomic number of about 164 (whose L radiation is identical with the Ni (K) rays). Compare Fig. 55.

absorption falls once more. In other words, the transparency reaches a maximum with a nickel screen and also with one whose L characteristic radiation is identical with the nickel K radiation. Thus the regular curve of increasing μ/ρ with atomic number of the absorber is modified by the addition of sudden drops at as many regions as there are elements having one or other of their characteristic radiations identical with the X rays which are being absorbed.

Similar curves are obtained for any other characteristic radiation : if the radiation is harder, all the maxima and minima are displaced to the right, and, if softer, to the left.

It will be remarked that Fig. 72 is the analogue of Benoist's curve (p. 107) for heterogeneous X rays.

Much light has been thrown on the subject by de Broglie's work on the absorption spectra of X rays. (See p. 249, and *J. de P.* for 1914 *et seq.*)

Absorption of Characteristic Radiations in Gases.

E. A. Owen (*P.R.S.* 1912) measured the absorption of a number of characteristic radiations in light gases. To get

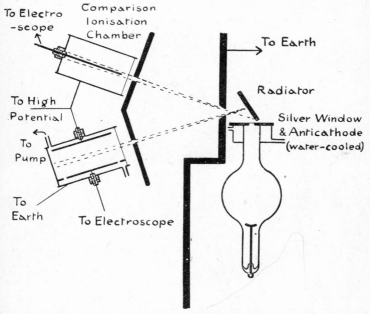

FIG. 73.—Owen's apparatus for measuring the absorption coefficients of characteristic X rays in gases.

over the difficulty of working with the feeble radiations generated by the ordinary method of placing the radiator at an angle to the path of primary X rays, Owen was led to employ the device of mounting a thin silver anticathode as a window in the discharge tube. The various radiators were placed near the outside of the window, and, by this means, intense characteristic radiations were obtained. Fig. 73 shows the apparatus. The anticathode was soldered to the glass, through the intermediary of an electrolytic deposit of copper ; and to prevent the fusion of the anticathode by the cathode rays, it was watercooled.

A pencil of characteristic (K) rays from a series of radiators ranging from iron to molybdenum entered an ionisation chamber through a parchment window. The pencil was sufficiently narrow to prevent it striking the electrodes, which, together with the whole of the inner surface of the chamber, were coated with paper. Both the nature and pressure of the gas in the chamber could be altered. A comparison chamber enabled the vagaries of the coil discharge to be overcome.

In some cases, e.g. SO_2, the absorption at atmospheric pressure was very great for the softer rays, and measurements had to be made at lower pressures. Owen first showed that the absorption coefficients of any of the characteristic radiations in a gas varied directly with the pressure, as, of course, would be anticipated for a homogeneous beam.

Further, the absorption coefficients of the different radiations in a particular gas proved to be proportional to the corresponding absorption coefficients in air, which goes to show that Barkla and Sadler's generalisation (p. 136) can be extended to gases. Owen was led to take the logarithms of the mass-absorption coefficients of the various radiations in a particular gas, and plot them against the logarithms of the atomic weights of the radiating metals. He found not only that the various observations all lay on a straight line, but that the different straight lines for the various gases were all parallel to each other. The slope of these lines showed that the absorption coefficient of a radiation is inversely proportional to the fifth or sixth power of the atomic weight (or atomic number) of the radiator. The curves for an aluminium absorber are shown on p. 119.

Barkla and Collier (*P.M.* 1912) have also worked at absorption in gases. Some of their results, as well as those of

TABLE XIII. ABSORPTION COEFFICIENTS OF CHARACTERISTIC RADIATIONS IN GASES.

Metal emitting Characteristic Radiation and Atomic Number.	Absorbing Gas (at 0° C. and 760 mm.).									
	Air.		CO_2		SO_2		C_2H_5Br		CH_3I	
	μ	μ/ρ	μ	μ/ρ	μ	μ/ρ	μ	μ/ρ	μ	μ/ρ
Fe (26)	0·0202	15·6	0·0456	23·1	0·24	83·3	0·512	105	2·16	339
Co (27)	0·0165	12·7	—	—	0·20	69·4	0·407	83·2	—	—
Ni (28)	0·0136	10·5	0·0319	16·1	0·166	57·6	0·325	66·3	1·80	282
Cu (29)	0·0109	8·43	0·0227	11·5	0·134	46·5	0·260	53·1	1·54	241
Zn (30)	0·0090	6·96	0·0184	9·31	0·112	38·9	0·215	43·9	1·27	198
As (33)	0·0053	4·10	0·00988	5·00	0·066	22·9	0·128	26·1	0·743	116
Se (34)	0·0044	3·40	0·00782	3·96	0·0546	19·1	0·110	22·4	0·619	97
Br (35)	0·0039	3·02	—	—	0·050	17·4	0·096	19·6	0·552	86·5
Sr (38)	0·0023	1·78	0·00420	2·12	0·0281	9·76	0·325	66·3	0·338	53·0
Mo (42)	0·00127	0·98	0·00281	1·42	0·0160	5·56	0·210	42·9	0·197	30·9
Ag (47)	0·00077	0·59	—	—	0·0079	2·75	0·108	22·0	0·113	17·7
Density, $\rho=$	0·00129		0·00198		0·00288		0·00490		0·00638	

K

Owen, are incorporated in Table XIII., which gives the absorption coefficients (in cm. gm. units) for air, carbon dioxide, and sulphur dioxide, ethyl bromide, and methyl iodide vapours.

CORPUSCULAR RAYS.

Curie and Sagnac (*C.R.* 1900) first showed that when a plate was struck by X rays, part of the secondary radiation was negatively charged. These corpuscular rays or electrons —as they have proved to be—are given off whenever a substance emits characteristic X rays.

The detection of these high-speed corpuscles is an easy matter, since the bombarded plate will charge up positively if it is insulated in a vacuum. By measuring the rate of charging, it would be possible to determine the number of corpuscles expelled per second ; while, by applying an electric force of suitable direction and magnitude, we could ascertain their speed. In actual practice, this method of measuring velocities, while convenient for slow-speed electrons such as are liberated, for example, by ultra-violet light, is not very practicable in the case of X rays, owing to the magnitude of the potentials required.

The magnetic-deflection method of measuring speeds may be employed if the electrons are sufficiently numerous.

Distribution of Corpuscular Rays.

The intensity of the corpuscular emission increases with the atomic weight.[1] The corpuscles preponderate in a direction at right angles to the beam of X rays, which accounts for the fact (Laub, *A.d.P.* 1908) that there are more corpuscles liberated by a glancing beam of X rays than by a normal one.

Furthermore, when X rays are sent through a thin metal plate more corpuscles are given off on the far or " emergence " side than on the near or " incidence " side. This is the more marked with hard X rays and with elements of low atomic weight. For example, Beatty (*P.C.P.S.* 1910) found with silver leaf, that while the excess amounted to no more than

---

[1] Moore (*P.P.S.* May 1915) finds that the atomic corpuscular radiation is proportional to the 4th power of the atomic weight of the radiator.

2 per cent. in the case of Fe X rays [1] (which are very soft), it attained 30 or 40 per cent. with the harder tin and aluminium rays. The speed is equally fast on both sides of the plate. On the other hand, Cooksey (*P.M.* July 1912) found that when the absorption of the exciting X rays in the layer of emitting metal is allowed for, the ratio of emergence to incidence corpuscular rays shows no certain variation either with the metal or the X ray. The excess emergence rays were of the order of 20 per cent. for both gold and silver plates, and for a range of rays extending from Cr X rays to Sn X rays—providing an eighty-fold variation of penetrating power.

It may be added that Kleeman (*P.R.S.* 1910) and Stuhlmann (*P.M.* 1911) found much the same value for corresponding experiments with ultra-violet light.

Velocity of the Corpuscular Rays.

Dorn in 1900 first measured the velocity of these negative rays, and in 1907 Innes (*P.R.S.*) made a more complete examination. In his experiments, the X rays fell on a metal sheet in a vacuum, and the corpuscles emitted passed in succession through a couple of slits in lead sheets and were recorded on a photographic plate. The whole of the apparatus was exhausted for the reason that the corpuscles are scattered at ordinary pressures, and their paths are too short to be followed. The velocity of the particles was ascertained from their deflection in a uniform magnetic field (produced by a pair of Helmholtz coils). Innes was able to establish the fact that the velocity of the corpuscle is independent of the distance of the X-ray bulb from the emitting plate—a most important result. The distance was varied some eight or nine-fold without discernible effect on the speed obtained. Nor did alteration of the frequency or magnitude of the current through the X-ray bulb produce any change in the speed.

But an increase in the spark-gap, *i.e.* in the potential applied to the bulb, evidenced itself at once by a speeding up of the corpuscles. This is plainly shown in Table XIV.

---

[1] *I.e.* the characteristic X rays from iron.

below. To derive absolute velocities from the measurements, it is necessary to assume a value for e/m for the corpuscles; this was taken to be $1·7 \times 10^7$ E.M.U.

TABLE XIV. VARIATION OF SPEED OF CORPUSCLES WITH LENGTH OF SPARK-GAP

Metal emitting Corpuscles.	Atomic Weight.	Spark-gap.	Velocity of Corpuscles.
Zinc - -	65	3·9 cm.	6·0 to 6·4 $\times 10^9$ cm./sec.
Silver - -	108	3·9	6·0 to 7·2 ,, ,,
,, - -	,,	19·0	6·1 to 8·0 ,, ,,
Platinum -	195	3·2	6·1 to 7·4 ,, ,,
,, -	,,	14·0	6·5 to 8·0 ,, ,,
Gold - -	197	3·4	6·1 to 7·5 ,, ,,
,, - -	,,	15·0	6·2 to 8·1 ,, ,,
Lead - -	207	5·1	6·3 to 7·8 ,, ,,
,, - -	,,	16·0	6·4 to 8·3 ,, ,,

It is apparent from the table that the nature of the material exerts little, if any, certain influence on the velocity of the corpuscles; but a more definite pronouncement is possible from the later experiments of Beatty (*P.M.* 1910) and of Sadler (*P.M.* 1910), both of whom used characteristic X rays.

Absorption of Corpuscular Rays by Gases.

Sadler has shown that the corpuscular radiation excited by characteristic rays is of uniform quality for any particular metal and follows an exponential law of absorption. This is true no matter what the metal or the characteristic rays. Thus, in each case, the corpuscular rays have a definite absorption coefficient, the value of which Sadler found to be proportional to the atomic weight of the metal whose characteristic rays were being employed.

Both Sadler and Beatty employed a method in which two parallel plates were mounted opposite each other with a saturating electric field between them. The high-potential plate was bombarded with characteristic X rays, and the resulting stream of corpuscles proceeded towards the insulated plate, ionising the intervening gas. This ionisation was measured. Sadler cut down the corpuscular rays by moving one electrode and so lengthening their path in the gas ; Beatty, on the other hand, raised the effective path by increasing the pressure of the gas, a method probably superior in accuracy.

The results of Beatty and Sadler are given in Table XV.

In spite of conflicting data for some of the elements, the table shows plainly that the absorption coefficient (and thus the velocity) of the corpuscular rays is constant throughout for the same X ray and the same absorber, no matter what the nature of the atom from which the corpuscles are emitted.

The velocity, however, does depend very greatly on the quality of the characteristic X ray. Sadler concluded from his experiments that the corpuscular rays are an invariable accompaniment when characteristic rays, and possibly also scattered X rays, are produced. The corpuscular rays from a substance increase very markedly as soon as the substance begins to emit its characteristic X radiation, and possibly the former rays are conditioned by the presence of the latter.

Whiddington (*P.R.S.* 1912) has shown that Beatty's results conform to the expression

$$\mu A^4 = \text{const.},$$

where μ is the absorption coefficient and A the atomic weight of the metal supplying the characteristic X rays.

It follows, as a deduction from the fourth power absorption formula for cathode rays (p. 10), that

$$\mu v_0^4 = \text{const.},$$

where v_0 is the velocity of a particle at the moment of projection from the plate.

Combining these expressions, we conclude that

$$v_0 \propto A ;$$

and, in fact, Beatty's measurements show that

$$v_0 = 10^8 . A.$$

But this is the value of the critical velocity which cathode rays must possess to generate a characteristic radiation (p. 133), and, therefore, it follows that the secondary corpus-

TABLE XV. ABSORPTION COEFFICIENTS (μ) IN AIR AND HYDROGEN (at 0° C. and 760 mm.) OF THE CORPUSCULAR RAYS PRODUCED BY VARIOUS CHARACTERISTIC X RAYS.

(To derive μ/ρ, multiply the values of μ below by **773** for air and **11,130** for H_2.)

Absorbing Gas.	Metal emitting Corpuscles (and at. wt.).	Exciting Characteristic X Radiation from										
		Fe (56)	Ni (59)	Cu (64)	Zn (65)	As (75)	Se (79)	Sr (88)	Mo (96)	Rh (103)	Ag (108)	Sn (119)
Air	Al (27)	—	—	—	—	29·6	—	20·0	15·2	—	8·90	6·54
"	Fe (56)	—	38·9	37·0	35·8	30·2	26·4	21·5	15·5	10·9	8·84	6·41
"	Cu (64)	—	—	—	36·2	30·4	—	20·8	15·2	10·8	8·81	3·67
"	Se (79)	—	—	—	—	—	—	16·1*	14·0*	—	8·8*	6·5*
"	Ag (108)	87·2*	—	51·9	{42·7* / 35·4}	{27·4* / 30·2}	—	21·2	15·4	10·3	8·78	{3·97* / 6·63}
H_2	Ag (108)	17·05*	—	9·55*	7·71*	—	—	—	—	—	—	0·51*

*Values marked * are due to Beatty; the rest are Sadler's.

cular rays from X rays have, at any rate approximately, the same velocity as the original generating cathode rays in the X-ray bulb—a result of great theoretical importance.

Barkla, Simms and Philpot have shown that in the gaseous absorption of X rays the amount of corpuscular radiation generated is proportional to the absorption co-efficient.

Barkla and Shearer (*P.M.* Dec. 1915) have further shown that the *K* and *L* groups of corpuscles ejected from a par-ticular substance by the action of X rays are emitted with approximately the same velocity, although the two groups are different in origin and association, being probably pro-duced by two separate rings of electrons in the atom (see p. 18).[1]

Fatigue Effect in Production of Secondary X Rays.

A number of experimenters, among them More (*P.M.* 1907), Gowdy (*P.R.* 1910), and Rieman (*P.R.* 1911), have obtained results which indicate that the output of secondary X rays from a metal diminishes with time, and that the metal exhibits a fatigue effect under the action of the X rays. It is now, however, pretty generally accepted that the effect is due largely, if not wholly, to chemical change of the surface by the action of the surrounding gas. A freshly prepared metal surface, obtained for instance by distillation *in vacuo*, shows little or no fatigue if the vacuum is continually maintained and any action due to gases thereby prevented.

---

[1] Much work is being done on this subject at the present time (1922), and some of the above results on corpuscular rays (pp. 147 *et seq.*) are now known to need correction. The electrons liberated by homogeneous X rays are not of uniform speed but consist of a number of groups, the velocity of each of which depends on the amount of energy expended in liberating the electron from one of the several rings of the atom. The nature of the atom is thus an important factor. See De Broglie, Whiddington, and Ellis, 1921 and 1922.

CHAPTER X.

FURTHER PROPERTIES OF X RAYS.

IONISATION BY X RAYS.

WHEN X rays pass through a substance they here and there intrude into an atom, and are able to expel from it a corpuscle and so ionise the atom. But the proportion of atoms thus affected is extremely minute. Even in favourable cases, only one atom in a billion (10^{12}) or more is ionised : the rest are passed over, presumably without receiving any energy or being influenced in any appreciable way.

Ionisation and Pressure.

The degree of ionisation depends greatly on the nature of the gas and on its pressure, as well as on the quality of the X rays. The ionisation produced in a gas by the passage of X rays should, in the absence of any secondary radiation, be proportional to the mass of the gas, that is, to the pressure (at constant temperature). But usually, secondary radiation is generated : if it is sufficiently penetrating to reach the electrodes, the ionisation it produces will be proportional to the square of the pressure. If the secondary radiation were absorbed before reaching the electrodes, the ionisation would be simply proportional to the pressure.

But numerous observers agree that in the great majority of cases where the pressure is not very low, the ionisation-pressure curve follows a straight line,[1] and the inference

[1] For example, Crowther (*P.R.S.* 1908) using ordinary X rays; and Owen (*P.R.S.* 1912) with homogeneous X rays. The conditions must be such that no characteristic radiations are generated.

would be that the ionisation is due either to the direct action of the X rays or to the easily absorbed corpuscular rays.

X Rays ionise indirectly.

It is now generally accepted that the ionisation produced by X rays is an indirect one and due solely to the corpuscular rays; in other words, the secondary corpuscles carry all the ionising power but not all the energy. Prof. Bragg was the first to insist on the fact that X rays spend little energy in their flight, and that they can therefore have little ionising action.

Beatty's results (*P.R.S.* 1911) on the ionisation of heavy gases—SeH_2, AsH_3, and $Ni(CO)_4$—gave great support to Prof. Bragg's theory. Beatty found that the quantity of the corpuscular rays was the same whether the substance was in the gaseous or solid condition. But indisputable proof of the correctness of Bragg's notion was given by C. T. R. Wilson from his condensation experiments (see p. 156).

More recent work by Barkla and Philpot (*P.M.* 1913) has established the additional fact that the relative ionisations produced by equal absorptions of X rays in gases are the same as those produced by the corpuscular rays.

Relative Ionisation in Various Gases.

Most of the early experiments on gaseous ionisation were vitiated by the corpuscles released from the impact of the X rays against the electrodes or the surface of the ionisation chamber. Crowther (*P.R.S.* 1908), in an investigation of the ionisation produced by heterogeneous X rays in a large number of gases, took steps to avoid this difficulty. Some of Crowther's results are given in Table XVI.

With the exception of hydrogen, and possibly ethyl bromide, the degree of ionisation is evidently not affected much by the quality of the X rays. Owen (*P.R.S.* 1912) [1] and Barkla and Philpot (*P.M.* 1913), working with a series of homogeneous X rays of a great range of quality, have

---

[1] Owen's apparatus is shown on p. 143.

TABLE XVI. RELATIVE IONISATION PRODUCED IN VARIOUS GASES BY HETEROGENEOUS X RAYS.

Gas or Vapour.	Density relative to Air=1.	Ionisation relative to Air=1.	
		Soft X Rays (6 mm. spark).	Hard X Rays (27 mm. spark).
Hydrogen, H_2	0·07	0·01	0·18
Carbon dioxide, CO_2	1·53	1·57	1·49
Ethyl chloride, C_2H_5Cl	2·24	18·0	17·3
Carbon tetrachloride, CCl_4	5·35	67	71
Nickel carbonyl, $Ni(CO)_4$	5·90	89	97
Ethyl bromide, C_2H_5Br	3·78	72	118
Methyl iodide, CH_3I	4·96	145	125
Mercury methyl, $Hg(CH_3)_2$	7·93	425	—

TABLE XVII. RELATIVE IONISATION PRODUCED IN VARIOUS GASES BY HOMOGENEOUS X RAYS.[1]

Element emitting Characteristic K Radiation.	Ionisation relative to Air=1.					
	H_2* (Beatty).	O_2 (B. & P.).	CO_2 (Owen).	SO_2 (Owen).	C_2H_5Br (B. & P.).	CH_3I (B. & P.).
Fe	·00571	1·37	1·58	11·3	41·2	
Ni		1·35	1·55	11·6	—	162
Cu	·00573	1·38	1·55	11·8	42	152
Zn	·00570	1·42	1·54	11·5	41·6	
As	·00573	1·27	1·51	11·7	42·2	158
Se		1·31	1·53	11·8	41·7	
Sr		1·28	1·53	11·8	153	
Mo		1·28	1·54	11·5	213	188
Ag		1·32			272	198
Sn	·04	1·29			335	205
Sb		1·28				—
I		—				211
Ba		—				251

B. & P., Barkla and Philpot.

[1] All the secondary radiations except scattered X rays were completely absorbed in the gas. With ethyl bromide and methyl iodide, however, this was not the case with the X rays which were hard enough to excite the characteristic radiations of bromine and iodine respectively.

* Shearer (*P.M.* Oct. 1915) obtains values of 0·0010 and 0·0016 for Cu and Sn rays respectively.

established the fact that the ionisation is independent of the hardness of the X rays. The one proviso is that no characteristic radiations shall be excited in the gas. If a characteristic radiation is generated, both the ionisation and absorption are usually increased. These results are apparent from Table XVII.

Total Ionisation in Various Gases.

Owen derived also the important result that the total number of ions produced by the complete absorption of a beam of homogeneous X rays in a gas is the same no matter what the hardness of the rays or the nature of the gas, so long as the characteristic radiations are not excited. This result was extended and confirmed by Barkla and Philpot (*P.M.* 1913), who also showed, in the case of corpuscular rays, that the total ionisation produced in a gas by a beam of homogeneous corpuscular rays is independent of the nature of the absorbing gas.

In regard to mixed gases the conditions are complicated, and the results are difficult of interpretation. It appears probable that an additive law does not hold (Barkla and Philpot, *P.M.* 1913), and that when a mixture of two gases is traversed by X rays the observed ionisation differs considerably from the sum of the ionisations that would be observed if the pencil of X rays went through the gases separately.

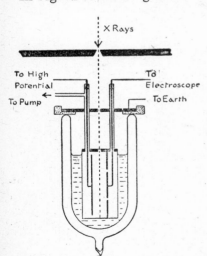

FIG. 74.—Crowther's apparatus for showing that the degree of ionisation by X rays in a gas is independent of the temperature. The guard-ring device will be noticed. The apparatus is here shown as arranged for liquid-air temperature.

Ionisation and Temperature.

In 1909 Crowther(*P.R.S.*) showed that the ionisation produced by X rays was independent of the temperature, provided the density was kept constant. In these experiments, Crowther used a range of temperature from about −180° to +184° C., and took especial care that the X rays did not strike the testing electrodes. His apparatus as arranged for liquid air temperatures is shown in Fig. 74.

C. T. R. Wilson's Condensation Experiments.

C. T. R. Wilson (*P.R.S.* 1912), in a series of remarkable experiments, has recently succeeded in rendering visible and photographing the tracks of the charged ions which are produced when a beam of X rays (or radium rays) passes through a gas. The method is based on the fact that supersaturated water vapour deposits on ions—just as it does on dust particles—and forms tiny drops. Thus the trail of a beam of X rays, itself invisible, becomes marked by a crowded line of cloud.

Wilson has been able to take instantaneous photographs of these condensation nuclei in the positions which they occupied immediately after their liberation by the X rays.

Fig. 75 shows the apparatus. The air within the shallow condensation chamber was kept completely saturated with moisture by means of water in the bottom of the vessel. Supersaturation was produced by suddenly increasing the volume of the chamber by exposing the under side of the movable bottom to a vacuum chamber. This was effected by a sharp pull (to the left) on the cord shown (in Fig. 75), which opened the valve below the condensation apparatus. After the release of the valve, the cord pulled up with a jerk, the heavy weight attached to it was thus suddenly arrested, and the fine thread below it carrying a steel ball, snapped and the steel ball fell. In its descent, the ball passed in succession through two spark-gaps. The first passage caused a Leyden jar flash through the X-ray bulb ; the second similarly excited the illuminating spark.

The arrangements were such that a horizontal beam of X rays crossed the centre of the chamber ; the illuminating spark flashed a pencil of light at right angles to the beam of X rays, and horizontally, or nearly so ; and the camera was usually mounted horizontally on the opposite side of the chamber to the illuminating spark. An electric field was maintained between the upper and lower faces of the expansion chamber.

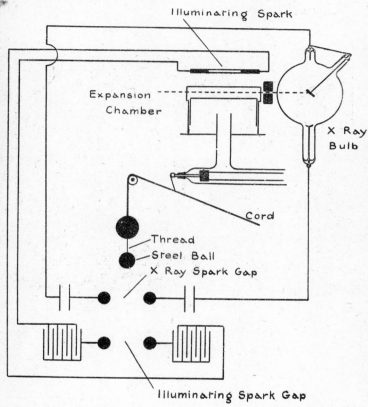

FIG. 75.—Diagrammatic representation of C. T. R. Wilson's apparatus for photographing the track of a beam of X rays in moist air.

The order of events in an experiment was, therefore, (1) expansion producing supersaturation, (2) X-ray discharge producing ionisation in the cloud chamber, (3) condensation of water on the ions, (4) passage of the spark for photographing the cloud tracks.

Wilson's instantaneous photographs (see Figs. 1 and 76)

show the tracks of corpuscles starting within the beam of
X rays and extending for some distance beyond it. There
is no indication of any activity on the part of the X rays
other than the production of corpuscles : and the track of
the X ray is not distinguishable otherwise than as being
the region in which corpuscles have their origin. The cloud

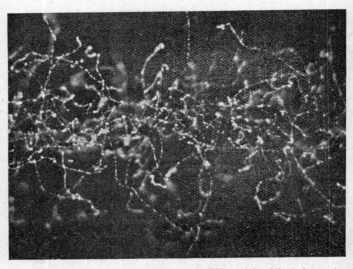

FIG. 76.—Photograph obtained by C. T. R. Wilson of the path of a beam of
X rays in air supersaturated with moisture (see p.156). The beam of rays,
about 2 mm. in diameter, traversed the air (from left to right of the picture)
immediately after the expansion which produced the supersaturation. The
axis of the camera was horizontal, and the magnification of the photograph
is 6 diameters.

trails show that the corpuscles start in all directions from
within the path of the primary beam : they do not appear
to exhibit preference for any particular direction.

The result is striking confirmation of the view which
Prof. Bragg has advocated for some years—that the X ray
is completely inoffensive and innocuous during its life, and
that only on its disappearance does the effective agent—
the corpuscle—come to life. Ionisation by X rays appears,
therefore, to be entirely a secondary process.

Fig. 2 shows a pencil of X rays passing obliquely through
a copper plate. The transmitted beam, though much less

dense than the initial beam, can be plainly seen. From the copper issue corpuscular rays in all directions ; these, which are responsible for the " halo " round the sheet, prove to be mostly of relatively long range. The characteristic copper radiation also excites corpuscular rays in the air, the majority of which have only a range of about 1 mm. at atmospheric pressure, and are to be found scattered throughout the vessel. This may be compared with the 1 cm. to 3 cm. tracks of corpuscles from the primary X-ray beam. If silver is used instead of copper, the secondary corpuscles have a much longer path. The clear space shown on both sides of the copper sheet in Fig. 2 is due merely to the heat of absorption of the X rays and the consequent formation of a region of air which is not saturated.

Wilson attempted to display the crystal-reflection of X rays (see p. 211) by means of the above apparatus, but, for some reason, the reflected beam was ineffective in producing ions, and the plan did not succeed.

Shimizu (*P.R.S.* 1921) has extensively developed and simplified the technique of Wilson's experiments.

VELOCITY OF X RAYS.

In 1906, Marx in Germany published the results of an ingenious and elaborate investigation on the speed of the Röntgen rays. He excited an X-ray bulb by means of electric waves from an electrical-wire system ; these waves also charged to a varying potential an insulated plate on which the X rays fell. The secondary corpuscles emitted from this plate were collected by a Faraday cylinder connected to an electrometer : the amount was obviously controlled by the phase-relation between the potential of the plate and that of the cathode of the Röntgen-ray bulb. If the various distances and the connecting wire lengths were adjusted so that the charge received by the Faraday cylinder was (say) a maximum, then it was found that if the distance of the X-ray bulb from the insulated plate was increased by a certain amount, the wire along which the waves travelled to the plate had to be lengthened by the same amount to restore the maximum. Thus, according to Marx, the Röntgen rays travel with the same velocity as electric waves along wires, and, therefore, with the velocity of light, at any rate to within 5 per cent.

Marx's experimental arrangements were subjected to severe criticism by Franck and Pohl, who, having repeated the experiments, doubted the validity of the method. In reply, Marx (*A.d.P.* 1910 *et seq.*) has since carried out a new series of experiments which, he claims, support his original result, but which nevertheless do not appear to have satisfied his critics (*A.d.P.* 1911).

All this work was carried out before the nature of the X rays was known ; and there is now no reason for believing that X rays travel with a velocity other than that of light.

CHAPTER XI.

PRACTICAL APPLICATIONS OF X RAYS.

X Rays and Medicine.

Radiography.

An extended treatment of this most important branch of the subject can be found in medical works ; Chapter XII. deals with a number of important points in connection with equipment and technique. A radiograph is, of course, nothing but a shadow picture, and naturally care must be taken to place the subject symmetrically with regard to the bulb, so as to avoid unnecessary distortion of the image. For perfectly sharp images, the X rays should obviously proceed from a single point on the anticathode, but this, as has been remarked, is impracticable, and so it is usually beneficial to stop down the rays as much as is feasible. For this purpose, lead tube diaphragms are often employed, and can, in some medical cases, be made to serve a double purpose—for example, the kidneys, which are in continual periodic motion, can be arrested temporarily, for radiographic purposes, by pressing down such a tube tightly into the abdomen.

The greater the distance of the bulb from the fluorescent screen or photographic plate, the more correct the picture ; in practice the distance is usually from 12 to 24 inches. For the bulk of medical work 6 to 8 inches spark-gap between points is an average, though higher values may be used for special purposes. If the X rays are too hard, photographic contrast suffers (as with γ rays).

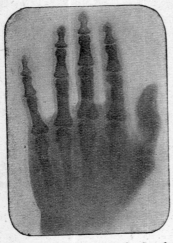

FIG. 77.—Early radiograph by Campbell Swinton, Jan. 18, 1896. Exposure 4 mins.

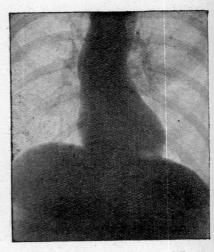

FIG. 78.—Instantaneous radiograph of thorax. Exposure about 1/100 sec. (Knox, 1915.)

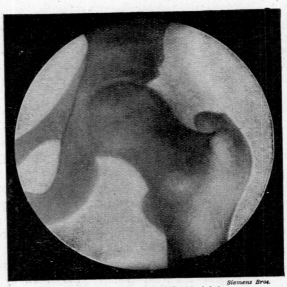

Siemens Bros.

FIG. 79.—Radiograph of the hip-joint

Photographic exposures naturally vary with the high potential generator and tube used. The latitude in exposure is large, though it is important to avoid under-exposure.

The photographic plates are placed with the film towards the bulb, and most photographers agree that slow development is useful for work such as this, where full detail is required.

The effects of scattered radiation have often to be guarded against, as they are prejudicial to definition. They can be lessened somewhat in the negative by generous exposure and short development.

The method of tank development and standardised procedure is gaining in popularity. Films are now preferred to plates by many workers.

Bismuth Radiography.

The alimentary system may be radiographed by rendering the required part temporarily opaque through the administration of bismuth salts or emulsions with the food. This produces contrast in the photograph. Fig. 80 shows a good illustration of the method. Thorium oxide and barium sulphate are also used. A word of caution should be added, for the pronounced and very soft secondary rays that bismuth and other heavy metals emit, may actually be injurious.

Stereoscopic Radiography.

In this work, two distinct pictures are taken in turn by moving the X-ray tube, between the exposures, 2 or 3 inches parallel to the surface of the plate, the distance between tube and subject being about 20 inches. The resulting photographs are examined in a stereoscope. The method affords a means of ascertaining the depth of a foreign substance in the body, and is often of great assistance in diagnosis. There are other types of localisers, some of which display much ingenuity of design; they can be found fully described in the makers' catalogues (see p. 205).

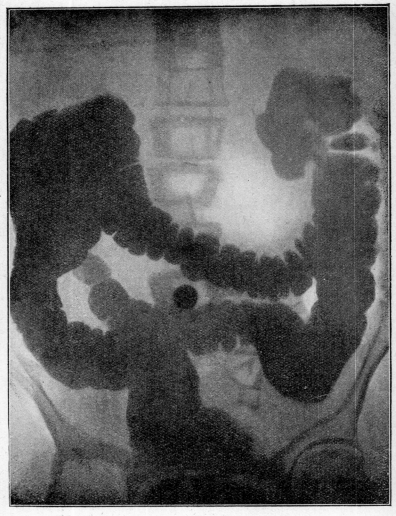

Fig. 80.—Bismuth radiograph of the intestines. The black circular spot near the centre of the picture is produced by a metal disc which is placed on the umbilicus as a "landmark."

Instantaneous Radiography.

It is a far cry from the prolonged exposures in the early days of X rays to the instantaneous work that is possible with modern apparatus. Nowadays, snapshots can be taken through any part of the body, and almost any of the moving organs can be radiographed. The worker who requires exposures short and frequent enough for, say, cinematograph films now experiences no difficulties out of the ordinary.

If a single rapid photograph is all that is required, it is possible to secure it by comparatively simple means, and to send through an X-ray tube momentary currents of a magnitude undreamt of a few years ago. One method for obtaining practically instantaneous radiographs is to join the primary of a modern heavy current induction coil, or other high-tension transformer, straight to the direct-current town-lighting mains using special " explosive " fuses. When the current is switched on, the fuses are immediately blown, and the consequent interruption of the current produces a powerful discharge through the secondary winding and the X-ray tube in circuit with it. For such rapid exposures a simple X-ray tube without cooling and regulating devices suffices. Dessauer in 1909, by using a type of explosive fuse for the break, was able to take single flash radiographs with exposures of the order of $\frac{1}{100}$ sec. The momentary current through the tube was some 200 milliamperes or more, and the alternative discharge in air consisted of a broad band of flame 40 to 50 cms. long.

Sir James Mackenzie Davidson a few years ago radiographed a bullet leaving the muzzle of a revolver. The bullet in its flight over the surface of a photographic plate broke the primary circuit of a coil somewhat after the fashion employed by Mr. Boys some thirty years ago in his flying-bullet photography. The resulting flash through a suitably disposed X-ray tube in the secondary circuit gave a shadow photograph of the bullet.

Perhaps even more remarkable were Dr. Worrall's experiments with a monster coil having a core weighing some 3 hundredweights. With a primary current of from 40 to 80 amperes at 240 volts, and the use of an explosion break, flash currents of the order of 1·4 amperes lasting for an interval of from $\frac{1}{200}$ to $\frac{1}{1000}$ second were sent through an

X-ray tube. The intensity of the discharge was such as to be capable of chiselling out a piece of metal from the anticathode and leaving a pit behind. Dr. Worrall has obtained very beautiful instantaneous radiographs by means of his apparatus.

The possibilities of the extension of such experiments as these are far from being exhausted. A transformer which weighs about half a ton was referred to by Duddell in his Presidential Address to the Institution of Electrical Engineers (1912). Given a closer co-operation between the medical profession and the electrical engineer, mammot' apparatus and extraordinary results may be looked for in the future.

Intensifying Screens.

But by the aid of intensifying screens (a device which dates back to 1897), instantaneous radiography is possible with a much less formidable equipment. The recent improvements in such screens have largely removed the defects of grain, etc., which formerly militated against their employment. The Sunic screen, for example, is coated with tungstate of calcium, which, fluorescing as it does with a very actinic bluish light, is capable of reducing an exposure twentyfold. The screen is placed in close contact with the film of the plate and the X rays are sent through the screen before reaching the plate. Owing to the after-luminescence, which persists for some minutes, the screen should either be removed immediately after the exposure or not be disturbed for some little time. Intensifying screens are more efficacious with hard rays than soft.

X-Ray Photographic Plates.

A photographic plate registers only about 1 per cent. of the X rays passing through it. Progress has mainly consisted in thickening the emulsion or richly loading it either with more silver or with heavier metals. Exposures may be shortened either by backing up the emulsion with a sheet of a heavy metal, such as lead, or, more appreciably, by

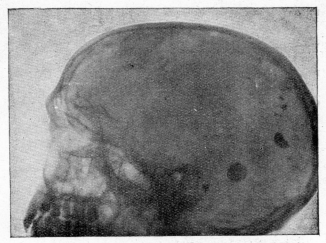

FIG. 83.—Shrapnel bullets and fragments of shell in brain. (N. S. Finzi.)

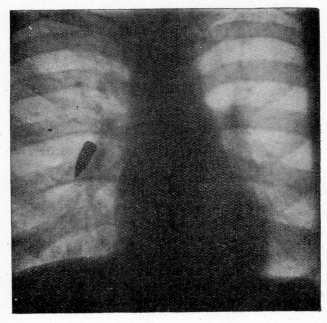

FIG. 84.—Bullet at hilum of right lung. The bullet had been there a month when this radiograph was taken. There was neither inflammation nor symptoms. (N. S. Finzi.)

In another direction the venous and arterial systems of the human body can, by the aid of suitable injections, be radiographed and displayed to the student.

H. Béclère has done excellent work in the production of X-ray finger prints. For the purpose the finger-tip is rubbed with red lead, and the resulting radiograph is peculiar to the patient, not only in the design of the finger print, but also in the shape of the bone (Fig. 85).

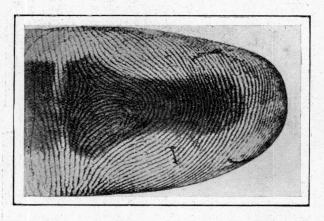

FIG. 85.—Radiograph of finger, showing finger print and bone. (H. Béclère.)

Radiotherapy.

The X rays possess a marked effect on animal tissue. The living cells have the power of resisting or responding to X rays, while malignant cells disappear with suitable "dosage." The treatment has, for example, been largely and successfully employed for rodent ulcers, and much attention is being paid to the cure of cancer.

In many skin diseases the X rays have proved to be of notable service. For example, they are now the accepted and certain means of curing ringworm. The "dose" is all important, for the sweat glands and hair follicles are also affected and, with excessive exposure, may even be destroyed, the result being baldness.

The red and white corpuscles of the blood appear to be

prejudicially affected by X rays, resulting in a form of aplastic anæmia. Certain of the internal organs are very susceptible to the rays, *e.g.* the spleen, the generative organs, etc.

Curiously enough, the rays seem to have little or no action on bacteria or their spores, and in this respect stand out in marked contrast to ultra-violet light.

Deep-seated organs are now successfully treated by X rays. In deep radiotherapy, more particularly for cancerous growths, modern technique is tending in the direction of administering massive doses of very short-waved X rays. The soft rays prejudicial to the skin are removed by using metal filters (Al or Zn) with a coating on the side nearest the skin of wood or leather, so that no characteristic radiation may play on the skin. Over-dosage of the skin is also avoided by employing multiple parts of entry, each of the various beams being properly directed at the deep affected tissue.

The chief hindrance to precise radiotherapy at the present time is probably the lack of a convenient and accurate means of measuring the dose of radiation absorbed by the particular region concerned, especially if it be at a depth in the body. On physical grounds, at any rate, it would seem that it is only those rays which are absorbed which can produce physiological changes, and only such rays should be included when speaking of a dose. It may be, of course, that selective action is present, and that only a restricted range of wave-lengths is appropriate for the conversion of energy in the correct spot. With this reservation it would seem that the degree of reaction should be a function of the absorbed and converted energy. The problem of dosage is complicated by the large amount of scattering which occurs and the lack of homogeneity of the primary beam.

It may be added that the therapeutic effect of X rays often manifests itself pronouncedly in the proximity of bones. This is probably due in part to characteristic radiations emitted by the calcium and other constituents of the bones.

Among the tragedies of the war few were more pathetic

than the ghastly disfigurements caused by shell wounds of the face and head. Fortunately, it was often possible, by the wonderful grafting operations of the surgeon, to restore at least a semblance of the patient's former appearance. Lips were renewed, new noses built up, eyelids replaced, cavities in the palate filled in by flaps taken from the skin or scalp. The scar-tissues and flaps were kept pliant and adaptable by "spraying" with X rays, which also served to depilate hair and to stimulate the healing process in both flaps and bone.

It may be remarked that in therapeutic work a sharp-focussed X-ray tube is not necessary.

X-Ray "Burns."

The dangers of indiscriminate exposure to X rays are now common knowledge, but some of the pioneers in X-ray work bought their experience at the price of their lives. Undue exposure results in severe dermatitis or skin disease, followed in chronic cases by large and cancerous ulceration, scaling and shedding of the nails. Unfortunately, the extremely painful progress of the disease does not appear to be arrested by avoiding further exposure to the rays. Nor is there any known means of hastening recovery, though, according to the late Sir James Mackenzie Davidson, some improvement has been obtained in superficial cases by the application of radium to the affected part in "doses" of some minutes at a time.

A further danger to the X-ray operator appears to consist in derangement of internal organs and impoverishment of the blood corpuscles.

X-Ray Protection.

It is now known that X-ray "burns" are mainly due to the absorption by the skin of the very soft rays; such rays are easily arrested by screening. The various protective devices (gloves, spectacles, aprons, etc.), now always employed for the safety of workers, rely mainly on the absorptive properties of lead or lead salts in some form or other, for example, lead-impregnated rubber, lead glass, etc.

The X-ray bulb should be enclosed as completely with adequate protective material, either in the form of a tube box or as a lead glass sheath. In some instances, the bulb itself is made of lead glass provided with a window of soda or lithia glass to allow the rays to get out. Fluorescent screens used for examination work should be faced with an adequate thickness of lead glass on the side remote from the bulb.

In view of the great public interest which the subject has excited, and the fact that complete safeguards are possible, the reports are given in Appendix V. of a representative committee which reviewed the whole question in the light of present-day knowledge. The recommendations are many-sided and cover most of the points which experience has suggested both in X-ray and radium practice.

It may here be remarked that with exciting voltages in the region of 200,000, 3 mm. of lead reduces the intensity of X rays over 10,000 times, 10 mm. of lead over 1,000,000 times. Good lead-impregnated rubber sheet is ordinarily equivalent to about $\frac{1}{4}$ to $\frac{1}{2}$ of the same thickness of lead sheet. For lead glass the corresponding figures are $\frac{1}{10}$ to $\frac{1}{5}$, although it is possible to obtain glass with a figure of $\frac{1}{4}$.

The dangers of scattered X rays should be realised, particularly with very high exciting voltages.

Glasses specially Transparent to Soft X Rays.

A bulb intended for skin treatment should be either made of a glass which is transparent to X rays or provided with a window of such glass. Schott in 1899 was the first to make up a glass of this kind—a silico-borate of soda and alumina—as the result of experiments on the transparency of various oxides and carbonates to X rays. His list reads in order of diminishing transparency—Li, B, Na, Mg, Al, Si, K, Cu, Mn, As, Ba, and Pb—a sequence which is that of atomic weight. Schott's glass was never put on the market, as at that time the radiographic properties of the X rays were the only ones considered, and in this respect the glass possesses no appreciable advantage over soda glass. C. E. S. Phillips' conducting glass (*P.R.S.E.* 1906), which is a mixture of silicate of soda and borax with a little lead glass, is also very transparent to X rays. Its coefficient of expansion is unusually high, but by the use of intermediate glasses, windows of it could probably be fused into X-ray tubes. Lindemann (1911) was the first to construct focus bulbs provided with windows of a glass of lithium borate, which, of all the glasses ever made, is probably the most transparent to soft X rays. This glass is not very permanent, however, but Messrs. Cossor have brought out a lithium glass which can be worked and permits joints with platinum, so that X-ray bulbs can be constructed entirely of it (Fig. 46).

Therapeutic Use of Characteristic Radiations.

It has been suggested that the various characteristic radiations would find application and lead to greater precision and efficiency in curative X-ray work. These radiations are each of uniform quality, and it is therefore only a question of choosing a suitably hard radiation for the purpose in hand. But characteristic X rays, as ordinarily generated, are so feeble that hours of exposure are required in place of the minutes necessary with primary X rays from a bulb. The writer showed, however (p. 126), that, under the right conditions, a large proportion of the rays from an anticathode may consist of its characteristic radiation. By this means, an intense beam could be obtained from a tube provided with a suitable metal for anticathode and a window of thin glass or aluminium. It is further advantageous to use a thin filtering screen of the same metal as the anticathode. Better still, perhaps, in some respects, would be to make the window itself of the metal whose radiation is desired and to use the window also as anticathode. Such a tube with a window soldered to the glass has been used by a number of experimenters.

Therapeutic Use of Cathode Rays.

If, as Prof. Bragg has long maintained, and, as is now generally believed, the X ray is in itself ineffective and owes all its activity—physical and chemical—to the electrons which it produces when arrested, then the only purpose the X ray serves in therapeutics is to plant the action deeper in the body. To produce therapeutic action at any particular point, there must first of all be transformation of the X rays into corpuscular rays, and then absorption of these corpuscular rays. If cathode rays themselves were simply discharged at the skin by means, say, of a Lenard tube (p. 5), they could not penetrate more than about $\frac{1}{50}$ mm., *i.e.* about the thickness of a cigarette paper. Possibly such a treatment might be valuable for some surface ailments, more especially as the radiation would certainly be accompanied by an abundance of very soft X rays from the aluminium window.

X RAYS AND INDUSTRY

In well-nigh every branch of industry the testing of materials has come to be of importance. With increasing knowledge and the stress of competition, a variety of testing methods have been evolved to ascertain quality and uniformity as determined by the several physical, chemical, and visual characteristics. Such tests are commonly conducted on samples which are selected to be as representative as possible. From the nature of things the value of the results is limited, and the engineer in particular is ever on the lookout for opportunities for further insight into the materials he employs.

The employment of X rays in the examination of materials lies at present in two main directions :

(1) X-ray crystallography or the study of crystal structure.

(2) Radiography or X-ray shadow photography.

X-Ray Crystallography.

We can only refer to the great potentialities of the results of X-ray analysis as applied to the structure of materials. As described in Chapter XIII., Laue in 1912 sent a heterogeneous beam of X rays through a thin crystal and showed photographically that a diffraction pattern was produced. The Braggs followed with the X-ray spectrometer in which monochromatic X rays are reflected from the several faces of a crystal. The examination of the resulting emission spectra served to disclose the atomic architecture of a large number of crystals. De Broglie also turned the method to account in connection with X-ray absorption spectra (p. 249).

The practical possibilities were greatly enlarged when Debye and Scherrer (at Zurich), and Hull (at the G.E.C. Research Laboratory, Schenectady) showed that large crystals were not essential, but that the method could be applied to an aggregate of finely powdered crystalline material, provided the orientation of the crystals was sufficiently random. This was a big step forward, for it enables the crystalline structure of a body to be examined even when the individual crystals are microscopic or ultra-microscopic in size. We now know that almost every solid substance when examined is found to possess crystalline structure; and it would seem that the various physical properties—elasticity, hardness, melting points, etc.—are all manifestations of the various atomic forces which reveal themselves in the crystalline form. The very formation of solids may be merely an outward and visible sign of crystallisation, and a definition of a " solid " may be so derived, which is, at any rate, as adequate as others which have been framed. Not only the growth but the decay, the change-points, etc., can all be followed and watched without harming the body in any way.

We have thus a new tool of research, which, although at present rather delicate and tentative in application, would seem to offer boundless possibilities. The metallurgist, to whom crystalline formation means so much, need no longer have to content himself with inferring from their external forms what the internal structure of the crystals in his metals and alloys may be. He may also find that the method will throw light on the fundamental nature of the effect of heat treatment, tempering, rolling, and ageing on steels and other crystalline metals and alloys. It has been shown that powdered graphite is fully crystalline; that colloidal gold and silver are made up of minute, yet perfect, crystals so small that they contain only a few score atoms. Even the particles "sputtered" from a cathode in a discharge tube are possible of examination and are found to be crystalline.

These are but a few of many examples which can be found in the extensive literature. There is a great opportunity for the metallurgist and physicist to get together. At present the main difficulties are those of technique, but they are being rapidly overcome.

Industrial Radiography.

As was anticipated by Röntgen and others, when the art of radiography had sufficiently advanced in medicine, it extended its scope to industry. The method of X-ray inspection has the outstanding advantage of not injuring a body in any way. Furthermore, it provides in many cases the only means of detecting concealed defects in a material, or of scrutinising in a structure the accuracy of assembly of component parts which are hidden from view.

While the general technique is much the same as in medicine, mention should be made of one of the chief experimental precautions in the X-ray photography of metals. Even in medical radiography the experienced worker is well aware of the effect of the scattered radiation which is generated whenever a beam of X rays strikes any particle of matter. Such scattered radiation, if allowed to reach the photographic plate, tends to fog the main image. The various surfaces of the bodies encountered are bad offenders, and even the air contributes its quotum (p. 113).

The effect is especially marked with metallic objects, which require penetrating rays and relatively long exposures. Worthless results will be obtained in the absence of suitable precautions. These consist in enveloping the photographic plate, back and front, with sheet lead (preferably with an inner lining of aluminium), a hole being left no bigger than necessary for the reception of the direct image of the object. If the object is continuous and flat, there is no difficulty, for it can be brought into close contact with the plate. If, however, the body is irregular in contour, it may conveniently be cemented with paraffin wax to the bottom of a cardboard or aluminium tray, and mercury, fine lead shot, lead powder or the like poured round it. Wax filling or plasticene is also necessary to fill up any pockets or cavities and to prevent the mercury or lead from straying into the path of the projected image.

Considerable gain may result from the use of the Bucky grid between the object and the plate. This consists of a rectangular lead grid, the faces being spherical in contour and the dividing cell-walls of the grid everywhere radial. The grid, while allowing direct X rays from the focus to pass, kills the majority of the scattered radiation. The grid is kept in slight motion to prevent its being registered on the photograph. Still greater freedom from the effects of secondary radiation may be obtained by using specially sensitive plates, and so shortening the exposure.

Naturally the orientation of the object with reference to the beam of X rays may make or mar a radiograph. Distortion may be reduced by avoiding undue obliquity of the rays, and to this end it is wise to keep the distance between the object and bulb as great as is expedient. For good definition the rays should be stopped down as much as possible.

The present practicable depths which can be penetrated in various materials are :—

  4-5 mm. of lead.
  12 mm. of tin.
  7·5 cms. of steel (carbon) or iron.
  10-15 cms. of aluminium and its alloys.
  30-40 cms. of wood.

The limiting factor in practice is the exposure which hitherto has been very protracted with the greater thicknesses. However, with the latest type of X-ray plate, the exposures are greatly reduced, and 1 inch of steel, for example, now requires an exposure of about a minute, using a voltage of about 130,000 and a few milliamperes through the tube.

Within the above limits we can, with considerable delicacy, hunt out anything which is so disposed as to cast a measurable variation in the shadow, provided the body is not too complicated in design to render the shadow too confusing to interpret. The method is surprisingly sensitive, for example, tool-marks and fine mould-marks often show up in a radiograph. The opacity is merely a measure of the number and weight of the atoms encountered, and so different qualities of a metal possessing different densities display different intensities in a radiograph, *e.g.* a wrought rivet in a casting of the same metal shows a darker image. For the same reason, equal thicknesses of carbon, nickel, and tungsten steels differ markedly in transparency, a property which has been turned to account.

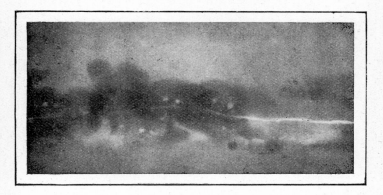

Fig. 86.—Radiograph of defective weld in steel plate ½ inch thick.

Electric and oxy-acetylene welding have come into great prominence during and since the war : an indifferent welder can turn out what appears on the surface to be an excellent weld, but is quite an unreliable job notwithstanding. There appears to be no adequate mechanical test for a weld, and in any event any such test, whether mechanical or microscopical, destroys the weld, good or bad. The X rays promise to be of great use in this connection. If the component parts are not actually fused together, a narrow dividing line comes out on the plate (Fig. 86). Blisters and blowholes show up as light spots. The amount of detail revealed is considerable, and the process compares favourably with that of photomicrography, which is only very local in its test, and, as already remarked, involves the destruction of the weld.

Hidden cracks in a metal, which are a bugbear to metallurgists, can often be detected, though if they are very fine or tortuous (hair cracks) the method is rarely suitable. Such cracks are sometimes the sequel to "pipes" or blowholes in the ingot, and it is easier to detect them in the ingot than after working.

In the case of alloys, the uneven distribution of any component results in a "patchy" or streaky radiograph. X-ray examination will often diagnose defective soldering or brazing, blowholes in castings, the substitution of one metal by another, hidden stopping or pinning, and so on. The method has also found application in detecting hidden corrosion (as in gas cylinders, in ferro-concrete, and the armouring of cables), in scrutinising steel turbine discs for segregations, etc., and so on.

Fig. 87.—Radiograph of silver (Sitka) spruce showing annual rings. (Knox and Kaye.)

Naturally enough the X rays found a great opening during the war in the manufacture of explosives and related devices. In some instances, *e.g.* the correct filling of liquid-gas grenades, the examination of opaque cordite, the interior detail of detonators, Stokes igniters, vent-sealing tubes and other pyrotechnic stores, no other method of inspection was possible. The X rays also proved of value in examining enemy ammunition of unknown design, where, for reasons of safety, it was desirable to ascertain the internal construction before opening up. They have also proved useful in checking the contents of packing boxes. Most of this work was carried out by the Research Department at the Royal Arsenal, Woolwich.

In the case of timber, the different varieties absorb X rays to different degrees. Peculiarities in the structure and path of the fibres (such as the contortions which produce "figure") are easily discerned. The denser heart wood is differentiated from the sap wood, the summer and

Fig. 88.—Radiograph (side and front views) of hollow aeroplane spar with plywood sides, showing badly-shaped end block split by screws. (Knox and Kaye.)

spring growths of the annual rings are readily identified (Fig. 87), and defects such as knots or grub-holes show up with astonishing clearness.

A method of utilising the X rays to examine the wooden parts of air craft was developed by Kaye and Knox on behalf of the Air Ministry during the war. At a time when the submarine was seriously endangering the country's supplies of high-grade timber from Canada and the States, designs for building up aeroplane parts from smaller timber were developed, using laminated or "box" structures. The workmanship required has to be of the finest, and much of it is hidden of necessity;` but the inspector now has a powerful ally in the X rays which unerringly reveal hidden faults such as knots, large resin-pockets, defective glueing, and poor workmanship (Fig. 88). Wood is very transparent to X rays, and thicknesses up to 18 inches or more can be dealt with, screen examination being possible in most cases.

X rays are also being turned to account by the tyre manufacturer in his efforts to improve the union between the rubber and the Egyptian cotton fabric. In the manufacture of golf balls, fine rubber tape is wound on a round core either of soft rubber or liquid. If care is not taken the core is distorted, becoming either roughly ellipsoidal or even dumb-bell shaped. The resulting ball is defective from the point of view of accurate flight, but such balls can be readily sorted out by the help of the X rays. The method is now in extensive use, no other being readily available (Fig. 89).

The help of the X rays has also been effectively sought by the manufacturer of carbon and graphite brushes and electrodes, to reveal mineral matter and internal cracks and flaws. The makers of electrical insulators—ebonite, built-up mica, fibre, paper, etc.—find the method invaluable for detecting the presence of foreign bodies.

The manufacture of optical glass became a key industry during the war, as hitherto we had relied wholly on Germany for our supplies. One of the greatest troubles which was encountered was the destructive action of the molten glass on the fireclay pot, in which the components were fused. It was found that the effect was caused by the presence of iron and other impurities in the clay. Recourse was had to the X rays, and it was found that on examining the pots before they were fired, those containing prejudicial foreign matter could readily be sorted out. In this way much expense can be saved. The "melt" of optical glass can also be examined for inclusions before working.

X-ray photographs are useful for displaying the arrangement of concealed wiring, for example, when embedded in
the interior of insulating panels or in radio apparatus.   In
much the same way, during the war, the X rays were useful
in scrutinising the wiring within the leather of aeroplane
pilots' electrically heated clothing.

Among the miscellaneous uses of the X rays we can only
make mention of the examination of oysters for pearls ;
the differentiation of lead glass jewels from the more transparent genuine gems ; the scrutiny of artificial teeth ; the
detection of contraband by the customs officials ; the sorting
of fresh from stale eggs ; the
detection of heavy elements
in minerals ; of metal particles in chocolate ; of weevils
in grain ; of mineral adulte-
rants in certain powdered
drugs (*e.g.* asafœtida); and of
moths in tobacco for cigars.

The internal diameter of
a tube can be measured
by filling it with mercury
and radiographing it in close
contact with a plate.   There
are no refraction effects to
allow for.

FIG. 89.—Radiograph of golf ball, showing
unsymmetrical core.

In quite a different direction an enterprising shoe store
has installed a screen outfit, so that the potential customer
can see his " footigraph," and satisfy himself visually
whether or not the shoe he is trying on is a good fit.

The application of the cinematograph principle to X-ray
photography offers wide possibilities.

We can only refer to the more academic applications of
the X rays by the conchologist to examine the interior of
shells and fossils, without in any way spoiling a rare specimen.
These have valuable educational possibilities.

The use of the X rays for revealing the interior of plant
life is comparatively recent.   Considerable differences exist
in the mineral content and density, and hence the trans-

parency of the different parts of a plant—root, stem, leaf, flower, fruit, seed, etc.—and thus it happens that even the most delicate structures of plants can be laid bare without tearing the plant to pieces in order to study it. Microscopic detail is, of course, not revealed. Long-waved X rays are required for such work (Fig. 90).

Radiomicrography of tiny objects has been successfully achieved by M. Goby (*A.Rt.R.* Dec. 1913). (See Fig. 91.)

X Rays and Old Masters.

In any picture we have to consider three media—(1) the surface which is painted on—usually canvas or wood,

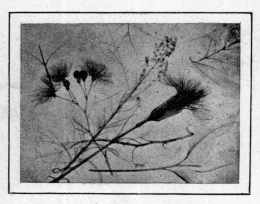

though paper, porcelain, or other materials may be used ; (2) the priming or sizing —nowadays almost always white lead, though formerly carbonate of lime and glue were employed ; (3) the actual pigments.

Fig. 90.—Radiograph of flowers, showing delicate structure. (Knox.)

Both wood and canvas are very transparent to the X rays, though different kinds of canvas vary a good deal. The white lead primer is much more opaque than carbonate of lime, and the former, moreover, penetrates much farther into the interstices of the canvas. This in itself is sufficient to show a marked difference under the X rays between modern and older pictures.

As to pigments, they vary greatly in X-ray opacity from the opaque salts of lead, zinc, and mercury to the transparent aniline derivatives and bitumen. Both modern and ancient whites are usually opaque, most of the blacks (new or old) are transparent, and modern reds are more transparent than the old reds. Most of the earliest pigments are mineral in origin, and opaque.

In a modern picture the sizing is very commonly more opaque than the pigments, and X-ray examination is, for

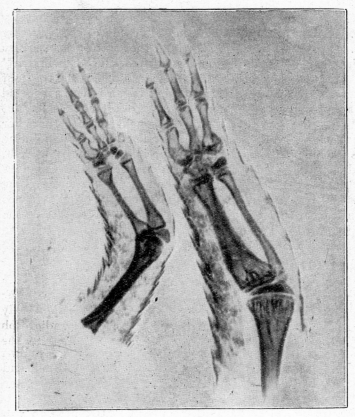

FIG. 91.—Microradiograph (magnified 17 diameters) of legs of a tiny lizard (*Seps tridactylus*). By Pierre Goby.

that reason, usually inconclusive. But, fortunately, in the pictures of the old masters the reverse conditions hold, and thus it is that with a little experience the X rays can be employed most usefully as a means of identifying a modern fake, or detecting alterations to an old picture. It is a practical certainty that, however skilfully the process has been carried out, the several materials used—whether canvas, priming, or pigment—will differ from those in the original painting and will, in consequence, be differentiated in the radiograph.

Notable work on this subject has been carried out by Dr. Heilbron of Amsterdam and, more recently, by Dr. Chéron of Paris. Among the sixteenth - century paintings examined by the former was the "Crucifixion" by Cornelis Engelbrechtsen, which contained in the right foreground the portrait of a woman which it was suspected was that of a former "donatrice," who (after a fashion not unknown in those days) had thus sought to perpetuate her association with the picture. A radiograph of the painting showed many "restorations," especially on the right half, and beneath the portrait of the donatrice was revealed the picture of a monk in surplice and stole, the head being smaller than that of the over-painted lady. The evidence was so clear that the picture was sent to be restored at the Rijks Museum in Amsterdam, the result being to bring to light once more the monk who had been hidden for 400 years.

Among the other paintings examined by Heilbron was a panel of the "Madonna" by Geertgen van St. Jans (c. 1500), which had always excited comment because of the apparently stiff and unnatural position of the arms. The radiograph showed that the presence of the Child in the arms of the Madonna fully explained their attitude. St. Jans is known to have painted his children disproportionately small, and the presumption is that this defect was the cause of some former owner having the Child painted out.

Dr. Chéron X-rayed a Flemish panel attributed to van Ostade, and showing a party of country dancers and revellers. The radiograph revealed only a farmyard scene containing peacocks, ducks, and chickens. The supposed van Ostade is almost certainly modern, since practically all its colours are transparent to the rays. The farmyard picture is apparently old, since the sizing is not opaque (Fig. 92).

Fig. 92.—(A) Ordinary photograph of a reputed van Ostade ; (B) Radiograph showing underlying farmyard picture. (Chéron.)

Future Developments of Industrial Radiology.

Our ideal should be to make the taking of an X-ray photograph as easy and silent as that of light.   The present limitations of industrial radiography are largely those prescribed by equipment and technique. Considerable improvements will have to come if the subject is to extend its scope and become an attractive commercial proposition in heavy engineering. If great thicknesses are to be tackled, means will have to be found so that exposures are not intolerably long. There appear to be two means to this end—(a) by using much heavier X-ray outputs at much higher voltages, or (b) by using much more sensitive screens, plates, or other detectors.

We have already considered the probable developments of the high-potential generator and, as we should anticipate, all experience agrees in demanding higher and higher voltages for work with metals. The ordinary Coolidge tube will, however, take no more than 150,000 volts, preferably less. This can be increased to 200,000 by lengthening the arms of the tube or completely immersing it in oil. If there is a demand for it, the electrical engineer will doubtless overcome the difficulties in the way of supplying half a million or more volts. Such transformers have already been made for other purposes, but their bulk, weight, and cost are formidable.

Heavier discharges will demand more elaborate cooling arrangements, and probably glass X-ray tubes will not stand up to the work. We may have to turn to metal tubes radically different in design, capable of absorbing 50 H.P. or more. Furthermore, we shall have to improve the very low efficiency of the whole outfit.

As regards fluorescent screens and photographic plates, great improvements are called for. No screen at present available is sensitive enough for thicknesses exceeding about $\frac{1}{4}$ inch steel, and only then with difficulty. Photography must be resorted to in such cases, and the time taken over the process may then become prohibitive, at any rate for routine " mass inspection."

For a more extended treatment of industrial radiology the reader is referred to the author's " Practical Applications of X-Rays " (Chapman & Hall).

CHAPTER XII.

X-RAY EQUIPMENT AND TECHNIQUE.

By W. F. Higgins, M.Sc.

The various types of apparatus employed in the production of X rays have been described in previous chapters, but a brief account of the installation and procedure for taking X-ray photographs may be of interest, more especially in view of the great importance the subject assumed in the late war. For a fuller treatment and for guidance in the interpretation of radiographs, the various medical treatises should be consulted, *e.g.* Knox's *Radiography and Radiotherapeutics* (Black), or Hirsch's *Principles and Practice of Rœntgen Technique* (Lewis).

The necessary installation may be conveniently described under the following headings :—

(*a*) High-tension generator.
(*b*) Control switchboard.
(*c*) Measuring apparatus.
(*d*) X-ray tubes.
(*e*) High-tension circuits.
(*f*) Tube-stands and couches.
(*g*) Photographic apparatus.

(*a*) **High-tension Generator.**

The high-tension generator consists either of an induction coil and its accessories, or of one of the more modern high-tension interrupterless transformers dealt with on p. 63 *et seq.* The latter type of apparatus is of particular value for instantaneous radiography, though it is possible to turn out the highest class of work of all kinds with an induction coil. In the late war, induction coils were almost exclusively used in the British base hospitals and in field and motor travelling outfits. For most purposes a 12-inch coil will suffice, but a 16 or 20-inch coil is better if ample power is desired. Moreover, although a potential corresponding to a 20-inch point-gap is not as yet required in X-ray practice, such coils give a much greater current-output (and less inverse current) at the lower voltages employed, and thereby enable reasonably short exposures to be given. Portable sets are often provided with smaller coils, with a view to reducing weight and expense, but their scope is necessarily limited.

The coil chosen should give a "fat" flaming discharge well up to its maximum sparking distance, and not a thin crackling spark such as characterises a small coil. As is remarked on p. 54, the attention of coil makers has been directed towards designs which yield a large current-output; and very efficient apparatus is now obtainable.

The condenser is joined in parallel with (or "across") the interrupter. In the case of an electrolytic break, no condenser is required. As mentioned on p. 55, modern coils are frequently provided with a subdivided primary winding. Suitable connections are then made according to the nature of the break employed.

Interrupters. The several varieties of interrupters are dealt with on pp. 66 to 70. The type most generally employed is the mercury-jet break, working in an atmosphere of coal-gas. The provision of a gas supply is usually of no great difficulty, as rubber gas bags may be used where no supply is laid on. In all but experimental installations it is much better for the gas supply to be brought close to the interrupter by permanently fixed gas-piping, and the final connection made by a short length of flexible metallic or stout rubber tubing. Rigid connection is undesirable, as many interrupters vibrate considerably, a tendency which may be checked by fixing the apparatus to a heavy base standing on a thick felt pad.

Before starting the coil, gas is allowed to flow through the interrupter for a few minutes to drive out the air. The exit tap is then closed, the inlet being left open in connection with the supply, as most mercury-gas breaks work better under a small excess pressure. Should the air not be entirely replaced by gas, the switching on of the current and the consequent sparking in the interrupter usually fires the mixture, and a small explosion results, to prevent any damage from which a simple safety valve is generally fitted to the apparatus.

In mercury-breaks the size of the contact plates against which the jet strikes is of importance, and these should be adjusted to suit the coil with which the break is to be used. To work an induction coil to the best advantage a regulating resistance is desirable in order to adjust the speed of the driving motor, and so control the rate of interruption.

For instantaneous radiography a Wehnelt electrolytic break is frequently employed. A very convenient arrange-

Fig. 93.—Mercury-gas interrupters. (See also Fig. 41.)

ment in a permanent installation is to provide a triple Wehnelt interrupter for instantaneous radiography as an alternative to a mercury-break for screening and general work. A throw-over switch is then mounted on the control switchboard, to permit a quick change from one break to the other.

(b) Control Switchboard.

The next important feature to be dealt with is the control switchboard, and it is largely on the design of this that convenience in the working of an installation depends. The first essentials are simplicity and accessibility, as adjustments often have to be carried out in a darkened room. These features may most readily be secured by arranging the essential switches, resistances and measuring instruments on a marble or slate panel carried at a convenient height on a light iron framework mounted on castors (see Fig. 36). This movable switchboard is connected to a fixed terminal board, installed near the coil, by cables which for protection may conveniently be grouped together in a length of flexible metallic tubing. The switch-table is brought close to the X-ray couch or stand, and the current can then be regulated without the operator having to move about in a darkened room among high-tension leads.

The essential controlling apparatus mounted on the switch-table consists of a main switch, an ammeter of suitable range, and an adjustable resistance for regulating the current through the primary of the coil. If it is desired to get a measure of the energy-input, a voltmeter will have to be added, in which case it is necessary to employ the shunt method of regulating the coil, as, otherwise, the voltmeter will merely indicate the voltage of the supply-circuit.

In the shunt method of regulation (see Fig. 94) the supply circuit is connected to each end of a resistance which plays the part of a potential-divider. The coil is connected to any point on this resistance by means of a moving contact, so that any desired voltage between zero and that of the main supply may be applied to the coil. To avoid the use of an inconveniently large number of studs, finer adjustment of the regulation may be secured by the inclusion in the shunt circuit of a small variable resistance in series with the coil. In designing the main resistance it should be remembered that the coils at one end will at times have to carry heavy currents ; furthermore, the individual coils of the resistance should be graded so as to ensure that the voltage applied to the coil may be increased by approximately equal steps as the contact is moved from one stud to the next.

The alternative method to the shunt connection just described is to connect the coil directly to the mains with a suitable resistance in series.

For carrying out screen-examinations a well-darkened room is necessary. The artificial light should be under control from the switch-table. Where much work of this nature has to be undertaken it is a great convenience to install a "foot-switch." By such means it is possible, by one movement of the foot, to switch off the room lights and simultaneously turn on the coil ; a second movement reverses the operation, cutting off the coil and again turning on the lights.

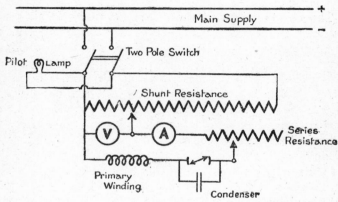

FIG. 94.—Shunt method of regulating an induction coil.

A pilot light is frequently fitted to the switch-table, this lamp being connected across the outgoing terminals of the main switch (see Fig. 94) so that whenever this switch is in the " on " position, the lamp is illuminated, and thereby indicates that the high-tension circuit is "live." To avoid interference with screen examinations, such pilot lamps are usually of small candle-power, and are of ruby or dark-blue glass. A pilot light is of particular value when working with a Coolidge tube, as this tube does not fluoresce.

The timing of an exposure is usually carried out by means of a stop-watch, a method which is quite the most satisfactory for ordinary work. For short exposures of only a few seconds or a fraction of a second, an automatic timing switch is a great convenience.

(c) Measuring Instruments.

Reference has been made in the preceding section to the provision of an ammeter and voltmeter in the primary circuit of the coil. These enable the energy put into the system to be determined. Of greater importance, however, to the radiologist is the measurement of the energy in the secondary circuit, since it is the current through the tube which controls the amount or intensity of the X rays generated, and the potential difference across the terminals which regulates the hardness of the rays.

The current through the tube (see p. 90) is almost invariably measured by means of a milliammeter. These instruments are usually of the moving-coil type. If any inverse current is present, the milliammeter records the difference between the direct and inverse currents.

A reliable milliammeter is undoubtedly a very convenient instrument for measuring exposures in radiography. Experience will show an operator the number of " milliampere-seconds " necessary to obtain a satisfactory radiograph of any particular subject, and this will afford useful data for future work with the same equipment. The values cannot, however, be applied, except as a very rough guide, to other installations.

Although it may be the case that the ordinary method of specifying hardness by means of the equivalent spark-gap is not completely satisfactory, its convenience, together with the wide latitude permissible in almost all X-ray work, leads to the well-nigh universal adoption of this method in radiography and radiotherapy.

The measurement is made by means of a spark-gap connected in parallel with the X-ray tube. The terminals of the gap are often a point and a plane (the latter consisting of a metal disc some 3 or 4 inches in diameter), or alternatively two spheres or points. The terminals are mounted on insulating pillars, which may be moved in a slide, an attached pointer and scale enabling the voltage or the length of the gap to be read directly.

In taking a reading, the gap is reduced until a spark just passes while the tube is running. The length of gap is then noted, and reference to a table such as that on p. 102 enables the voltage on the tube to be determined. Greater accuracy can be obtained by allowing the spark to take place between balls of definite size. For the same voltage the spark gap between balls is much smaller than between points (as Table V. reveals), and this is one reason why

FIG. 95.—Qualimeter of Bauer type. (See p. 110.)

the point and point, or point and plane have been generally used, the longer distance being easier to measure.

Hardness comparisons should be made for specified currents through the tube, and it must be again pointed out that the equivalent spark-gap may not be a true measure of the hardness of the X rays, as, for a given voltage, the composition of the rays emitted may vary very considerably from tube to tube. If, however, this is borne in mind, a radiographer will find the measurement of spark-length of great practical value as soon as he becomes accustomed to the particular apparatus under his control.

The alternative to measuring the voltage on the X-ray tube is to determine directly the hardness of the rays emitted. The several types of penetrometer used for this purpose are dealt with on pp. 108 to 110, and require no further description here. A penetrometer of the Bauer type is illustrated in Fig. 95.

(d) X-ray Tubes.

Reference to makers' catalogues will show numerous varieties of X-ray tubes. The main features of the various types have been considered in detail in Chapters IV. and VI.

If gas tubes are preferred, a battery of six or more heavy tubes will be found useful. By having a number of tubes at one's disposal, a suitably conditioned bulb may be chosen for the required purpose. Each tube possesses its own characteristics, and it is only by actual experience with the individual tubes that the most satisfactory choice of tube may be made for a particular purpose. X-ray bulbs which work erratically may frequently be restored to good condition by being rested for a month or two. In this connection reference may be made to Chapters VI. and VII.

All gas tubes are fitted with vacuum regulators; the type chosen is mainly a matter of personal predilection. In this country the "occlusion method" (p. 78) is very largely employed. Continued use of this regulator should be avoided as far as possible, as this tends to make the tube unsteady in its running. Most gas tubes will ordinarily run for long periods for some definite values of current and hardness without much regulation. It is for this reason that the method of keeping a number of bulbs in current use is advocated.

(e) High-tension Circuits.

The connecting up of the X-ray tube to the secondary circuit of the induction coil or transformer is a point worthy of some consideration. It is obvious that, in order to carry out an X-ray examination of any part of the human body the X-ray tube must be capable of being placed in a variety of positions. In all these positions it must be possible for the high-tension leads to be brought to the tube without coming within sparking distance either of each other or of any metal parts of the tube-stand, etc. The safety of both patient and operator must also be considered by keeping the leads taut and as remote as possible.

The plan now very largely adopted is to instal an overhead circuit, consisting of a pair of stout conductors tightly stretched from one side of the X-ray room to the other. These wires or rods are sufficiently far apart to prevent any possibility of sparking across. To reduce the brush discharge which always tends to take place, sharp points and edges to all parts of the high-tension conductors should be avoided. The system is insulated at each end by ebonite or fibre rods from 10 to 12 inches long. Wire strainers may be fitted to enable the conductors to be kept taut.

The overhead circuit is connected at one end of the room to the high-tension generator, the milliammeter and valve-tube being conveniently inserted in these connections. The supply to the X-ray tube is then brought down from the overhead circuit at any desired point by spring connections hooked on to the wires. A convenient spring connector is of the self-winding type, resembling closely a small self-winding steel measuring tape. By such means slack connections are avoided, and the danger of accidental sparking is greatly reduced.

The several kinds of valve-tubes and rectifiers are dealt with on pp. 70 and 71. Care must be taken that these are connected in the circuit in the correct polarity. A useful accessory to show whether inverse current is present or not is a small vacuum tube

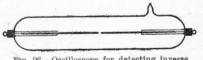

Fig. 96.—Oscilloscope for detecting inverse current.

known as an oscilloscope (Fig. 96). When this is connected in the high-tension circuit one of the electrodes (the cathode) is covered with a blue glow. If, however, inverse current is present, the other electrode will also show this appearance. The length of glow is a rough measure of the current passing at any moment (p. 2), and when viewed by a revolving mirror or equivalent device the shape of the current wave is revealed, as in an oscillograph.

(f) Tube-stands and Couches.

The examination of a patient by X rays may be carried out either by the use of a fluorescent screen or by the taking of photographs. In most cases it is usual to combine these methods, a preliminary screen examination being made to enable the photographic plate to be placed in the most advantageous position. In order that this examination may be carried out rapidly and conveniently, it is necessary that the X-ray tube should be supported in such a way that it may be readily adjustable while the patient occupies some convenient stationary position. The various forms of apparatus by which this is accomplished may be divided into two classes—upright screening stands and horizontal couches. Certain of these stands are convertible from one type to the other, while other more complicated forms constitute combined X-ray examination couches and surgical operation tables. We can only deal here with the main features of each type.

Upright Screening Stands. In this form of apparatus the patient under examination stands or sits in contact with a vertical partition, behind which the X-ray tube is supported. The tube is carried in a protective box on a framework capable of motion in both transverse and vertical directions. Ease in working is obtained by the provision of a counter weight, while either movement may be arrested at will by means of clamping devices. The partition is of thin wood or of tightly stretched canvas, so as to be practically transparent to the X rays.

The fluorescent screen is supported in front of the patient. It may either be carried by an arm rigidly fixed to the tube-holder and capable of moving with it in both directions, or it may be carried on a separate support, the two motions being again provided for. The former plan, of tube and screen moving simultaneously, is more satisfactory. The

fluorescent screen must, in addition, be capable of movement to and from the partition, and a clamp should be
provided to maintain it at the right place. This adjustment further enables a slight pressure to be applied to the
patient while an examination is being made, and so helps

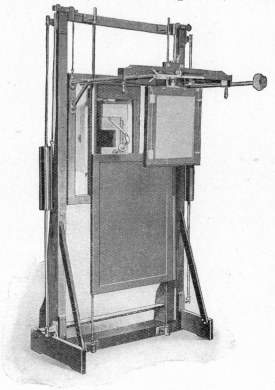

Fig. 97.—Upright screening stand (Watson).

to prevent movement of the part which is being photographed.

If, now, a photograph is desired (the adjustment of position
having been made), the screen is removed from the supporting frame and replaced by a holder containing the photographic plate. A second method which may often be
conveniently employed is to slip the plate contained in a

black-paper envelope between the object to be photographed
and the fluorescent screen without the latter being removed.
The envelope is then held in position while the exposure is
made. Fig. 97 shows a modern type of upright screening stand.

FIG. 98.—Mackenzie Davidson X-ray couch, showing tube-box in position.   Protective screen
removed.

Horizontal X-ray Couch.   In a horizontal couch the patient
is examined in a recumbent position on a horizontal table.
The apparatus is of more general application than are the
upright screening stands just described, as the physical
condition of the patient is frequently the deciding factor.
The X-ray tube must be capable of motion in either direction

in a horizontal plane, but its position may be either above
or below the patient.   For screen examinations the " below
position " is naturally more convenient, while for photographic work the over-couch position is usually preferred,
and in some cases is the only practicable course.   Some of
the methods for the localisation of foreign bodies are more
easily carried out in the " over " position, while the com-
pression necessary to prevent movement of the subject
in photographing, for example, the kidney region is more
readily possible in this position.   Fig. 98 illustrates a modern
X-ray couch.   Where facilities are limited, an X-ray couch
may be replaced by a plain table (or a stretcher on trestles)
and a tube-stand.

X-ray couches should be constructed, as far as possible,
of wood.   With the all-metal type there is liability of electric
shock both to patient and operator through faulty insulation or inattention to the position of high-tension wires.
Such a shock may not be actually dangerous, but is always
unpleasant, and the use of wood will greatly reduce the risk
of its occurrence.   The employment of metal in the tube-
support should also be as restricted as possible, and in
any case it must not be in contact with or close to the X-ray
bulb, otherwise sparking and perforation of the bulb may
occur, particularly with a hard tube.

Protection of Operator and Patient.   The X-ray tube itself
must in all cases be surrounded by some form of protective
cover or box, which will effectually prevent the passage
of X rays in every direction other than that in which
they are required.   In this connection it may be remarked
that all forms of X-ray stand or couch should be provided
with an adjustable diaphragm, by means of which the cross-
section of the beam of rays may be controlled.   This may
be either a circular iris-diaphragm or rectangular with a
separate adjustment in either direction.   In both types
the movable leaves should be effectively opaque to the
rays in order to afford protection for the operator.   An
adjustable diaphragm is of great assistance in searching
for foreign bodies as it enables one to improve the definition
by stopping down the rays.   (See p. 174.)

For couches in which the tube is carried under the table, it is possible to fit a box which will completely enclose the tube. This box is covered with lead-impregnated rubber, or in some instances with sheet lead. In the latter case it is important that ample space should be provided to avoid the danger of puncturing the X-ray bulb by sparks passing from the tube to the sides of the box. Further, the bare metal should be covered by thick paper, felt or leather, etc., to absorb the very soft but dangerous secondary rays produced.

In the case of field sets, or where considerations of size and weight are important, the use of a box of this nature

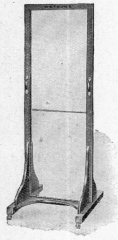

Fig. 99. — Lead-glass shield mounted on castors (Watson).

is not possible. The protection in such cases consists of a shield either of lead-glass or built up of protective rubber. Such shields may be satisfactory, but are rarely completely so. It is important that the quality of the material should be good, and the opinion of the National Physical Laboratory should be sought in cases of doubt. (See p. 289)

The fluorescent screen should be covered with lead-glass of proved quality, as otherwise the radiation falling on the operator's face may have dangerous results if much screening is carried out. In some installations, arrangements are made for viewing the screen from the side by reflection in a mirror; the face is then entirely protected from direct radiation.

The latest types of horizontal couch are provided with a shield, which supplements and moves with the tube-box. The shield increases the protection afforded to the operator, who has perforce to stand within a short distance of the tube. A convenient type of lead-glass screen which can be wheeled about the room is shown in Fig. 99.

(g) Photographic Apparatus.

The purely photographic apparatus required for the production of radiographs comprises very little beyond the ordinary equipment of a dark room. Provision must be made for carrying on operations with photographic plates up to 12 by 15 inches, and adequate drying arrangements should be fitted, as finished prints may be required within an hour or two of taking the negative.

The plate is generally exposed in two black-paper envelopes, which protect it from the action of light, while if an intensifying screen (p. 166) is used, a special holder to take both screen and plate is necessary.

The question of the suitable placing of the photographic plate is too large to be considered here. The reader is referred to medical books on radiography. The question of the time of exposure of the plate can only be settled by the operator himself after the various factors concerning the individual characteristics of the installation and the nature of the subject to be photographed have been taken into account.

A warning may be given against storing unexposed X-ray plates in the neighbourhood of an X-ray installation, as continued use of the apparatus may lead to slight fogging of the plates, quite sufficient to mask some of the finer details which are looked for in a good negative. If exigencies of space render it necessary to store the plates in or near the X-ray room, they should be protected by a lead-lined box.

Localisation.

The difficulty of the interpretation of radiographs arises from the fact that such photographs merely record the positions of shadows which do not necessarily correspond in shape and size with the image that would be produced in an ordinary camera.

This will be clear from a consideration of Fig. 100, in which suppose GHK represents a body resting on a fluorescent screen or photographic plate (EF), and A represents the source of X rays. On examination of the screen or

developed plate, the images of foreign bodies situated at
B and C will be indicated at L and M respectively.

It will be seen at a glance that the distance from L to M
is not a measure of the distance between the bodies at
B and C, while, if attention is turned to a third body at D,
it will be seen that its shadow coincides with that of B,
and there is nothing to distinguish the one from the other.
It is apparent that the position of the shadow merely indicates the *line* on which the foreign body is situated and
not its actual position.

Suppose now the X-ray tube is moved to a point A',
all else remaining unchanged, the shadows of B and C will

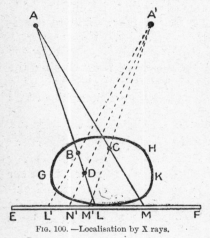

FIG. 100.—Localisation by X rays.

move to L' and M', while
a new one corresponding
to the body D will be seen
at N'; it no longer coin-
cides with the shadow of B.

Thus the new position
of the tube marks out a
new set of lines cn which
the bodies are situated.
This suffices to give the
exact position of each of
the bodies, namely the
points of intersection of
each pair of corresponding
lines. The foregoing em-
bodies the fundamental

principle of practically all the existing methods of localisation, of which that due to Sir J. Mackenzie Davidson
was one of the first introduced.

In practice, the points A and A' are maintained at the
same vertical distance from the plate (EF); the triangles
ABA' and LBL' are then similar, and from simple geometrical considerations the height of the foreign body at
B above the plate can be readily calculated if the distances
AA', LL', and the height of A or A' above the plate are
known. LL' is the distance through which the image of
the foreign body moves when the tube is moved through

the distance AA'. The various methods which have been suggested for carrying out the process of localisation are merely devices for solving geometrically or analytically the above simple exercise in trigonometry. In some cases the several distances are actually measured and the calculation performed by the aid of tables or some mechanical device. For these methods a couch must be employed such that the tube may be readily adjusted to any desired position, and can then be moved through a measured distance without upsetting the adjustments.

In other methods an auxiliary object of known dimensions is photographed simultaneously with the foreign body whose position is required, and the shift of the tube and its distance from the plate are determined from the two images of the auxiliary body.

Full details of most of the present-day methods of localisation are given in the various issues of the *Journal of the Röntgen Society* for 1915 and 1916.

Stereoscopic methods of localisation are referred to on p. 163.

CHAPTER XIII.

DIFFRACTION OF X RAYS BY CRYSTALS.

Early Attempts to diffract X Rays.

From time to time, a good deal of ingenuity has been exercised by various experimenters in testing whether there are, on the boundaries of the shadows cast by small obstacles, variations in the intensity of the X rays corresponding to optical diffraction fringes. Röntgen (1898) could not satisfy himself on the point. Haga and Wind (*Wied. Ann.* 1899-1901) experimented with a V-shaped slit, a few thousandths of a millimetre broad at its widest point, and obtained, in their photographs of the slit, broadenings of the narrow part of the image : if the effect were due to diffraction, the same amount of broadening with light would be associated with a wave-length of about 1.3×10^{-8} cm.

It must be confessed that the result is in accordance with those recently obtained by crystal-reflection methods (pp. 240-41), but Walter and Pohl (*A.d.P.* 1908), who repeated Haga and Wind's experiments, found that the width of the image of the slit was largely affected by secondary effects in the photographic plate depending on the amount of energy sent through the slit, with the result that different times of exposure gave rise to images of different widths. They concluded that the diffraction effect was not proven, and that their own experiments went to show that the wave-length of an X ray does not exceed 10^{-9} cm.

Attempts to refract X Rays.

Many attempts have also been made to refract X rays. Röntgen, for example, tried prisms of a variety of materials such as ebonite, aluminium, and water. He also attempted to concentrate the rays by lenses of glass and ebonite. Chapman (*P.C.P.S.* 1912) experimented with a prism of ethyl bromide vapour—a substance which is strongly ionised by X rays. Two distinct experiments were conducted, in which the conditions might have been expected to favour a positive result. In one, the X rays were such as to stimulate markedly the radiation characteristic of bromine (p. 139) ; in the other, the rays were of a type that was selectively absorbed by the vapour. In neither case, however, could any trace of refraction be discovered.

Reflection Experiments.

Many fruitless efforts have also been made to reflect X rays. We now know that the obstacle in the way of success to such experiments was the extreme shortness of the wave-length of the X rays. The specular reflection of ordinary light waves is rendered possible by the fact that the irregularities remaining in a polished surface are small compared with the wave-length of light. But irregularities negligible for light waves become all important with X rays, and a reflecting surface, such as mercury or plate glass, deals with X rays in much the same way as a surface covered with innumerable facets scatters light rays in all directions with no trace of regular reflection as a whole.

Diffraction of X Rays.

It was Prof. M. Laue of Munich who, believing that X rays were short light rays with wave-lengths of an atomic order of magnitude,[1] conceived in 1912 the notion that the regular grouping of the atoms in a crystal, which modern crystallography affirms, should be capable of producing interference effects with the X rays, in a way analogous to that in which diffraction gratings deal with light waves. Laue's theory was at once put to the test and triumphantly justified by Friedrich and Knipping (*A.d.P.* 1913). It will be inter-

---

[1] Planck's theory of radiation had led Wien in 1907 and Stark in 1908 to values of 0.7×10^{-8} and 0.6×10^{-8} cm. respectively for the wave-length of an X ray.

esting to trace in some detail the historical development of these crystal experiments, which have also been pursued from a different standpoint in this country (see later).

Laue's Theory.

Crystallographers have gradually developed the theory introduced by Bravais in 1850, which contemplates the atoms of a crystal as residing at the angular points of a "space-lattice." In a crystal, like atoms are regarded as forming a perfectly regular system of points in space, each and every kind of atom present in the crystal conforming to its own independent system. These different point-systems, of course, interpenetrate, the result being a parallel net-like arrangement of points, to which the term "space-lattice" is applied. Thus the crystal naturally divides itself up into a large number of precisely identical elements, in all of which the same relative positions of the atoms are maintained. This elementary volume is, in a sense, the brick from which the crystal pattern is built up everywhere after the same plan.

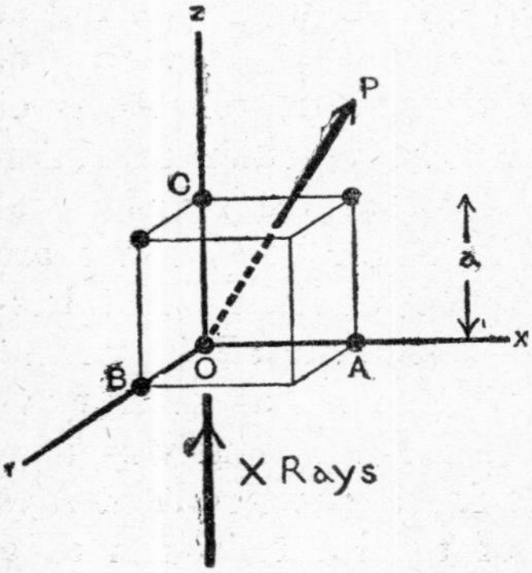

Fig. 101.—Representation of the diffraction of X rays by the atoms at the corners of an elementary cube of a cubic crystal.

The several atoms thus repeat themselves at definite intervals, and Laue's notion was that the resulting regular avenues of atoms should be capable of acting as a three-dimensional diffraction grating for rays of suitably short wave-lengths.

Laue first considered the case of a simple cubic crystal, and assumed that the atoms were arranged at the corners of little elementary cubes—this being the simplest cubic point-system possible. As the incident X rays pass through the crystal, they influence the atoms *en route*, and a secondary wavelet spreads from each atom as a wave passes over it. Let us take for convenience axes of reference parallel to the sides of a cube and an origin at the centre of one of the atoms, O. (Fig. 101 shows the atoms in the xz and yz planes of the lattice.) For simplicity, consider a beam of X rays to enter the cube in the direction of the z axis. Let us ascertain the conditions which will ensure that the wavelets from all the various atoms in the lattice shall co-operate or "be in phase" in some particular direction OP, whose direction cosines are α, β, and γ.[1]

It is sufficient for the purpose to take the cases of the nearest atoms to O on the axis, viz. A, B, and C, and express the conditions that the wavelets from these atoms shall be in phase with that from O. These conditions are

$$\left. \begin{array}{l} a\alpha = h_1 \cdot \lambda, \\ a\beta = h_2 \cdot \lambda, \\ a(1 - \gamma) = h_3 \cdot \lambda, \end{array} \right\} \dots\dots\dots\dots\dots\dots(1)$$

where a is the distance between neighbouring atoms (i.e. one side of the cube), l is the wave-length of the X rays, and h_1, h_2, and h_3 are integers representing the number of complete wave-lengths that the waves from A, B, and C respectively are ahead of the wave from O.

From (1) we obtain

$$\frac{a}{h_1} = \frac{\beta}{h_2} = \frac{(1 - \gamma)}{h_3} = \frac{\lambda}{a},$$

and therefore α, β, and $(1 - \gamma)$ ought to be in a simple numerical ratio.

From a consideration of the other cubes grouped round the z axis, it is apparent that there is a number of other points of maximum intensity situated precisely like P with reference to the z axis, so that if a photographic plate is placed to receive the transmitted X rays, there should appear, where the waves co-operate, a group of spots of fourfold symmetry.

The Experiments of Friedrich and Knipping.

Laue's theory was put to the test of experiment at Laue's request by Friedrich and Knipping (*A.d.P.* 1913). All that

[1] That is, α, β, and γ are the cosines of the angles which OP makes with the axes of x, y, and z respectively.

was required was to arrange that a parallel beam of X rays should, after traversing a crystal, be received on a photographic plate, so that any directions showing " interference maxima " would be registered as spots. The apparatus used is shown in Fig. 102.

The X rays emitted from the bulb were cut down by lead stops, so that a narrow pencil of rays fell on the crystal, behind which a photographic plate was placed a few cms. distant. The first crystal that was tried gave the result anticipated from the theory. The photographic plate showed an intense undeflected spot round which was grouped a

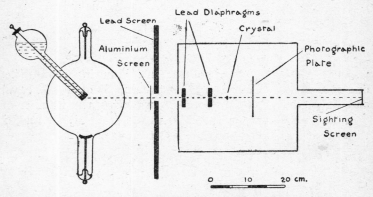

Fig. 102.—Friedrich and Knipping's apparatus for showing diffraction of X rays by transmitting them through a crystal.

number of diffracted spots, some of which were deviated by as much as 40° from the original direction of the rays (see Figs. 103 and 105). If the crystal were moved parallel to itself, the grouping of the spots was unaffected. By altering the distance of the photographic plate from the crystal, the spots, while showing but little alteration in size, increased or diminished their displacement from the centre. Further, if the crystal was rotated so as to make a different angle with the primary beam, the pattern on the plate was affected : by careful adjustment, it was possible to obtain positions in which the spots grouped themselves quite symmetrically round the centre spot.

The results were generalised for a number of different

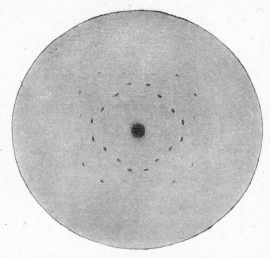

Fig. 103.—Pattern of Laue spots obtained by Friedrich and Knipping when X rays are diffracted by a zinc-blende crystal. The incident rays are parallel to a cubic axis of the crystal.

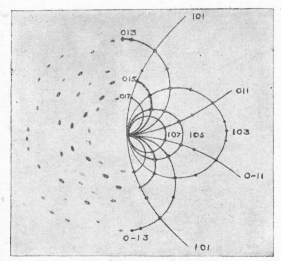

Fig. 104.—W. L. Bragg's construction to explain the position of the Laue spots shown in Fig. 103 (see p. 221). (From the *Proceedings of the Cambridge Philosophical Society.*)

crystals. It was found that exposures of some hours were necessary to obtain good results, since by far the greater proportion of the rays was unaffected and undeviated by the crystal. Shorter exposures, however, sufficed to reveal the more intense spots.

Laue's Results for Zinc-blende.

Figs. 103 and 105 are reproductions of the results obtained in the case of zinc-blende when the rays travel along two different axes of symmetry in the crystal. Knowing the coordinates of any spot on the photographic plate relative to rectangular axes having their origin at the point where the primary beam strikes the crystal, we can get at once the direction cosines, a, β, and $(1-\gamma)$ of the ray which gives rise to that particular spot, and hence we can deduce the values of the parameters h_1, h_2, and h_3. Now, as remarked above, since h_1, h_2, and h_3 are whole numbers, these values of a, β, and $(1-\gamma)$ should be in a simple numerical ratio. This was actually found to be the case in all the photographs. In no instance was it necessary to assume a number for h_1, h_2, or h_3 greater than 10 to give the values of a, β, and $(1-\gamma)$ a whole number ratio. This in itself is strong confirmation of the theory that the spots are due to interference.

Each spot has its own values of h_1, h_2, and h_3. These have to conform to equations (1). The associated values of a, β, and γ have further to obey the relation

$$a^2 + \beta^2 + \gamma^2 = 1,$$

and so it follows that there is only one value which λ/a can have to satisfy all the equations for each spot. Thus every spot gives a different wave-length, since the values of h_1, h_2, and h_3 are different for the different spots. It is here that an important distinction arises between a crystal grating and a line-grating. In a line-grating an interference maximum is always possible, no matter what the wave-length ; that is to say, the grating yields a continuous spectrum with incident white light. But in the case of a three-dimensional grating, certain wave-lengths only are eligible

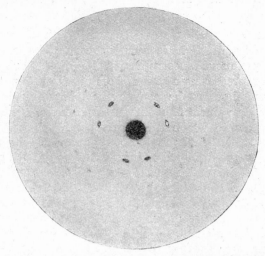

FIG. 105.—Pattern of Laue spots obtained by Friedrich and Knipping, when X rays are diffracted by a zinc-blende crystal.   The incident rays are parallel to a trigonal axis of the cubic crystal (*i.e.* diagonal-wise through centre of cube).

FIG. 106.—W. L. Bragg's method of stereographic projection, applied to the case in Fig. 105 (see p. 222).

to form interference maxima, so that a continuous spectrum is impossible. A similar effect may be imitated by mounting half-silvered parallel plates in front of an ordinary line-grating. If white light is now thrown on the grating, the former continuous spectrum will be replaced by a line spectrum representing a series of definite wave-lengths.

The Laue photographs seem to show that while, in general, the larger the values of the integers h_1, h_2, and h_3, the fainter are the spots to which they correspond, yet, at the same time, the smallest integers do not represent the most intense spots as one would be led to infer by analogy with a diffraction grating, for which the low-order spectra are generally the brightest. Not only that, but certain spots associated with simple values of h_1, h_2, and h_3 are absent altogether. But if the pattern were the most general possible, then all values of the integers, at any rate up to a certain limit, should be represented on the plate.

A satisfactory theory must account for these anomalies, and Laue sought to explain them by assuming that the primary beam was made up of a limited number of independent homogeneous constituents, the absence on the plate of a spot with simple parameters being ascribed to the absence of the particular wave-length, which alone is capable of forming the spot in question. It was pointed out above that any fixed values of h_1, h_2, and h_3 gave a definite value for λ/a, but it is evident that if we took the same multiples of all these values, say, nh_1, nh_2, and nh_3, the equations (1) on p. 211 would still be satisfied, but now by a wave-length λ/n instead of λ. By adjusting the values of h_1, h_2, and h_3 in this way, Laue was able to account for all the spots in the photographs by assuming the existence of only five different wave-lengths in the incident beam.

The explanation is not, however, entirely satisfactory, because these five wave-lengths should give many other spots which do not appear in the photographs.

The Laue Spots for a Zinc-blende Crystal.

A zinc-blende crystal belongs to the cubic system, and crystallography distinguishes between three elementary point systems of cubic symmetry, namely those containing :

(1) points at each corner of the elementary cube,
(2) points at each corner and one at the centre of the cube, and
(3) points at the corners and at the centres of the cube faces.

Laue assumed that zinc-blende belongs to the first system, but in point of fact it almost certainly belongs to the third, as Pope and Barlow have shown from other considerations. W. L. Bragg (*P.C.P.S.* 1912) was led to examine the Laue spots of zinc-blende from this point of view.

Adopting this view of the structure, Bragg supposed, as before, that axes are taken with origin at an atom O (Fig. 107 shows the atoms in the xz and yz planes), and that when the various atoms are stimulated by the X rays (incident along the z axis), O emits a wavelet which in the direction OP is h_1

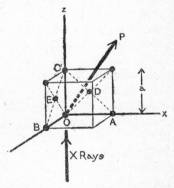

FIG. 107.—Representation of the diffraction of X rays by the atoms at the corners and face-centres of an elementary cube of a cubic crystal.

wave-lengths behind that from atom A on the x axis, and so on. The equations (1) on p. 211 ensure that all the corner atoms (including that at the origin) shall emit wavelets which are in phase along OP. It is necessary to obtain the corresponding conditions for the centre-face atoms (such as D and E), so that their wavelets also shall be in phase with those from the corner atoms.

The difference in phase between the wavelets from D and O will be $\left(\dfrac{h_1}{2} - \dfrac{h_3}{2}\right)$ wave-lengths, since D is situated in the middle of the face of the cube. This must be a whole number of wave-lengths to give an interference maximum along OP ; and it follows that h_1 and h_3 must either be both odd or both even. The same must also hold for h_2 and h_3. This at once explains why the complete series of values of h_1, h_2, and h_3 for the Laue spots is not represented on the photograph.

Consider first of all the set of spots in the appropriate Laue photograph of zinc-blende (Fig. 103), which have h_3 = unity. The corresponding wave-lengths prove to have every possible value greater than a limiting wave-length of $\lambda = 0.034a$, where a is the length of the side of an elementary cube. The sets of values corresponding to wave-lengths approaching $\lambda = 0.06a$ are responsible for the two very intense spots in the inner square of the pattern ; all other wave-lengths smaller or greater than $0.06a$ give fainter spots until, for the limiting wave-length $0.034a$, they are barely visible. Bragg accordingly concluded that the X rays utilised in this particular Laue pattern formed a continuous spectrum, with a maximum intensity in the region of $l = 0.06a$.

Exactly similar results are obtained for the sets of numbers having $h_3 = 2$. There are two very intense spots which form the outer square, and, in addition, a few others considerably fainter. Similarly for $h_3 = 3$, in which series there are still fewer spots.

In Table XVIII. is displayed a typical set of values of λ/a for the different spots corresponding to $h_3 = 1$.

The table is very interesting because of its completeness ; within a certain range of wave-lengths, every spot anticipated from theory is registered on the photographic plate.

Thus Bragg's results afford strong support to the atomic grouping which Pope and Barlow claim for the zinc-blende space-lattice. In later work, Bragg has shown that the zinc-blende diffraction pattern is due almost entirely to the heavier zinc atoms. The sulphur atoms are situated on a similar parallel lattice, which may be reached by stepping along one quarter of the diagonal of the elementary cube of the zinc-lattice.[1]

---

[1] See Braggs' *X Rays and Crystal Structure* for a complete account.

TABLE XVIII.

Zinc-blende crystal; incident X rays parallel to a cubic axis. Values of wave-length for $h_3 = 1$.

Value of h_2.	Values of λ/a, for $h_3 = 1$.				
	$h_1 = 1$	$h_1 = 3$	$h_1 = 5$	$h_1 = 7$	$h_1 = 9$
1	(off the photograph)	0·178 (m)	0·073 (v)	0·039 (v)	0·024 (invisible)
3	0·178 (m)	0·104 (v)	0·057 (v)	0·034 (f)	0·022 (invisible)
5	0·073 (v)	0·057 (v)	0·039 (m)	0·027 (invisible)	—
7	0·039 (f)	0·034 (f)	0·027 (invisible)	—	—
9	0·024 (invisible)	0·022 (invisible)	—	—	—

[The letters v, m, and f indicate the intensity of the spots—" v " signifying very intense, " m " moderately intense, and " f " faint.]

W. L. Bragg's Theory of the Laue Spots.

Bragg was led to bring forward an alternative explanation of the Laue interference phenomena from the point of view of the parallel and equidistant planes of atoms which can be pictured in a crystal. Many systems of planes can, of course, be chosen, but we can confine the choice to the relatively few systems in which the planes are rich in atoms.

Contrary to the view of Laue, Bragg (as mentioned above) supposed that the incident beam of X rays contained (like white light) every possible wave-length over a wide range, and thus formed a continuous spectrum of rays. Imagine then that such a beam falls on a crystal, and let us assume that when it strikes a system of parallel planes of atoms a small amount of energy is reflected by each plane. The wave front of the reflected beam from a particular plane is formed by the wavelets sent out by the individual atoms in the plane. If the distance between successive planes is d, and the glancing angle of the rays is θ, the train of waves reflected from the different planes in the system will follow each other at intervals of $2d \sin \theta$; and if the wave-length is such that this distance is equal to a whole number of wave-lengths, the waves will reinforce each other, and we shall get an interference maximum in that direction. Hence in this case, when the incident beam contains every possible wave-length, a particular system of planes in the crystal picks out, so to speak, the right wave-lengths, and the result of the simultaneous working of all the various systems of planes is to resolve the beam into its constituents. If the angle of incidence is altered, then different wave-lengths will in general be selected to form the interference maxima.

On this view, the different intensities which the various spots exhibit might be due either to an unequal distribution of the energy in the spectrum of the incident X rays or to a difference in the closeness of packing of the atoms in the various reflecting planes.

Bragg's method of regarding the interference is, of course, analytically equivalent to that of Laue. The reflection-method has the great advantage of being more readily pictured, especially in considering what happens when a crystal is rotated, in which event the pattern of spots is distorted exactly as it would be if the spots were reflections in plane mirrors. By changing the angle of incidence, we alter the phase difference $(2d \sin \theta)$ between waves from successive planes ; and so a spot produced initially by a certain wave-length continues to represent without break a sequence of the wave-lengths present in the incident beam. If, as Laue imagined, certain wave-lengths only were present in the incident X rays, then as the crystal was slowly tilted spots would suddenly appear and disappear on the plate ; but, on the contrary, when the experiment is tried, the same spots can be traced continuously across the plate. It is also interesting to notice that some spots are very much changed in intensity as the crystal is tilted. One spot, for instance, which is barely visible in the symmetrical pattern, becomes, in another position of the crystal, the most intense of all, because its new wave-length now coincides with the maximum in the spectrum of the X rays.

The elliptical shape of the Laue spots is a direct consequence of the fact that the incident pencil of X rays is not strictly parallel but slightly conical, and so the reflected pencil, which is obliquely received on the photographic plate, shows an elliptical section.

Elliptical Loci of Laue Spots.

With prolonged exposures, many more spots appear on the photographic plate than can be detected in Fig. 103. As Fig. 104 shows, the various spots group themselves naturally on ellipses of various sizes, all of which pass through the

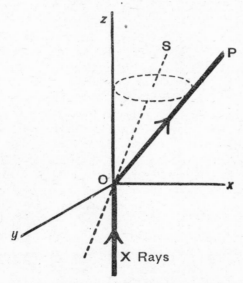

FIG. 108.—Construction demonstrating elliptical loci of Laue spots.

central spot. These ellipses, which are nearly circular, are sections of circular cones having the incident beam as a generator. The elliptical locus is a consequence of the fact that the various systems of parallel planes which can be selected in a crystal may have all manner of orientations : the atoms are grouped on parallel straight lines as well as on parallel planes, and each of these rows has a set of planes parallel to it. For example, suppose as before that a beam of X rays travels along the z axis, and consider a closely packed plane of atoms passing through the line OS (Fig. 108), S being a point in the xz plane. If this plane of atoms contains the y axis, then the reflected beam will pass along OP. But there is a family or "zone" of planes of atoms which can also be selected as passing through OS, and as we pass in rotation from one of these planes to another, the reflected beam OP will sweep out a circular cone with OS as "zone-axis." The trace on the photographic plate (which is at right angles to the z axis) will accordingly be an ellipse which passes through Oz and touches the yz plane.

Similarly, if the plane is rotated about a zone-axis which is in the yz plane and passes through the origin, the ellipse passes through the z axis and touches the xz plane. Now suppose that there is a plane of atoms in the crystal which contains both these zone-axes, then the reflected beam from this plane will give a spot at the intersection of the two ellipses obtained as above.

We can in this way, by drawing ellipses corresponding to rotations about various axes through the origin, locate almost all the Laue spots. This is done in Fig. 104, which graphically displays a key to the spots for zinc-blende when the incident rays traverse a cubic axis of the crystal.

The ellipses are marked in each case with the co-ordinates of the atom nearest the origin through which the axis of rotation passes. The scales of co-ordinates are measured in terms of a unit equal to half the distance between consecutive points along the axes. This unit is chosen because the only system competent to account for all the Laue spots in the case of zinc-blende, is that in which there are points both at the corners and face centres of the elementary cube (see p. 217).

Stereographic Projection of Laue Spots.

In representing a Laue pattern diagrammatically, it is tedious and inconvenient to draw the various elliptical loci. A much easier method is, however, possible without unduly distorting the pattern.

Suppose the X-ray beam *AO* (Fig. 109) traverses the crystal at *O*, the undeviated beam striking the photographic plate *ZD* at *Z*. Let *OS* be a "zone-axis"; the rays reflected in the family of planes which pass through this zone-axis lie on a circular cone, of which *OS* is the axis and *OZ* and *OP* are two generators. This cone cuts the sphere of which *OZ* is a radius, in a circle of which *ZB* is a diameter. The projection of this circle on the plane *ZD* from the "pole" *A* is also a circle, of which *ZP'* is a diameter and *S* is the centre.

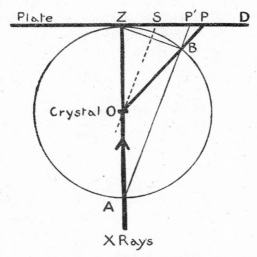

FIG. 109.—Geometrical construction to explain stereographic projection of Laue spots.

Thus, if we consider the Laue pattern which is formed on the surface of the sphere *ZBA*, and then project this pattern on the plane *ZD* from the pole *A*, we shall have a new projection in which the ellipse with *ZP* as major axis is replaced by the circle on *ZP'*. The distortion of the pattern of spots by the transformation is very small except in the regions remote from the centre; and we now have the convenience of drawing circles instead of ellipses. It is easy to calculate the positions of the centres of the circles, such as *S*, from the dimensions of the pattern when the crystal is symmetrically placed.

An application of this method of projection to the case of zinc-blende is shown in Fig. 106. It will be observed how closely the diagram follows the corresponding photograph obtained by Friedrich and Knipping (Fig. 105).

Display of Laue Spots by Fluorescent Screen.

Terada (*Proc. Math.-Phys. Soc. Tokyo*, Ap. 1913) found that by the use of a sufficiently transparent crystal and a not too narrow beam of X rays,[1] he could detect the Laue spots visually by means of a fluorescent screen.

On rotating the crystal, the elliptical loci of spots referred to above are strikingly displayed.

The fluorescent method is likely to be especially useful for a rapid initial examination of a crystal. It is also of value for watching the progressive behaviour of a crystal which is being subjected to physical or chemical treatment. For instance, it was found that on heating a crystal of borax, the spots remained visible until the crystal was almost entirely melted.

Interference by Metallic Crystals.

The method has been applied to metallic crystals Keene (*P.M.* Oct. 1913) found that if a beam of X rays was passed through freshly rolled metal sheets, a symmetrical pattern was formed on a photographic plate placed behind the sheet. The axis of symmetry of the pattern was parallel to the direction in which the sheet had been rolled. A rotation of the sheet in its own plane produced a corresponding rotation of the spots in the pattern. If the sheet were heated and allowed to cool, the pattern was replaced by a number of radial streaks arranged in a circular band around the undeflected spot. A very old specimen of metal gave the same result. These radial streaks are undoubtedly due to reflection from small crystals formed in the one case by age and in the other by annealing.

The subject was also investigated by Owen and Blake (*N*. Feb. 19, 1914), who adopted a reflection method. A piece of copper was cut in two and one of the pieces was

[1] 5 to 10 mm. diameter.

annealed, while the other was untreated. A beam of X rays was allowed to fall in turn on each of the samples, with the result that a large number of spots were obtained on a photographic plate in the case of the annealed specimen, while no effect was produced with the other specimen. The difference is, in the one case, to be accounted for by the presence of innumerable small crystals variously oriented, each of which reflects its quotum of the original beam, while in the unannealed specimen there is an absence of crystalline structure and regular atomic grouping.

W. L. Bragg (*P.M.* Sept. 1914) examined native copper crystals with the X-ray spectrometer (see below) and found that the atoms are arranged in simple face-centred cubic lattices. Vegard (*P.M.* Jan. 1916) obtained the same result for crystals of native silver. Many other elements have since been examined.

THE X-RAY SPECTROMETER.

In the preceding portion of this chapter we have followed for convenience the development of the subject of X-ray diffraction from the historical point of view. It will have been remarked how completely and satisfactorily the various Laue phenomena are interpreted on W. L. Bragg's view of reflection from planes of atoms. Bragg was led, at the suggestion of C. T. R. Wilson, to ascertain whether X rays were regularly reflected from cleavage planes in crystals : such planes are known to be very rich in atoms. Mica at once suggested itself, and the experiment, when tried, proved immediately successful, only a few minutes' exposure being required to give a visible impression on a photographic plate.

We have spoken of "reflection," but it is apparent that the crystal in such experiments is playing the part of a diffraction grating. Prof. W. H. Bragg and his son, W. L. Bragg, attacked the subject from this point of view, and devised the X-ray spectrometer in which the crystal is used as a reflection grating. Their work, which has received international recognition, is described in their book on *X Rays and Crystal Structure* (Bell), to which the reader is referred,

P

Experiments on similar lines were conducted at the same time by Moseley and Darwin at Manchester, and later by Moseley, who also obtained results of the first importance.

FIG. 110 —Photograph of Bragg's X-ray spectrometer. *B* is a lead box containing an X-ray bulb. S_1 and S_2 are adjustable slits which direct a beam of X rays on to the face of the crystal *C*. The reflected beam passes through the slit S_3 into the ionisation chamber *I*, where it is recorded by the tilted electroscope in the metal box *E*. *K* is an earthing key ; *M*, a mirror for illuminating the electroscope. *C* and *I* can each be rotated about the axis of the spectrometer.

X-ray Spectrometer.

Bragg's X-ray spectrometer is illustrated and described in Fig. 110. As will be seen, the apparatus is similar to an optical spectrometer in arrangement, an ionisation chamber taking the place of a telescope. The strength of the ionisation current measures the intensity of the reflected beam. Moseley, de Broglie, and others have used a photographic instead of an ionisation method of registering the rays.

The crystal is mounted with wax on an adjustable mounting fixed on the table of the spectrometer. The X-ray bulb should be very " soft," and a pencil of X rays is employed which leaves the anticathode at a grazing angle, a plan which diminishes the evil effect of the wandering of the cathode spot, and with it the variation in the angle of incidence of the X-ray beam.[1] The ionisation chamber is filled with a heavy gas or vapour (SO_2 or methyl bromide) so as to yield a large ionisation.

A variation of the photographic method was used by de Broglie (*C.R.* 1913 *et seq.*) in which the crystal is caused to revolve slowly and uniformly by clockwork. In a second method, camera and crystal move together, the former at twice the rate of the latter. De Broglie and Lindemann (see Gorton, *P.R.* 1916) have employed a concave reflection grating consisting of a sheet of mica bent to a cylindrical shape.

X-ray Spectra.

From what has been said already of crystal structure, we can picture a series of planes of atoms parallel to each natural face of a crystal. When X rays fall on this face, they appear to be reflected from the face itself, although in point of fact it is within a thin layer inside the crystal that reflection is occurring, at depths usually not exceeding one millimetre.

If a train of X rays all of the same wave-length (λ), falls on the crystal, it is only when the glancing angle (θ) has certain values that " reflection " takes place. These values are given by

$$\lambda = 2d \sin \theta_1,$$
$$2\lambda = 2d \sin \theta_2, \text{ and so on,}$$

where d is the distance apart of the atomic planes. The reflection at θ_1 gives the first order spectrum, that at θ_2 the second order, and so on. At other angles there is, in general, no reflected beam. The above equations give us a relation

---

[1] A Coolidge tube in which the cathode stream is normal to the anti cathode offers many advantages for X-ray spectrometry.

between λ and d ; and so, by employing the same crystal face, the wave-lengths of different monochromatic X rays can be compared ; or by using the same wave-length, the spacing d can be compared for different crystals or different faces of the same crystal.

We thus have the means not only of analysing a beam of X rays, but of investigating the structure of crystals. The X-ray spectrometer (which is the exact analogue of the optical spectrometer) has given us a measure of both the atomic spacings of crystals and the absolute wave-lengths of monochromatic X rays.

In the case of general (or white) X rays, however the crystal is oriented there is always some value of θ which fits in with the possible values of d and λ. Every set of planes reflects somewhat, but the amount of reflection diminishes with the complexity of the plane. Thus at every angle of reflection, a certain amount of reflected radiation can be detected, the quantity increasing very greatly as grazing incidence is approached.

But with monochromatic rays the effect is more restricted, and it is at only a few special angles (given by the equations above) that reflection can be detected. Thus with a mixture of monochromatic and general radiation (such as is ordinarily emitted by an X-ray bulb), if the strength of the reflected beam is plotted against the glancing angle, the X-ray spectrum consists of a background or smooth curve of white radiation, superposed on which are " peaks " corresponding to the monochromatic spectrum " lines." The position and form of these peaks depend only on the metal of the anticathode of which they are characteristic.

It appears to be the case that the independent radiation referred to above is the exact equivalent of white light in the visible spectrum, and that it is represented by a perfectly continuous spectrum of rays.

It would be anticipated that the spectrum lines would be present in the " secondary " X rays produced by the original " reflection " method of Barkla. On trying the experiment de Broglie (*C.R.* May 1914) had no difficulty in detecting the lines.

Fig. 111 is the curve obtained by the Braggs for the rays from a platinum anticathode. The reflector in this instance was a rock-salt crystal, though the general form and relative proportions were found to be the same for all the crystals examined. The curve shows three prominent peaks (marked A, B, and C in the figure) thrice repeated. The rays corresponding to each of these peaks are found to be homogeneous when tested by the usual absorption method. Correspond-

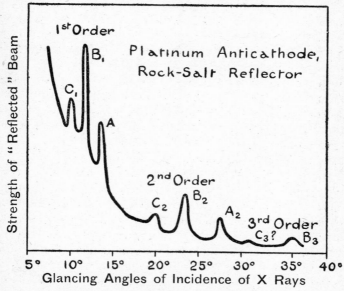

FIG. 111.—Showing intensity-distribution of spectrum of X rays from platinum. There are three main spectrum lines, and a large proportion of "white" or general X rays.

ing peaks in the different series prove to be closely related : not only are the absorption coefficients of the rays producing, for instance, B_1, B_2, and B_3 identical, but the sines of their reflection angles are in simple ratio. For example, the several angles of reflection of the B peaks are

$$11°·55, \quad 23°·65, \quad \text{and} \quad 36°·65.$$

The sines of these angles are

$$0·200, \quad 0·401, \quad \text{and} \quad 0·597,$$

which are very nearly in the ratio of 1, 2, and **3**.

There can be little doubt as to the interpretation of these results.   The peaks A, B, and C represent three different sets of homogeneous rays which appear as first, second, and third order spectra.   The three groups of rays are not manufactured in the crystal, for their properties prove to be the same, no matter what crystal is used.   The incident X rays consist, in fact, of " independent " rays of all wave-lengths with an admixture of homogeneous radiations characteristic of the platinum anticathode (compare Kaye and Beatty's results on pp. 36 and 134).   It is clear, moreover, that the characteristic rays consist not of a single homogeneous constituent, but of several groups of component rays of different wave-lengths.

Moseley and Darwin (*loc. cit.*), using rather more refined apparatus, similarly detected five homogeneous constituents in the platinum radiation : peaks B and C are, in fact, close doublets.   The proportions of these constituents appeared to depend on the state of the X-ray bulb.

The allied metals, osmium and iridium, yield X-ray spectra similar to that of platinum.   Each contains three main groups of homogeneous rays, together with a good proportion of general radiation.   The spectra of palladium and rhodium are very similar to each other ; each is very nearly homogeneous, at any rate with a soft bulb (see p. 126), and contains little general radiation.   On this account, both radiations have been employed a great deal by the Braggs in their later crystal experiments.   Fig. 112 shows the rhodium spectrum, the principal line of which is in point of fact a very close doublet.

It needs to be pointed out that Figs. 111 and 112 are examples of X-ray spectra of which the general form depends on the circumstances.   While it is true that the spectral lines themselves are invariable in position, their relative intensity and that of the general radiation are modified by such factors as the hardness of the X-ray bulb, the presence of any filtering screens, the type of discharge, and, of course, on the resolving power of the spectrometer.   The chemical nature of the crystal also exerts a marked effect on the distribution of the energy.   Bragg has shown that this is due to the selective absorption by the atoms of the crystals of the various components of the X rays.

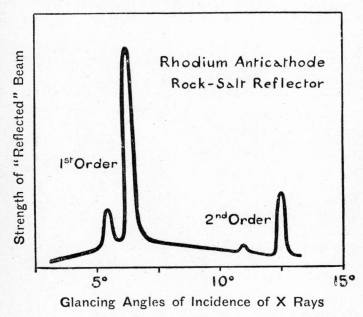

FIG. 112.—Spectrum showing distribution of energy in X rays from rhodium. There is a large proportion of monochromatic radiation, and very little "white" or general radiation.

Suitable Crystals for X-ray Analysis.

In the analysis of X-ray spectra, the choice of crystal is important. Experience has shown that defects in crystals are of common occurrence, and that perfect crystals are relatively rare. The diamond is a very perfect and intense reflector: it can, moreover, although very hard, be readily cleaved. Calcite is nearly as good as diamond, but the reflection is not so intense. Rock-salt, which was used largely in the pioneer experiments, is often imperfect. Iron pyrites and zinc-blende reflect more truly than rock-salt.

CRYSTAL-STRUCTURE.

We must now refer, if only briefly, to the important work which has been done during the last few years by W. L. Bragg (*P.R.S.* 1913 *et seq.*) on the structure of crystals.

In order to arrive at the structure of a crystal and the dimensions of its space-lattice, we require to determine

(1) to what point system it belongs ;

(2) what are the several distances separating the atomic planes parallel to the different crystal faces.

On these lines, Bragg attacked, first of all, the problem of the structure of the halogen salts of the alkaline metals, all of which form cubic crystals.

(1) Nature of the Space-Lattice.

The salts dealt with were the chlorides of sodium and potassium, and the bromide and iodide of potassium. The Laue patterns were obtained for each of these when the X rays fell normally on a plate cut parallel to a cube-face. On *a priori* grounds, we might anticipate that these chemically similar bodies would all belong to the same point system and give identical Laue patterns. On the contrary, when the tests were made it was found that

(1) potassium chloride gave rise to a simple pattern such as would be produced by a simple cubic lattice of the first kind (p. 217);

(2) potassium bromide and iodide each produced the pattern characteristic of the face-centred lattice of the third kind (p. 217);

(3) sodium chloride gave a third pattern more complex than either of the others, and apparently intermediate between them.

The most obvious and plausible explanation of this dissimilarity is that the relative masses of the two constituents affect the diffracting ability of the molecule. It is reasonable to infer that a heavy atom would form a better diffracting centre than a light one, and, if we assume this to be the case, the apparently strange results become rational. In the case of potassium chloride, the atomic weights of potassium and chlorine (39·1 and 35·5 respectively) are sufficiently close for the atoms to be equally efficient as diffracting centres. The disparity in the atomic weights of sodium and chlorine (23 and 35·5) complicates the rock-salt pattern, while with potassium iodide (39·1 and 127) and bromide (39·1 and 79·9) one atom is so much heavier than the other that the system consists in effect of only one kind of atom on a simple space-lattice.

We have now to conceive a grouping of metal and halogen which, though common to all four salts, will bring out the

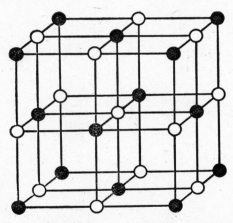

FIG. 113.—Representation of two types of diffracting centres in a cubic crystal.

points of difference. Following Bragg's notation, let us distinguish between the two kinds of diffracting centres in a salt by calling one black and the other white. Then the points must be arranged in such a way that

(1) there are equal numbers of black and white ;

(2) the arrangement of points, black and white, taken all together is that of the first cubic space-lattice, viz. points at the corners only of each elementary cube (p. 217);

(3) the arrangement of blacks alone or of whites alone

is that of the third cubic space-lattice, viz. points at the corners and face-centres (p. 217).

An arrangement which gives this result is shown in Fig. 113. The space-lattice formed by the whites is the same as that formed by the blacks, each of the two being the third system. If black and white centres become identical, as in KCl, the lattice becomes the simple cubic one of the first type.

The evidence for this arrangement of the atoms in these halogen salts seems very weighty, but we are still unable to say with certainty whether the diffracting unit at each point of the system contains only one atom or more. Bragg has, however, brought strong support in favour of the view that single atoms are associated with each centre. Laue photographs were obtained for three such different substances as zinc-blende (ZnS), fluorspar (CaF_2), and calcite ($CaCO_3$); in each case the X rays traversed the crystals along the trigonal axes.[1] The patterns proved to be identical, which points to the fact that the diffracting centres are arranged on precisely similar space-lattices in all three cases.

But, since a space-lattice is an arrangement in which each point is situated relatively to its neighbours in exactly the same way as every other point, it would be impossible to arrange complex molecules in a space-lattice unless only one point in each molecule were effective. We are led to infer that, at any rate in the above cases, each molecule acts as a single point, by reason of the fact that it contains one atom much heavier than the rest; and that it is the lattice of the heaviest atom in the molecule which is responsible for the diffraction pattern observed.[2]

Thus far, well and good, but to complete the argument in support of the view that each diffracting centre contains only one atom, we need to know the comparative dimensions of the lattice of the several crystals. This we can get by the X-ray spectrometer, as we will now proceed to indicate.

---

[1] *I.e.* diagonal-wise through the centre of the cube.

[2] Bragg's later work leads him to the conclusion that the scattering power of an atom is proportional to its atomic weight.

(2) Separation-Distances of Atomic Planes.

A knowledge of the angles at which the various X-ray
"peaks" are reflected in the spectrum of an element,
enables us to find the distance between the planes of the
reflecting system in terms of the wave-length of the X rays
concerned.   By measuring the first-order value of the
glancing angle θ in

$$\lambda = 2d \sin \theta$$

for the reflection curves from the three primary planes of
the crystal, we can derive the several values of $\dfrac{d_1}{\lambda}, \dfrac{d_2}{\lambda}, \dfrac{d_3}{\lambda}$
for the three principal directions.   We can thus deduce
both the form of the elementary parallelopiped and the
value of $\dfrac{d_1 d_2 d_3}{\lambda^3}$ or $\dfrac{V}{\lambda^3}$, where V is the volume of the parallelopiped.   Now, if ρ is the density of the crystal, the mass
associated with each parallelopiped, and so presumably with
each diffracting centre, is $V\rho$.   If M is the molecular weight
of the substance, the number of molecules associated with
each centre is $\dfrac{V\rho}{M}$, which we may write $\lambda^3\left(\dfrac{V}{\lambda^3} \cdot \dfrac{\rho}{M}\right)$.   If, in a
series of comparative experiments, λ is kept constant, then
the expression within the brackets is proportional to the
number of molecules per centre, and can, moreover, be
evaluated by experiment.   Bragg proceeded to do this for
a number of different crystals, each of which contained one
heavy atom, viz. zinc-blende (ZnS), fluorspar (CaF_2), calcite
($CaCO_3$), iron pyrites (FeS_2), and rock-salt (NaCl).   Using
in every case the homogeneous rays of the B peak of Pt,
he found that the value of the quantity was, within a few
per cent., the same for all substances.   His results are put
out in Table XIX.

Thus the number of molecules associated with each diffracting centre is the same, and if we take into consideration
the very different constitution of these crystals, this fact
seems to point to the association of one molecule, and one
alone, with each diffracting centre.   By combining this
result with the deductions on p. 234, it would seem that,

since there is only one heavy atom in each molecule, the pattern obtained with the various crystals is due to a space-lattice formed by the association of only one heavy atom with each centre.

It will be noticed that potassium chloride gives a value for $V\rho/\lambda^3M$ equal to half that for the other crystals, the explanation being that the two atoms, being of nearly the same weight, are equally effective as diffracting centres, and that a parallelopiped with half the side is now the crystal unit.

The above argument is obviously not a complete proof of this important point, but the probability of the truth

TABLE XIX.[1]

Crystal.	Lattice.	Density ρ	Mol. Wt. M	Face.	θ	$\dfrac{d}{\lambda}$	$\dfrac{V}{\lambda^3}$	$\dfrac{V\rho}{\lambda^3 M}$
Sylvine, KCl	Simple cubic	1·97	74·5	(100)	10·2°	2·86	23·4	0·605
				(111)	18·0	1·62	22·2	
Rock-salt, NaCl	Face-centred cubic	2·15	58·5	(100)	11·4	2·53	32·5	1·22
				(110)	16·0	1·82	33·9	
				(111)	9·8	2·95	33·5	
Zinc-blende, ZnS	Face-centred cubic	4·06	97·0	(110)	16·5	1·76	30·8	1·28
Fluorspar, CaF$_2$	Face-centred cubic	3·18	78·0	(100)	11·7	2·46	29·8	1·18
				(111)	10·3	2·79	28·3	
Calcite, CaCO$_3$	Rhombo-hedral	2·71	100·0	(100)	10·5	2·74	44·8	1·22
				(111)	11·2	2·60		
Iron pyrites, FeS$_2$	Face-centred cubic	5·03	120·0	(100)	12·1	2·39	27·3	1·15

[1] In this table—

θ = glancing angle of Pt B peak, first order.

λ = wave-length of Pt B peak.

d = distance between planes parallel to the face investigated.

V = volume of elementary parallelopiped, calculated from this value of d and a knowledge of the nature of the lattice.

of the assumption that each centre represents a single atom has been strengthened by each and every one of the many varieties of crystals subsequently examined.

In later work, Bragg has been able to allocate the positions of both the light and heavy atoms in many types of crystals, and has studied the motions of the atoms with heat. (See Braggs' *X Rays and Crystal Structure.*)

Dimensions of Space-lattice and Wave-length of X Rays.

If the arrangement assigned to the alkaline salts is correct, we are now in a position to calculate the wave-length of the B peak, Pt radiation, for

$$\lambda^3 \left(\frac{V}{\lambda^3} \cdot \frac{\rho}{M} \right) = 1.$$

Take the case of rock-salt (NaCl),

Molecular weight, $M = 58\cdot5 \times 1\cdot64 \times 10^{-24}$ grammes.

Density, - - $\rho = 2\cdot15$ gm./c.c.

$V/\lambda^3 = 33\cdot3$ (experimentally determined).

$\therefore \ \lambda^3(33\cdot3 \times 2\cdot15) = 58\cdot5 \times 1\cdot64 \times 10^{-24}$;

whence $\qquad\qquad \lambda^3 = 1\cdot34 \times 10^{-24}$

and $\qquad\qquad \lambda = 1\cdot10 \times 10^{-8}$ cm.,

which gives us the wave-length of the homogeneous radiation of the B peak of platinum.

From the values of d/λ given in Table XIX., we can calculate the lattice-constants for the several crystals. (See p. 240.)

Platinum L Radiation.

The mass-absorption coefficient in Al of the rays constituting the B peak of platinum was measured by Bragg and found to be 23·7. From Fig. 60 this value corresponds either to a K characteristic radiation from an element of atomic weight 72·5 or an L characteristic radiation from one of atomic weight 198. The atomic weight of platinum is 195 : the agreement is too close to be fortuitous, and there can be little doubt that the B peak is due to the L radiation.

We have the means of deriving further relations. From Whiddington's rule for K radiations (p. 133) we can calculate that the cathode-ray energy necessary to excite the K radiation from an atom of weight 72·5 is about 2×10^{-8} ergs. This energy should be equal to the energy of the X ray excited, which, if Planck's radiation formula holds in this connection, is given by $h\nu$ [1] or hV/λ. h is Planck's constant $(6·55 \times 10^{-27}$ erg sec.), ν is the frequency of the radiation, and V is the velocity of light. Now we have just shown that Pt L radiation has a wave-length of $1·10 \times 10^{-8}$ cm., and therefore

$$\frac{h.V}{\lambda} = \frac{6·55 \times 10^{-27} \times 3 \times 10^{10}}{1·10 \times 10^{-8}}$$

$$= 1·78 \times 10^{-8} \text{ ergs}$$

—which is in fair agreement with the calculated value.

Moseley's Experiments.

Moseley ($P.M.$ Dec. 1913, April 1914) examined photographically the X-ray spectra of a large number of elements and obtained remarkable and important results. The elements were mounted as anticathodes (Kaye's form of apparatus, p. 36, was first used), the X rays being analysed by means of a crystal of potassium ferrocyanide. The discharge tube was provided with an aluminium window (0·0022 cm. thick), which in those cases where the radiation was very soft was replaced by one of goldbeater's skin. In some instances, the whole spectrometer had to be enclosed in an evacuated box, since the rays were too soft to penetrate more than 1 or 2 cms. of air.

In the majority of cases the pure elements were used as anticathodes, but if the elements were rare or volatile, oxides, salts, or alloys were employed. There was usually no difficulty in such cases in sorting out the spectrum lines.

Fig. 114 illustrates the X-ray spectra obtained by Moseley for some of the lighter elements which emit strong K characteristic radiations. The spectra are placed in approximate register in the photograph. It will be noticed that

---

[1] $h\nu$ is the energy of a quantum, according to Planck's theory.

the wave-length increases as the atomic weight diminishes, and that the spectrum consists in each case of two lines, of which the longer wave-length (the α line) is the more intense.

The *L* characteristic radiations were found to be made up of at least five lines, α, β, γ, δ, ε, reckoned in order of decreasing wave-length and decreasing intensity.

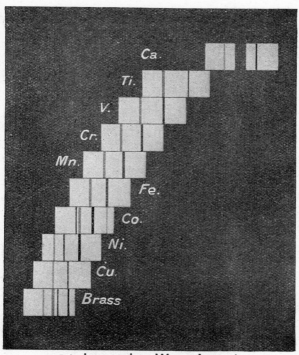

⟶ Increasing **Wave Length**

Fig. 114.—Moseley's photographs of the X-ray or high-frequency spectra of a number of metallic anticathodes. The spectra, which are in the third order, are placed approximately in register in the figure. The wave-lengths are given on pp. 240-41. For each metal, the more intense line, with the longer wave-length, is the *K* characteristic radiation. The brass shows the Zn and Cu lines ; the cobalt contained both nickel and iron as impurities.

Later work has shown that the principal line of the two-line *K* spectrum is really a close doublet ; and with both the *K* and *L* series there are a good many other fainter lines which are now being examined.

Table XX. Wave-lengths of Lines in X-ray Spectra.

Up to now, about 16 lines have been found to be associated with the characteristic X-ray spectrum of each element. Three series of lines are known at present—the K, L, and M, of which the K has the highest frequency. A J series has also been claimed to exist, but the evidence needs confirmation. The K series contains at least 4 lines—α_2, α_1, β, and γ—of which the γ line has the highest frequency. The L series contains probably 3 groups of lines, each group similar to the K series. The values of the wave-lengths of the principal lines are given below in Angström units. It should be noted that all the values rest on W. L. Bragg's estimate of the lattice constant of rock-salt (see below).

Lattice Constants of Crystals.

Crystal.	Lattice Constant.	Observer.
	$\times 10^{-8}$ cm.	
Rock-salt, NaCl - - -	2·8140	W. L. Bragg, Roy. Soc. Proc., 1913.
Calcite (cleavage face), $CaCO_3$	3·0290	Siegbahn, Phil. Mag., 1919.
Potassium ferrocyanide, K_4Fe $(CN)_6 \cdot 3H_2O$	8·408	,, ,,
Gypsum, $CaSO_4 \cdot 2H_2O$ - -	7·621	,, ,,

K Series.

At. No.	Ele- ment.	α_2	α_1	β_1	β_2	Observer.
		$\times 10^{-8}$ cm.	$\times 10^{-8}$ cm.	$\times 10^{-8}$ cm.	$\times 10^{-8}$ cm.	
11	Na	—	11·95	—	—	Siegbahn & Stenström, P.Z., July 1916.
12	Mg	—	9·92	9·48	—	,, ,,
13	Al	—	8·36	7·99	—	,, ,,
14	Si	—	7·13	6·76	—	,, ,,
15	P	—	6·17	5·81	—	,, ,,
16	S	—	5·36	5·02	—	,, ,,
17	Cl	—	4·7187	4·39	—	Siegbahn, P.M., June 1919.
19	K	—	3·7339	3·4474	—	,, ,,
20	Ca	—	3·3519	3·0879	—	,, ,,
21	Sc	—	3·0253	2·7745	—	,, ,,
22	Ti	2·746	2·742	2·509	2·492	Siegbahn & Stenström, P.Z., July 1916.
23	V	2·502	2·498	2·281	—	,, ,,
24	Cr	—	2·2852	2·0814	—	Siegbahn, P.M., June 1919.
25	Mn	2·093	2·093	1·902	1·892	Siegbahn & Stenström, P.Z., Feb. 1916.
26	Fe	—	1·9324	1·7540	—	Siegbahn, P.M., June 1919.
27	Co	—	1·7852	1·6176	—	,, ,,
28	Ni	—	1·6547	—	—	,, ,,
29	Cu	—	1·5374	1·3895	—	,, ,,
30	Zn	1·437	1·433	1·294	1·281	Siegbahn & Stenström, P.Z., Feb. 1916.
32	Ge	1·261	1·257	1·131	1·121	,, ,,
39	Y	—	0·833	—	—	Moseley (corrected), P.M., April 1914.
40	Zr	—	0·790	—	—	,, ,,
41	Nb	—	0·746	—	—	,, ,,
42	Mo	—	0·717	—	—	,, ,,
44	Ru	—	0·635	—	—	,, ,,
45	Rh	0·6164	0·6121	0·5453	0·5342	Duane & Hu, P.R., 1919.
46	Pd	0·589	0·583	0·516	—	Bragg.
47	Ag	0·562	0·557	0·495	—	
48	Cd	—	0·537	0·475	—	Siegbahn, D.P.G.V., 1916.
49	In	—	0·506	0·454	—	,, ,,
50	Sn	—	0·486	0·432	—	,, ,,
51	Sb	—	0·469	0·416	—	,, ,,
52	Te	—	0·456	0·404	—	,, ,,
53	I	—	0·437	0·388	—	,, ,,
56	Ba	—	0·388	0·344	—	,, ,,
74	W	0·2135	0·2089	0·1844	0·1794	Siegbahn, P.M., November 1919.
92	U	—	0·15	0·10	—	,, ,,

At. No.	Element	α_2	α_1	β_1	β_2	γ_1	Observer.
		$\times 10^{-8}$ cm.	$\times 10^{-8}$ cm.	$\times 10^{-8}$ cm.	$\times 10^{-8}$ cm.	$\times 10^{-8}$ cm.	
30	Zn	—	12·35	—	—	—	Friman, P.M., November 1916.
33	As	—	9·701	9·449	—	—	,, ,,
35	Br	—	8·391	8·141	—	—	,, ,,
37	Rb	—	7·335	7·091	—	—	,, ,,
38	Sr	—	6·879	6·639	—	—	,, ,,
39	Y	—	6·464	6·227	—	—	,, ,,
40	Zr	—	6·083	5·851	—	5·386	,, ,,
41	Nb	5·731	5·724	5·493	5·317	—	,, ,,
42	Mo	5·410	5·403	5·175	—	—	,, ,,
44	Ru	4·853	4·845	4·630	—	—	,, ,,
45	Rh	—	4·596	4·372	—	—	,, ,,
46	Pd	4·374	4·363	4·142	3·903	3·720	,, ,,
47	Ag	4·156	4·146	3·929	3·698	3·515	,, ,,
48	Cd	3·959	3·949	3·733	3·514	3·331	,, ,,
49	In	3·774	3·766	3·550	3·335	3·160	,, ,,
50	Sn	3·604	3·594	3·381	3·172	2·999	,, ,,
51	Sb	3·443	3·434	3·222	3·021	2·849	,, ,,
52	Te	3·299	3·290	3·074	2·881	2·712	,, ,,
53	I	3·155	3·146	2·934	2·750	2·583	,, ,,
55	Cs	2·899	2·891	2·684	2·514	2·350	,, ,,
56	Ba	2·786	2·776	2·569	2·407	2·245	,, ,,
57	La	2·674	2·665	2·461	2·307	2·146	,, ,,
58	Ce	2·573	2·563	2·359	2·212	2·052	,, ,,
59	Pr	2·472	2·462	2·259	2·120	1·958	,, ,,
60	Nd	2·379	2·369	2·167	2·036	1·875	,, ,,
62	Sa	2·210	2·200	2·000	1·884	1·725	,, ,,
63	Eu	2·131	2·121	1·918	1·810	1·662	,, ,,
64	Gd	2·054	2·043	1·844	1·744	1·597	,, ,,
65	Tb	1·983	1·973	1·775	1·682	1·531	,, ,,
66	Dy	1·916	1·907	1·709	1·622	1·470	,, ,,
67	Ho	1·854	1·843	1·646	1·568	1·415	,, ,,
68	Er	1·794	1·783	1·586	1·514	1·367	,, ,,
70	Yb	1·681	1·670	1·474	1·414	1·267	,, ,,
71	Lu	1·629	1·619	1·421	1·368	1·224	,, ,,
73	Ta	1·528	1·518	1·323	1·280	1·135	Siegbahn & Friman, P.M., July 1916.
74	W	1·4845	1·4735	1·2792	1·2419	1·0955	Siegbahn, P.M., November 1919.
76	Os	1·398	1·388	1·194	1·167	1·021	Siegbahn & Friman, P.M., July 1916.
77	Ir	1·360	1·350	1·154	1·133	0·989	,, ,,
78	Pt	1·323	1·313	1·120	1·101	0·958	,, ,,
79	Au	1·283	1·271	1·080	1·065	0·922	,, ,,
80	Hg	1·251	1·240	1·049	1·042	0·896	,, ,,
81	Tl	1·215	1·205	1·012	1·006	0·864	,, ,,
82	Pb	1·186	1·175	0·983	0·983	0·842	,, ,,
83	Bi	1·153	1·144	0·950	0·954	0·810	,, ,,
84	Po	—	1·109	0·920	—	—	,, ,,
88	Ra	—	1·010	—	—	—	,, ,,
90	Th	0·969	0·957	0·766	0·797	0·654	,, ,,
92	U	0·922	0·911	0·720	0·756	0·615	,, ,,

M SERIES.

At. No.	Element	α	β	γ	δ	Observer.
		$\times 10^{-8}$ cm.	$\times 10^{-8}$ cm.	$\times 10^{-8}$ cm.	$\times 10^{-8}$ cm.	
79	Au	5·838	5·623	{ 5·348 { 5·284	5·146 } 5·102 }	Siegbahn, D.P.G.V., 1916.
81	Tl	5·479	5·256	—	4·826	,, ,,
82	Pb	5·303	5·095	4·91 ?	4·695	,, ,,
83	Bi	5·117	4·903	{ 4·726 { 4·561	4·532 } 4·456 }	,, ,,
90	Th	4·139	3·941	{ 3·812 { 3·678	— } — }	,, ,,
92	U	3·905	3·715	3·480	{ 3·363 } { 3·324 }	,, ,,

The wave-lengths of the more intense lines of the K, L, and M series are given in Table XX., together with the lattice constants of a number of crystals.

Moseley's Law.

But the outstanding feature of Moseley's work is the relationship which he established between the X-ray spectrum and the order of an element in the periodic table. In

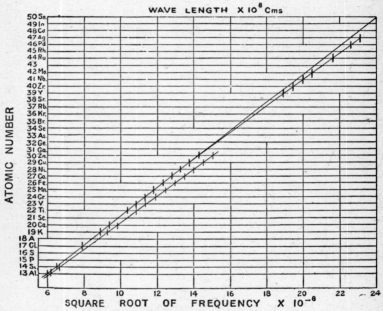

Fig. 115.—Moseley's relation between atomic numbers and frequency of K radiations (Braggs' *X Rays and Crystal Structure*).

brief, he plotted the atomic number (*i.e.* the number which represents the order of the element in the periodic table) against the square root of the frequency of the X ray, and found that the points for the different elements lay extremely well on a smooth line which was almost straight. In other words, the wave-length of the X ray is inversely proportional to $(N-a)^2$ where N is the atomic number and a a constant. Fig. 115 shows the result for the K radiations, and Fig. 116 for the L radiations. The several curves refer to corresponding lines of the various elements.

It will be observed that no element is unprovided for in the scheme, and the harmony of the relationship is such as to justify the assertion that the spaces which have been necessarily left are awaiting elements as yet undiscovered. Perfect regularity over the region extending from hydrogen

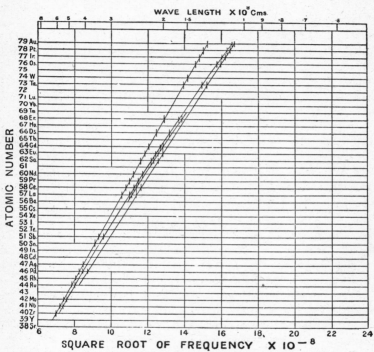

FIG. 116.—Moseley's relation between atomic number and frequency of *L* radiations (Braggs' *X Rays and Crystal Structure*).

(At. No , 1) to uranium (At. No., 92) can only be retained by allowing spaces for seven new elements with atomic numbers 43, 61, 75, 85, 87, 89, and 91 respectively. These elements, four of which are in the radioactive group, remain to be discovered.

The order of atomic numbers is that of atomic weights, except in the cases of argon, cobalt and tellurium. If in Figs. 115 and 116 atomic weights are employed instead of atomic numbers, the relationship is seen to be not nearly as perfect. A table of atomic numbers is given on p. 282 ; it will be noticed that the atomic number is approximately half the atomic weight.

It is apparent from Moseley's experiments that the atomic number is something more than a mere integer : it evidently represents some fundamental attribute of the atom. Now several quite different methods of experimental attack all agree in indicating that the atomic number agrees closely with the number of positive charges carried by the nucleus of the atom, or, alternatively, the number of electrons in the atom (see p. 22). We may well suppose that the wavelength of a characteristic radiation depends directly on the magnitude of the nuclear charge.

In passing we may note the development of a remarkable view that the same atomic number may be borne by each of several substances which may have different atomic weights (and in the case of the radioactive substances, different stabilities), but which may be quite inseparable by ordinary chemical or physical tests. Soddy calls the members of such a group of elements bearing a single atomic number and occupying therefore a single place in the periodic table " isotopes." That which is common to them all is the positive nuclear charge—adopting Rutherford's theory of atomic structure. (See pp. 18 and 22.)

From what has already been said, it would be expected that isotopes would yield the same X-ray spectrum. To take an example, RaB, ThB, RaD, and lead are all isotopes (in spite of the fact that their atomic weights range from 214 to 207), and, when put to the test by Rutherford and Andrade ($P.M.$ 1914), the spectrum of the soft γ rays from RaB proved to be identical with the L characteristic radiation of lead.

Bohr ($P.M.$ 1913 et $seq.$) has developed Rutherford's theory of the constitution of the atom with remarkable success ; and linked it up quantitatively with the quantum theory (p. 245) and Moseley's experimental results.

Moseley's work has been amplified by Siegbahn with Friman ($P.M.$ Ap. Jy. 1916 et $seq.$) and with Stenström ($P.Z.$ 1916). They have extended the K series down to Na, and the L series down to Zn ($\lambda_a = 1.2 \times 10^{-7}$ cm.) and up to U (see Table XX., pp 240-41).

X rays with wave-lengths as long as 12 Ångström units are extremely absorbable in character, and Siegbahn's work with such radiations was only possible with the aid of the vacuum spectrometer, a difficulty which was shared by workers on the extreme boundary of the ultra-violet, some four octaves away.   Further progress in the work of extending the X-ray spectrum towards the ultra-violet was halted for some time because the wave-lengths were becoming too long for the crystal gratings to deal with.

The gap was filled eventually by a number of workers: Millikan, *Astrophy. J.*, 1920; Richardson, *P.M.*, 1921; Kuth, *P.R.*, 1921; Hughes, *P.M.*, 1922; who, using indirect photoelectric methods, traced X-ray spectrum lines of

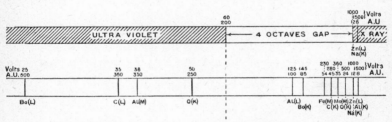

Fig. 117.—Showing some X-ray spectrum lines in the former gap between ultra-violet light and X rays.

various elements right across the gap and into the already explored ultra-violet.   Fig. 117 shows some of these lines.

Developments of X-Ray Spectrometry.

The subject of X-ray spectrometry has become so great and the literature so extensive that only a restricted account is possible here.   Measurements have become increasingly precise and now parallel in exactness those in optical spectrometry.   The technique has been developed in various directions, and the subject now claims an army of workers in many countries.   Both photographic and ionisation methods are in use, the former providing a permanent record and possessing certain conveniences, while the latter is more sensitive and offers advantages when intensity measurements are required.

The spectrometer and the oscillograph have thrown light on a number of problems which have been obscure in the past. The spectrometer reveals the composition of a beam of rays with an accuracy impossible by the older methods,

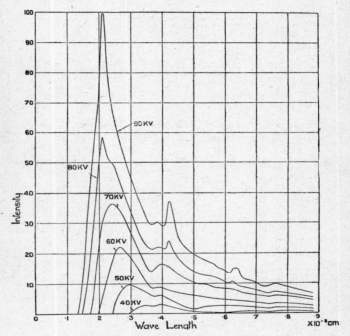

Fig. 118.—X-ray spectrum of tungsten at various voltages and same milliamps; no filter ; NaCl crystal.

such as those based on absorption. For example, Fig. 118, due to Hull at Schenectady, shows the spectral curves of tungsten at a variety of exciting voltages. At the lower voltages the curves indicate only continuous spectra of general radiation, but at the higher voltages we see the gradual development of peaks indicative of the presence of characteristic spectrum lines.

Another feature to be remarked is the definite position of

the quantum-limit or the shortest wave-length present in the various spectra, and its gradual shift to the left as the voltage is raised. The connection between the two has already been dwelt upon (p. 99). It may be added that Seemann has devised a direct reading spectrograph (Fig. 119) which enables the position of the short-wave boundary to be readily ascertained. Incidentally such spectrographs form very convenient and accurate voltmeters which indicate the actual maximum voltage effectively operating an X-ray bulb.

Spectral curves have a further value in that the areas of the curves are a measure of X-ray output. For example, if we ignore characteristic radiations, we find that in Fig. 118 the X-ray output is proportional to the square of the

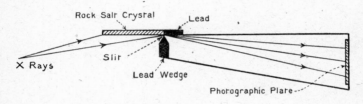

FIG. 119.—Seemann's spectrograph.

exciting voltage. If we obtain similar spectral curves keeping the voltage (V) constant and varying in turn the current (i) and the atomic number (N) of the anticathode, we find that the output is proportional to NiV^2, a result already arrived at in previous chapters. If we carry out such measurements with both gas and hot cathode X-ray tubes, we normally find the former to be somewhat more efficient.

Fig. 120 shows some X-ray spectra obtained by Müller at the Cavendish Laboratory. The L lines of platinum and lead and the K lines of copper are shown. The position of the quantum limit in each spectrum is indicated by a small dot. The gradual shift in position with voltage and the fact that the position does not depend on the nature of the metal are clearly indicated.

With reference to the determination of crystal structure, it happens that the great majority of substances do not yield individual crystals which are large enough to be conveniently handled singly in the X-ray spectrometer. As already referred to on p. 178 the utility of X-ray spectrometry was greatly increased when the method was found by Debye and Hull independently to be applicable to powders

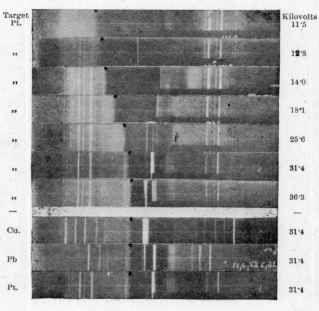

Target Pt.		Kilovolts 11·5
,,		12·8
,,		14·0
,,		18·1
,,		25·6
,,		31·4
,,		36·3
—		—
Cu.		31·4
Pb		31·4
Pt.		31·4

FIG. 120.—X-ray spectra showing spectrum lines and position of quantum limit (Müller).

and other aggregations of minute crystals. The one condition is that the orientation of the crystals shall be completely random. If a narrow tube of the powder is placed normally in the path of a pencil of homogeneous X rays, then among the large number of minute crystals will be a small proportion which are rightly disposed to be capable of reflecting the X rays just like a bigger crystal in the X-ray spectrometer. It is true that the great majority of the crystals will be incapable, through wrong orientation, of giving any reflection at all, but the only effect of this will be to waste a large fraction of the X-ray energy, and so to lengthen exposures. The reflected rays are received on a strip of photographic film bent into a semicircle with the rod of material as centre, and the resulting photograph shows a central spot surrounded by bands characteristic of the atoms in the material.

Bragg (*P.P.S.* 1921) has shown that it suffices to paste the powdered crystals on to a flat surface such as cardboard, and mount it on the spectrometer table just as one would a single crystal. Exposures are much shortened as homogeneous rays need not be used.

X-Ray Absorption Spectra.

The phenomena of absorption of characteristic radiation have already been referred to (p. 137), but they may usefully be recalled in connection with X-ray absorption spectra. If we pass X rays through a sheet of metal and gradually diminish the wave-length, we find that the rays are transmitted with steadily increasing facility until a critical value of the wave-length is reached. At this stage there is a large increase in the difficulty of passing the sheet, and at the same time all the lines of the characteristic series of the metal are generated. If the shortening of the wave-length of the primary beam is continued, the ease of transmission is resumed once more, but the former facility is not recovered until the wave-length has been greatly diminished.

These facts have a bearing on the behaviour of the silver in the emulsion of a photographic plate when an X-ray spectrum is thrown on it. We find that at one point—to be exact, wave-length 0·485 A.U.—there is a sharply defined boundary, known as the absorption edge. On the one side of the edge, the shorter wave-lengths are more absorbed, and affect the plate far more than the longer waves on the other side. The position of the edge at this particular wave-length is an infallible indication of the presence of silver and of no other element.

Let us now attempt to obtain the absorption spectrum of

a material by interposing a sheet of it as a filter in front of the photographic plate. A new absorption edge is formed in a position corresponding to the critical wave-length of the atom in question, shorter waves being so highly absorbed by the sheet that they are not recorded on the photographic plate, while longer waves are.

The distance between the two absorption edges depends on the difference between the atomic number of silver and that of the atom under discussion. Fig. 121, due to de Broglie, shows an example of the method.

We see, then, that the positions of the several absorption

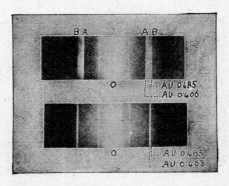

Fig. 121.—X-ray absorption spectra. Upper spectrum showing absorption edges of silver (A) and antimony (B); lower spectrum, absorption edges of silver and cadmium. (de Broglie.) (From the *Journal* of the Röntgen Society.)

edges in a spectrum afford a precise indication of the presence and identity of the corresponding elements in the absorption screen. The success of the method is not affected by the physical or chemical conditions of an element, so that salts or solutions may be utilised if convenient.

Reference should be made to the work of de Broglie (*J. de P.*, 1914 *et seq.*), who has developed the technique of the method to a fine degree.

Homogeneous X Rays.

An ideal of the radiologist has always been a means of producing homogeneous X rays, so that, among other things, a precision dose can be the better formulated in

therapy.   While all X-ray beams are heterogeneous, they
tend to become less so as the voltage is raised and the rays
are filtered by the right choice of substance of a suitable
thickness.   This may be seen either from absorption curves
or, more accurately, from spectral distribution curves.   The
nearest approach to homogeneity can be reached by
operating the X-ray bulb at a voltage somewhat above one

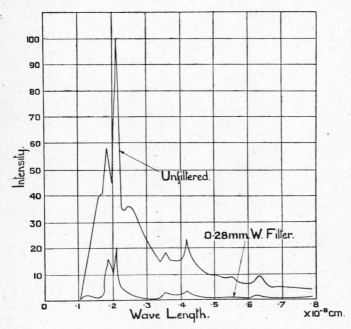

Fig. 122.—Intensity distribution of X-ray spectrum of tungsten, 110,000 volts.

of the critical values necessary to generate one of the
characteristic radiations of the anticathode, and then
filtering by a screen either of the same element as the
anticathode (as was first shown in Kaye's experiments,
p. 126), or, preferably, by an element of slightly smaller
atomic number.   We have already remarked that above the
critical voltage the characteristic radiations are generated
more copiously than the general radiation.   The voltage

should not be too high, however, or short-wave general radiation will begin to make its appearance, and will not be removed by filtration. There is, in fact, an optimum voltage. For example, while the critical voltage for the K radiation of tungsten (At. No. = 74) is about 70,000 volts, the optimum voltage is about 100,000 volts. A filter of tungsten (Fig. 122, Hull), or tantalum (At. No. = 73), 0 15 mm. thick, removes most of the general radiation, but leaves both the β and α components of the K radiation. An equally thick filter of ytterbium (At. No. = 70) would leave only the α component, with an intensity at least thirty times that of the remaining general radiation. Similarly for molybdenum (At. No. = 42) the optimum voltage is about 30,000, and the best filter zirconium (At. No. = 40). Tungsten would be a good filter for platinum radiation (At. No. = 78). Thus, if we have a battery of X-ray tubes each with a different anticathode a variety of homogeneous rays can be obtained. Unfortunately, such beams are of feeble intensity for radiological purposes.

The Three Methods of Analysis.

To recapitulate, there are then three methods of crystal-analysis depending on X rays.

(1) The Laue transmission method, which uses the independent, heterogeneous (or " white ") X rays that commonly constitute the greater part of the output from an ordinary bulb. The crystal plays a part somewhat like that of a " crossed " transmission grating, and the structure of the crystal controls the pattern of the diffracted spots.

(2) The Bragg spectrometer method, which employs the homogeneous X radiations and uses the crystal as a reflection grating. The structure of the crystal evinces itself in the distribution and intensity of the spectrum lines of the various orders. The Bragg method gives the data by which the dimensions of the lattices of crystals can be compared, and the X-ray spectrometer has already proved itself a powerful instrument for examining crystal-structure. The Laue method, on the other hand, can only supply information

concerning the nature of the lattices, and that in a limited degree.   The Bragg method is also applicable to an aggregation of minute crystals.

(3) The absorption spectrum method and the measurement of the absorption edge.

Relation between Wave-Lengths and Absorption Coefficients.

Table XXI. gives a series of comparative values of wavelengths and absorption coefficients in aluminium, derived from the results of Rutherford, Bragg, Moseley, and Barkla. A scrutiny of these results shows that if μ is the absorption coefficient and λ is the wave-length, then, except in the region of a characteristic wave-length,

$$\mu = k\lambda^{n},$$

where k is a const. for each material, and n lies between $\frac{5}{2}$ and 3.   But from Moseley's law (p. 242), we have approximately

$$\lambda^{1/2} \propto 1/N,$$

where N is the atomic number, and therefore, taking

$$\mu = k\lambda^{5/2},$$

we have

$$\mu \propto 1/N^{5},$$

which, if we replace atomic number by atomic weight, agrees with the relation referred to on p. 121.

Hull and Rice (*P.R.* 1916) have, however, shown that absorption results are not a reliable guide for deducing wave-lengths, at any rate for high frequencies, on account of the predominance of scattering over true absorption. (See p. 114.)

TABLE XXI. WAVE-LENGTHS AND ABSORPTION COEFFICIENTS.

Wave-length, λ.	μ/ρ_{Al}.	Wave-length, λ.	μ/ρ_{Al}.
1×10^{-9} cm.	0·04	12×10^{-9} cm.	22
2 ,,	0·21	13 ,,	28
3 ,,	0·57	14 ,,	35
4 ,,	1·20	15 ,,	43
5 ,,	2·10	16 ,,	51
6 ,,	3·3	17 ,,	61
7 ,,	4·8	18 ,,	72
8 ,,	6·6	19 ,,	83
9 ,,	8·9	20 ,,	95
10 ,,	12·2	21 ,,	108
11 ,,	16·5	22 ,,	120

Wave-lengths of γ Rays.

Rutherford and Andrade (*P.M.* May 1914 and August 1914) carried out an investigation on the diffraction of γ rays. They used as the source of their γ rays a thin-walled a-ray tube containing 100 millicuries of radium emanation.[1] The γ rays are given off by the products of the emanation, viz. RaB and RaC. A pencil of rays was allowed to fall on a crystal of rock-salt, just as in the X-ray spectrometer, the reflected beam being examined photographically.

About 30 lines were investigated, extending over a range of glancing angles of from 44′ to 14°.

The values of the wave-lengths of the various γ rays were found to lie between $1·365 \times 10^{-8}$ cm. and $7·1 \times 10^{-10}$ cm., the smaller values being much less than any X-ray wave-length hitherto recorded. The wave-lengths of the most penetrating rays of RaC are probably much smaller still, and will doubtless be very difficult to measure.

Rutherford and Andrade also employed an ingenious trans-

---

[1] A millicurie is the amount of emanation in equilibrium with 1 mgm. of radium

mission method of measuring the small angle of reflection (about $1\frac{1}{2}°$) of the γ ray.

A point source of radium emanation was placed centrally in front of a crystal of rock-salt, a photographic plate being set up behind the crystal (Fig. 123). The γ rays find their own reflecting planes at *A, A*, in the crystal and meet the photographic plate at *B, B*. The reflecting planes

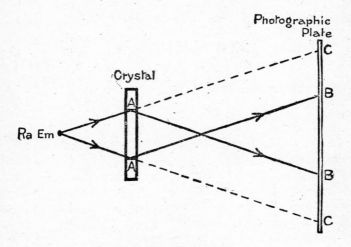

Fig. 123.—Reflection of γ rays.

also cast absorption shadows at *C, C*, since the transmitted beam is weakened by the loss of the rays that are reflected.

A similar reflection occurs at two planes parallel to the paper, and as a result the photographic plate shows a square pattern made up of both dark and light lines as in Fig. 124, from which the angle of reflection of the γ rays can be readily and accurately obtained.

Wide Range of Electromagnetic Waves.

With the addition of X rays to the list of electromagnetic waves already known, the table of wave-lengths is extended greatly in one direction. At the other end of the scale are the waves which were originally discovered by Hertz and are now used in wireless telegraphy. The longest wave-length generated up to the present is about 25,000 metres, or roughly fifteen miles : the shortest is a few milli-metres. The waves ordinarily used in " wireless " are a few thousand metres long, *e.g.* the wave-length of the wire-less time signals from the Eiffel Tower is 2000 metres ; of the Navy signals, from 600 to 1800 metres ; of trans-Atlantic signals, 7000 metres or more.

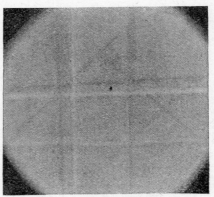

FIG. 124.—Reflection of γ rays.

Next to Hertzian waves, in order of magnitude, come the infra-red or heat rays, the greatest wave-length yet observed being $\frac{1}{5}$ mm. We pass from these right through the visible spectrum to the ultra-violet rays, which have been explored photographically by Schumann, Lyman, and Millikan as far as wave-length 2×10^{-6} cm. An extreme form of ultra-violet rays is probably represented by the " Entladungstrahlen " which are emitted from electric sparks, or the negative glow in a discharge tube (see Laird, *P.R.* 1911).

Next come X rays with wave-lengths of the order of 10^{-8} cm., and beyond them the most penetrating of all—the γ rays. As already remarked (p. 245) the range of the X rays now extends up to the ultra-violet.

The various wave-lengths, as at present known, are summarised in Table XXII.; they cover, as will be seen, the amazing range of about ten thousand million million fold. The only break in the sequence is a small gap between Hertzian waves and infra-red rays.

TABLE XXII.   WAVE-LENGTHS OF ELECTROMAGNETIC RADIATIONS.

Kind of Wave.	Wave-length in cms.
Hertzian waves - -	2×10^6 to 0.2
Infra-red rays - -	0.031 to 7.2×10^{-5}
Visible light rays - -	7.2×10^{-5} to 4.0×10^{-5}
Ultra-violet rays - -	4.0×10^{-5} to 2×10^{-6}
X rays - - - -	5×10^{-6} to 6×10^{-10}
γ rays - - - -	1.4×10^{-8} to 1.0×10^{-10}

CHAPTER XIV.

THE NATURE OF THE X RAYS.

THE discovery of the X rays by Röntgen, and their immediate application in surgery, excited the popular interest to an astonishing degree. Geissler tubes, no matter what their suitability, were in immediate demand by a strangely interested public. The scientific journals of 1896 bear witness to the many workers, who turned, if only for a time, from their usual pursuits, eager to test the extraordinary properties of the new rays. Naturally enough, among such an army of enthusiasts, speculation as to the nature of the rays was not marked by noteworthy restraint; a few of the responsible suggestions may be briefly recalled.

Röntgen, Boltzmann, and others regarded the rays as longitudinal ether-vibrations of short period and great wavelength : Jaumann added to this a transverse component : Goldhammer, Sagnac, and many others believed that the new rays were extremely short transverse ether-waves akin to ultra-violet light ; on the other hand, Re took the view that the wave-length, far from being short, was infinitely long : Sutherland considered X rays to be due to internal vibrations of the electrons within the atom : other workers held that the rays were a manifestation of the breaking up of molecules into atoms at the target : Michelson suggested that Röntgen rays were ether vortices : Stokes put forward a theory of irregular pulses in the ether ; and finally, many physicists, including at one time, Röntgen, and at a later period Sir Wm. Bragg, inclined to the view that the rays were flights of material particles which resembled strongly, and were possibly an extreme though electrically-neutral form of the parent cathode rays.

It is only within the last few years that controversy has been stilled by the discovery that X rays can be reflected and diffracted by crystals. There is no doubt now that X rays are identical with ultra-violet light of extremely short wave-lengths; wave-lengths, many of them of the order of the diameter of the atom.

There is, however, an obscure factor, while it seems certain from the extreme precision observed in the reflection experiments that X rays are regular light waves and occur in trains of great length, yet it is found that in many of their properties the rays behave strangely like streams of discrete entities, the effects of which are localised in space in much the same way as are the effects of rifle bullets. The difficulty is not, however, unique ; it is now known to be common to all forms of radiation. The Newtonian laws implying perfect continuity and infinite divisibility of time and space have, until recently, found complete credence ; but in the very nature of things they do not seem to be reconcilable with modern experiment, which suggests that energy radiation is essentially discontinuous and must take place by finite " jumps." As to the mechanism by which this is accomplished, it is at present obscure and still a matter for speculation.[1]

To meet the difficulty, J. J. Thomson, in his nucleated pulse theory, has suggested that all the various light radiations consist of concentrated and localised electromagnetic impulses which travel with the speed of light in some one direction through the ether (see p. 267). Planck's quantum theory, as developed by Einstein and Stark (*P.Z.* 1909 and 1910) similarly argues that X radiation (in common with all radiation) is made up of definite and indivisible increments which can travel without loss or alteration of form, the energy of these " bundles " being proportional to the frequency of the radiation (p. 268). The same difficulty was felt by Bragg when he put forward his corpuscular or neutral-

[1] For an excellent treatment of this subject see N. R. Campbell, *Modern Electrical Theory*, 2nd ed. 1913. Also *Rep. Brit. Assoc.* Sect. A, 1913.

pair theory of the X ray. This theory, which regarded an X ray as a neutral corpuscle, was conspicuously successful in predicting and interpreting the energy transfers met with in the inter-relations of electrons and X rays.

On the other hand, almost all the well established results of the undulatory theory of light seem to be irreconcilable with entity views such as these. Nucleated light does not appear to conform to the accepted explanation of interference and diffraction, which Young and Fresnel founded on a theory of spreading waves, nor does it obviously lead to the general laws of reflection and refraction which are apparently obeyed by all waves, from the shortest X rays to the longest Hertzian.

Points of Resemblance between Light Rays and X Rays.

The essential identity of X rays and light rays cannot be denied, in view of the work on crystal-reflection, but, notwithstanding, it will be useful and not without interest to summarise the points of resemblance which previous experiment had revealed between X rays, γ rays, and light rays. In many cases it had already been found that the effects differed only in degree. For example, the ionising effect of ultra-violet light on gases (first established by Lenard in 1900, and more recently and completely by Hughes, *P.C.P.S.* 1911) is relatively feeble when contrasted with the more vigorous activity of X rays.

Again, all three agencies cause the ejection of electrons from metals, and experiment has shown that:

(1) The intensity of the incident rays does not affect the speed, but merely the number of the ejected electrons (p. 147).

(2) The maximum speed of the electrons is controlled by the quality of the rays [1] (pp. 148 and 151). [With

---

[1] In the case of ultra-violet light, Hughes (*P.T.* 1912) finds experimentally that the energy rather than the speed of the fastest electrons is proportional to the frequency of the light. This confirms a deduction from Planck's quantum theory (p. 268), which regards the photoelectric effect as due to a quantum handing over its energy to an electron. Hughes found the velocity of emission to vary from metal to metal. (See footnote, p. 151.)

ultra-violet light the range of speeds is from about 10^7 to 10^8 cms. per sec. ; with X rays, 10^9 to 10^{10} ; with γ rays, 10^{10} to $2\cdot99 \times 10^{10}$.]

(3) The ejected electrons tend to continue in the line of flight of the original rays (p. 146).

(4) There is a pronounced emission of electrons for certain wave-lengths of the rays (pp. 124 and 149).

These results are common to all three rays.

There are further points of resemblance. As was noticed on p. 113, if an element is exposed to X rays, then, in general, two different classes of X rays are given out by the substance. Of these, one is identical in nature with the incident rays, and may be regarded as so much scattered radiation ; the other is a radiation characteristic of the element, and does not depend at all on the nature of the exciting rays, provided only that they are harder than the characteristic radiation. This latter feature at once recalls Stokes' law of fluorescence. Apart from some exceptions, Stokes' law— that the frequency of the exciting light is always greater than that of the fluorescent light—holds generally for light rays. The analogy with X rays is complete.

An even more striking similarity is presented if the distribution of the two secondary X radiations is compared with the distribution of light in kindred circumstances. When light is allowed to fall on minute particles in suspension, as in a fog, it is found that the scattered light is not uniformly distributed, but varies in amount in different directions. The scattered light emitted parallel to the original beam is double that at right angles ; the intermediate intensities are proportional to $(1+\cos^2\theta)$, where θ is the angle measured from the original beam. But if the particles emit fluorescent light as well as scattered, the fluorescent light is equally intense in all directions.

In just the same way, it is found (p. 115) that the intensity of the scattered X rays obeys, at any rate approximately, a $(1+\cos^2\theta)$ law over a considerable angular range ; and that the " fore and aft " intensity is very roughly twice that at right angles. And, to complete the parallel, the characteristic X radiations show a uniform distribution just as fluorescent light does.

Other points of resemblance between X rays and light rays have been noticed from time to time in the preceding pages. One point of difference is provided by the phenomena of absorption. In the case of light, it is known that many of the dark lines in the absorption spectrum of a body are in the same position as the bright lines in its emission spectrum : in other words, a body, under suitable conditions, is capable of absorbing strongly its characteristic light radiations. But, with X rays, on the contrary, we find that an element is especially transparent to its characteristic X radiations (see p. 137), and it is only for slightly harder rays than these that the absorption becomes abnormally large.

We may now consider the case for the restricted entity hypothesis. It will be convenient first of all to recall the main features of Stokes' famous theory of the X rays.

The Ether-Pulse Theory of Stokes.

Sir George Stokes promulgated the pulse theory of the X rays in the Wilde Lecture before the Manchester Literary and Philosophical Society, on July 2, 1897. He considered that " when the charged molecules [1] from the cathode strike the target, it is exceedingly probable that by virtue of their charge they produce some sort of disturbance in the ether. This non-periodic disturbance or ' pulse ' would spread in all directions, so that, on this view, the Röntgen emanation consists of a vast and irregular succession of isolated and independent pulses starting from the points and at the times at which the individual charged molecules impinge on the target. We know of no reason beforehand forbidding us to attribute an excessive thinness to the pulses " ; and to the narrowness of these pulses Stokes attributed some of the differences between ordinary light and X rays, which,

[1] This was in the days when the cathode rays were thought to be molecules.

apart from this, resemble each other closely [1] : both consist of electric and magnetic forces at right angles to each other and to the direction of propagation, but in the X rays there is not that regular periodic character occurring in trains of waves of uniform wave-length.

Thus a Röntgen pulse on Stokes' theory is somewhat analogous to the crack of a whip when it is suddenly stopped, or the flash of flame when a projectile strikes a target. Briefly, the theory claims that the energy of an X ray is contained within a thin spherical shell which travels outwards with the speed of light in all directions, from the place where the speed of a cathode ray is suddenly changed. The faster the cathode ray and the more abrupt the change in its speed, the thinner and more energetic the pulse. By the laws of electrodynamics, such pulses of intense electric and magnetic forces are inevitable when rapidly moving electrified particles are suddenly stopped or started.

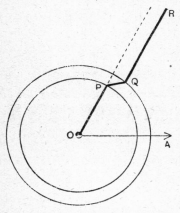

FIG. 125.—Representation of spreading pulse, showing kink in line of force *OPQR* attached to the charged particle *O*, the velocity of which has been suddenly altered.

The Polarisation of X Rays.

The polarisation of X rays (p. 115) follows as an immediate deduction from the pulse theory. The theory contemplates secondary radiation as owing its origin to the disturbances produced in the corpuscles when the primary X rays pass over them. While the X rays are thus accelerating the corpuscles, each gives out a pulse of electric and magnetic

---

[1] It should here be mentioned that, as a result of the work of Rayleigh, Schuster, and others, our notions of the nature of white light have been modified in recent years, and it is now generally accepted that white light (like " independent " X rays) consists of irregular pulses which are capable of being transformed into trains of sine-waves by the various diffracting or refracting instruments.

force—the secondary Röntgen pulse. A single primary pulse may produce a great number of secondary pulses with properties which depend on the grouping, etc., of the corpuscles. Thus, on this point of view, there is, to use Sir J. J. Thomson's apt comparison, much the same difference between the primary and secondary rays as there is between the sharp crack of lightning and the reverberations of thunder.

The argument in the polarisation experiments is that since in an X-ray tube the cathode rays are all travelling in the same direction, then in the resulting pulses the electric forces (which are at right angles to the direction of motion of the cathode rays) will lie in planes passing through that direction, and not at right angles to it (see Fig. 58). In other words, the particular pencil of X rays which is employed will be concentrated in the plane which contains both X rays and cathode rays.

Hence the motion of the excited corpuscles in the radiator will also be mainly in this plane, and so the intensity of the secondary radiation will be a minimum in this plane, and a maximum at right angles to it, a result which agrees with that actually found. The fact that the X rays are only partially polarised, may be ascribed to the fact that the cathode rays in the X-ray tube are not stopped in a single collision, but describe many directions before finally coming to rest.

Modification of Spreading-pulse Theory necessary.

But as has already been remarked above the theory of the spreading pulse needs extensive modification. It will be profitable to review the trend of the results (to some of which we have already referred), that have led to the theory in its modified form. Categorically these are :

(1) When X rays encounter a gas, only an exceedingly small fraction—less than one in a billion—of its molecules become ionised [1] (p. 152).

---

[1] The same difficulty occurs in understanding why, when ultra-violet light falls on metals which show photoelectric properties, such a very small proportion of the particles are liberated.

(2) The extent of this ionisation is unaffected by temperature (p. 155).

(3) When X rays encounter a metal, the electrons ejected have assorted velocities, the maximum of which

  (a) does not depend on the intensity of the X rays, and so is independent of the distance of the metal from the X-ray bulb (p. 147),

  (b) increases continuously with the hardness of the X rays (p. 147),

  (c) does not depend on the nature of the metal (p. 148); see, however, footnote, p. 151,

  (d) is equal, or nearly so, to the velocity of the cathode rays in the X-ray bulb (p. 149).

(4) These ejected electrons are not evenly distributed, but tend to pursue in the main the original direction of the X rays. The effect is most pronounced with metals of small atomic weight and hard X rays (p. 146).

In considering the first result, we may recall that according to the ether-pulse theory in its original form, all the molecules of a gas are equally exposed to the X rays, and we are led to infer that those few which become ionised must have been in a state very far removed from the average. Their abnormal condition cannot be attributed to an exceptionally high kinetic energy, for the kinetic theory of gases would then require that the ionisation should vary rapidly with the temperature—and we are immediately confronted with result (2).

We might, however, claim that the ionisation is controlled by the internal conditions of the different atoms, rather than by their kinetic energy. The phenomena of radioactivity lead us to believe that atoms possess large stores of internal energy which are not readily unlocked by outside agencies ; and if it should be the case that the possession of an exceptional amount of internal energy means weakened stability, then it might easily happen that only abnormal atoms would be ionised by X rays. Or, again, it might be that an atom is capable of collecting energy from many X rays until it has enough for one electron. On either view, the ejection of electrons from a metal subjected to X rays is interpreted as the outward sign of a sort of radioactive explosion of some of the atoms rendered temporarily unstable. The X ray thus acts merely as a trigger to start the explosion; the electrons come from the atom, and owe their energy to it alone. That their velocity should be independent of the intensity of the X rays follows at once, and is in accord with result (3a).

We have now to explain why the maximum speed of the electrons is dependent on the quality of the X rays (result (4)). Why should the velocity be greater when the X rays are hardened, if their only effect is that of a trigger action? and further, why should the path of an electron be influenced by the direction of the X ray, if the latter merely precipitates the disintegration of the atom? On the explosion theory, neither result could be anticipated; nor should we be unreasonable in expecting that the disintegration of different metals would lead to very different velocities of the ejected electrons. The reverse is the case. We are, in fact, left with no alternative but to suppose that the energy of the electron is derived from that of the X ray.

Now, result (3a) remarks that the energy of the corpuscle is independent of the distance of the X-ray tube. But, for reasons similar to the above, the X ray must derive its energy directly from the parent cathode ray, and, according to the pulse theory, it distributes this energy over an ever-enlarging surface. The argument is fatal to the spreading-pulse theory. The energy of the X ray must, it is evident, be confined within very narrow bounds which do not widen as the X ray travels.[1] Combining this result with (3d) above, we are led to conclude that the X ray is a minute entity whose energy is not frittered away along its track, ıt may be handed over completely or in part to an electron n suitable encounter with an atom. (See footnote, p. 151.)

This is a statement of the case for the entity hypothesis, and the difficulty remains of reconciling it with the ordinary electromagnetic theory of Maxwell. Of the attempts which

[1] Sommerfeld (1911) maintains that the pulse theory is competent to explain part, at any rate, of this localisation of energy.

have been made, we may refer briefly to Sir J. J. Thomson's nucleated pulse theory and Planck's quantum theory.

The Nucleated or Localised Pulse Theory of J. J. Thomson.

Sir J. J. Thomson's theory of the X ray assumes a fibrous structure in the ether, and pictures a corpuscle as the seat of a tube of force which stretches out into space. When a cathode ray has its velocity altered, the radiated energy runs along this tube, as a kink runs along a stretched wire. The energy is confined to the region of the kink, and it is not given up until it strikes an electron, to which it can then transfer its energy without waste. The nucleated pulse is equivalent to Stokes' pulse, with the exception that instead of spreading out uniformly in all directions, it is confined to one direction only.

Professor Thomson further believes that the energy of light is distributed in analogous fashion ; that individual light waves are not continuous, but correspond to a collection of wires along which the various disturbances travel ; and that if a wave-front could be made visible we should get, not continuous illumination, but a series of bright specks on a dark ground. The energy is not, therefore, uniformly distributed throughout the whole volume of the waves, but is concentrated in " bundles."

The rays diminish in intensity with increasing distance owing to the greater separation of the " batches," and not to the enfeeblement of individual units. The distribution of energy thus resembles that contemplated by the Newtonian emission theory of light, according to which the energy was located on moving particles sparsely disseminated throughout space.

In the case of X rays the phenomena are sharply defined, but with light rays they are much more involved. The discontinuous wave-front theory, in fact, regards X and γ rays as light in its ultimate simplicity. This agrees with experiment : the general laws covering the behaviour of X rays are obeyed with fewer exceptions than is the case with light.

Planck's Quantum Hypothesis.

The quantum theory, which has been applied to many branches of physics, originated in an attempt to account for the spectrum of black-body radiation. The development of the theory and the evidence for its physical basis are excellently set out by Jeans in a *Report on Radiation and the Quantum Theory* (Physical Society, London).

Briefly the theory assumes that all matter contains large numbers of vibrators which can emit ether waves of different frequencies, but only spasmodically and in such a way that the quantity of energy emitted is an exact multiple of a certain unit or " quantum " (ϵ). The amount of this quantum of energy increases with the frequency of vibration (ν), or the energy, $\epsilon = h\nu$, where h ($= 6 \cdot 5 \times 10^{-27}$ erg. sec.) is a constant of nature, now known as Planck's constant.

On Planck's theory the energy of an X ray is proportional to its frequency ; and the generation of secondary corpuscular rays and photoelectrons is due to a quantum giving up some or all of its energy to an electron. In the same way the maximum frequency ν of the independent radiation generated in an X-ray bulb can be calculated from the relation $Ve = h\nu$, where V is the voltage and e is the electronic charge. (See p. 130.) This important result has been verified experimentally by Duane and Hunt (*P.R.* 1915) and later Hull and Rice (*P.R.* 1916), for voltages as high as 150,000. In the case of the characteristic radiations, the various lines of a series appear simultaneously at a critical voltage corresponding closely to the line with the shortest wave-length. (See Webster, *P.R.* 1916.)

Thus the quantum theory contemplates a certain discreteness or atomicity of an entity which is measured by h or some function of h. It may be noted that the physical dimensions of h are those of angular momentum, an identity which is of great importance in Rutherford's theory of the nucleated atom as developed by Bohr.

It is probable that the atomicity of h is associated with the atomicity of the electronic charge, e, and in such event, a physical explanation of the quantum theory may be based on the atomicity and possible discrete existence of Sir J. J. Thomson's tubes of force or corpuscles of radiation referred to above. Arising out of this is the degree of substantiality of the ether, whether, as some of the modern school of British physicists contend, the ether is the primary real substance of the universe, or whether as the extreme relativity school hold, the ether has no reality at all.

Whatever rôle is assigned, however, to the ether, the main difficulty about the quantum theory is, as already mentioned, that of reconciling it with the well-established results of the undulatory theory of light.

"Fluctuation" Experiments with γ Rays.

Experimenters have naturally sought to establish by direct means the presumed discrete nature of light rays and X rays.

As is well known, the spinthariscope of Sir Wm. Crookes exhibits for the α rays of radium fluctuations both in time and space. Similarly, the effects predicable for β rays have been observed ; and since 1910 a number of workers, among them von Schweidler (1910), E. Meyer (1910), Laby and Burbidge (1912), and Burbidge (1913), have endeavoured to detect corresponding fluctuations in the ionisation produced by γ rays in a gas. For this kind of work, a steady source of rays is absolutely essential, and so γ rays have been worked at rather than X rays.

Laby and Burbidge (*P.R.S.* 1912) used two ionisation chambers, identical in all respects, and disposed them symmetrically about and equidistant from the radium emitting the γ rays. If the γ radiation has a spherical wave surface, then the ionisations in the two chambers will have a constant ratio. If, on the other hand, the γ rays are circumscribed entities, emitted in random directions, as α rays are, then the number entering each chamber in a given time will fluctuate. There is one outstanding difficulty : if Prof. Bragg's view as to the indirect process of ionisation by γ rays is correct (p. 153), the fluctuations might be produced by a variation in the number of β rays generated by each γ ray. The fluctuations which Laby and Burbidge actually observed in their experiments cannot, therefore, be interpreted with certainty.

Subsequently E. Meyer (*A.d.P.* March 1912), using somewhat similar apparatus, finally concluded that a single γ ray can produce ionisation in more than one direction and on more than one occasion : the numbers of γ rays emitted by the same source in two different directions do not appear to be independent. Meyer's experimental arrangements have been criticised by Burbidge (*P.R.S.* 1913). Meyer's results are, however, in accord with those of Rutherford (*P.M.* Oct. 1912), who has recently found reasons for supposing that a swift β ray may give rise to several γ rays in escaping from an atom, and still retain part of its original energy. We may here refer to the work of J. J. Thomson (*P.P.S.* Dec. 1914) and Chadwick (*P.M.* 1912), who have shown that positive and α rays are able to excite X and γ rays when they fall on matter. This would suggest that it is kinetic energy rather than velocity which is the determining factor.

"Fluctuation" Experiments with Light Rays.

N. R. Campbell (*P.C.P.S.* 1909, 1910) attacked the problem of light emission by the "fluctuation" method, with the object of discriminating between the ordinary and entity light hypotheses. Unfortunately the difficulty of finding a source of light which is very intense and also extremely constant proved insurmountable.

Taylor (*P.C.P.S.* 1909) approached the problem from a different standpoint. All ordinary optical phenomena are average effects, and are therefore incapable of differentiating between the usual electromagnetic theory of light and a restricted entity type. If, however, the intensity of light in a diffraction pattern were so greatly reduced that only a few of the indivisible bundles of energy could occur at once on a zone, the ordinary phenomena of diffraction would be modified or disappear altogether. Taylor's method of attack was to photograph the shadow of a needle under various illuminations, and with exposures chosen such that the total energy supplied was constant. Exposures ranging from a few seconds to three months were employed, but no variation in the sharpness of the diffraction pattern could be detected in the different photographs.

Thus the more direct attempts to confirm the "discontinuous" nature of light and of X rays have not met with success.

The Outstanding Problem of Radiation.

It will be apparent that the problem of the nature of the X ray cannot yet be dismissed. We have succeeded in establishing the essential identity of X rays and light rays, and the interest has, accordingly, shifted its ground. The difficulties, conspicuous with the X rays, have merged into those which all classes of electromagnetic waves are found to present in greater or less degree, and the full secret of the nature of X rays will doubtless be revealed when we find the key to the overshadowing problem of the mechanism of radiation in general. We have seen that the problem of the transference of energy by ether-waves involves us in the conception of a "quantum" of energy-radiation travelling undissipated through space. The reconciliation of the idea with the older and well-founded conception of spreading waves remains. The experimental evidence seems to indicate that both theories are true simultaneously : that radiant energy is both concentrated and indivisible, and at the same time spreads and is divisible. The keynote of the old mechanics is, in fact, continuity ; of the new mechanics, discontinuity. Any hope of a compromise between the two theories appears to involve concessions fatal to either. We are left confronted with the riddle of modern physics.

APPENDIX I.

IN connection with Röntgen's discovery, Sir James Mackenzie Davidson has been kind enough to write down for me his recollections of an interview with Prof. Röntgen not very long after the discovery of the X rays.

"While travelling on the Continent in 1896 I made a pilgrimage to Würzburg, and called at Professor Röntgen's house in the evening, and was kindly granted an appointment for the following morning. I presented myself about 11 a.m., and was shown into a laboratory which contained a coil and a small cylindrical-shaped X-ray tube. Professor Röntgen, a tall man with dark bushy hair, a long beard, and very kindly and expressive eyes, received me cordially. He could not speak much English ; I was still worse at German. However, by means of English and some Latin we made ourselves intelligible to one another. He excited the tube and showed me various shadows on a fluorescent screen. On each of the terminals of his coil he had a small aluminium ball, 1 cm. in diameter, which he told me he used as an alternative spark-gap to test the hardness of the tube. He incidentally remarked that he found a tube had its maximum photographic effect when it was working just at 2·5 cms. alternative spark—a fact which I have always found to be correct. I asked some blunt questions as follows :

Q. " ' What were you doing with the Hittorf tube when you made the discovery of the X rays ? '

A. " ' I was looking for invisible rays.'

Q. " ' What made you use a barium platino-cyanide screen ? '

A. " ' In Germany we use it to reveal the invisible rays of the spectrum, and I thought it a suitable substance to use to detect any invisible rays a tube might give off.'

" He then detailed how he made the discovery. He said he had covered up the Hittorf tube with black paper so as to exclude all light, and had the screen (which was simply a piece of cardboard with some crystals of barium platino-cyanide deposited on it) lying on a table 3 or 4 metres from where the covered tube was situated, ready to be used. He excited the tube to ascertain if all light was excluded. This was so, but to his intense surprise he found the distant screen shining brightly !

" I asked him, ' What did you think ? ' He said very simply, ' I did not think, I investigated.'

" Incidentally, he told me how he had taken a photograph through a pine door which separated two of his labora-tories. On developing the negative, he found a white band across it, which, he ascertained, corresponded to the beading on one of the door panels. He stripped the beading off, and found the band of shadow was due not to the increased thickness of wood but to the ' plumbum ' (white lead really) the doormaker had employed in attaching the strip of wood.

" He seemed amused at my remonstrating with him about keeping *the* ' screen ' lying about in his laboratory. I told him it was a ' historical screen,' and should be pre-served in a glass case ! I hope he has carried out this suggestion. For the sudden shining of that ' screen ' un-doubtedly led to one of the greatest discoveries in modern times."

J. M. D.

APPENDIX II.

THE PRODUCTION OF HIGH VACUA.

A BRIEF notice may be taken of the present methods of exhausting vacuum tubes. The very highest vacua can be got by making use of the extraordinary absorptive powers for gases of charcoal (*e.g.* cocoanut charcoal) when immersed in liquid air—a remarkably quick and effective method we owe to Prof. Dewar. Oxygen, nitrogen, water vapour, etc., are absorbed to large extents, hydrogen rather less so, helium and neon least of all. It is essential that the charcoal should be previously heated *in situ* [1] and the emitted gas pumped off before applying the liquid air. Angerer (*A.d.P.* 1911) records a pressure of 8×10^{-7} mm. Hg by the use of charcoal and liquid air.

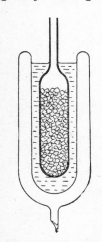

FIG. 126.—Tube containing charcoal immersed in liquid air.

The great majority of the various mechanical pumps for the production of vacua employ the plan of repeatedly abstracting and isolating, by means of a solid or liquid "piston," a certain fraction of gas from the vessel to be exhausted, and delivering it elsewhere. An exception is a strikingly ingenious "molecular pump" first introduced by Gaede.[2]

---

[1] As a practical precaution, a plug of glass-wool should be inserted above the charcoal, to stop the small carbon particles, which are expelled when the charcoal is heated, from passing over into the apparatus.

[2] See *Engineering*, Sept. 20, 1913.

It depends for its success on the viscous dragging of gas by the surface of a cylinder rotating within a second cylinder at a speed comparable with the velocities of the molecules of the gas, which are accordingly impoverished in one direction and accumulated in the other. The pump is extremely rapid in action, but requires the initial pressure to be reduced to a few mms. of mercury by an auxiliary pump. There is no piston, but always free communication, through the molecular pump, between the vessel to be exhausted and the auxiliary pump. With a speed of rotation of 12,000 revs. per min., and an initial vacuum of $\frac{1}{20}$ mm., Gaede records the remarkably low pressure of 2×10^{-7} mm. It is very interesting to note the susceptibility of the pump to the molecular velocity of the gas present. For the same velocity of the cylinder, a lower pressure is attainable with air (molecular velocity 500 metres/sec.) than with hydrogen (molecular velocity 1800 metres/sec.), as may be shown by scavenging the vacuum with one or the other gas. The pump shares with the cooled-charcoal method the advantage of not requiring any drying agent—vapours are sucked away as readily as gases. For such a rapid type of pump the connecting tube must not be restricted in bore ; the remark, indeed, applies to all low pressure pumps. Half-inch diameter tubing should be regarded as a minimum size.

In 1914 Gaede put on the market a hand-driven piston pump, which can produce very high vacua with great rapidity.

Next come the various types of mercury pumps—the Töpler and Sprengel in a variety of modifications, some of them designed to be automatic in action. The rotary mercury pumps, such as the Gaede, have come into extensive use, and possess the great advantage that they can be motor-driven—a feature commending itself to all who have worked with the hand-manipulated Töpler. In regard to mercury (and oil) pumps it is well to remember that they will not pump vapours,[1] and that the vapour pressure of mercury

---

[1] To obtain high vacua it is, therefore, necessary to remove water vapour by means of a drying agent such as phosphorus pentoxide. Other vapours can be frozen out by means of liquid air.

at ordinary temperatures is about $\frac{1}{1000}$ mm. mercury—a fact which does not always tally with the claims advanced.[1]

The most recent development is the mercury vapour (condensation) pump, which is remarkable for its simplicity of design and the rapidity and efficiency of its performance no matter what the gas. A liquid-air trap is necessary.

For the earlier stages of exhausting there is available a variety of oil-pumps which can be motor-driven, and some of which can deal with large quantities of gas. Ordinary heavy engine-oil works well in these pumps and has a low vapour pressure. A drying chamber should be used in conjunction with an oil-pump, or the oil may emulsify and the efficiency of the pump will suffer.

Gas held by Walls of Tube.

A great deal of gas—mostly hydrogen and moisture—is held by the electrodes and the walls of a vacuum tube. To liberate the gas, the discharge should be run for some time to suit the conditions under which the tube is intended to be used.[2] This, of course, ought to be done by the maker before the tube is sealed off from the pump. The walls of the tube hold this surface gas tenaciously—it appears to be largely moisture which is held bound as a condensed surface layer. To get rid of it, the tube has to be heated to between 300° and 400° C., at which stage there is a great evolution of gas. If this is pumped off while the tube is hot, the vacuum will be found to improve greatly when the tube is cooled, and will deteriorate less rapidly with time.

"Finishing-off" Processes.

There are one or two "finishing-off" processes to follow a pump, which are well known to research workers. Cocoanut charcoal, when used as anode, or the liquid alloy of potassium and sodium, when used as cathode, absorb

---

[1] It is, however, possible for a pump to exhaust somewhat lower than the vapour pressure of the liquid used. A really good water injector (filter) pump will exhaust to about 7 mms. of mercury, whereas the vapour pressure of water at atmospheric temperatures is some 12 to 15 mms.

[2] At higher pressures, more current can be passed through the tube, and the electrodes can be made hotter than at very low pressures.

ordinary gases, if the discharge is not too heavy. Yellow phosphorus is converted to red by bombardment with cathode rays ; the change is accompanied by a diminution in pressure, due partly to the lower vapour pressure of the red allotrope, and partly to the fact that under the discharge the red phosphorus combines with any oxygen, nitrogen or hydrogen present, forming compounds with very small vapour pressures. This latter method is used in exhausting the Lodge vacuum valve (p. 71) : the presence of the phosphorus compounds is further useful in regulating the vacuum during the subsequent use of the valve. Merton (*Chem. Soc. Journ.* 1914) finds that " precipitated copper " heated *in situ* to about 250° C. absorbs gases and vapours with great readiness on cooling.

In the earlier stages of exhausting a bulb, much time can generally be saved by omitting the usual constriction (for sealing-off purposes) in the connecting tube to the pump. When the exhaustion has reached a satisfactory stage, carefully dried air is admitted, the constriction put in and the re-exhaustion proceeded with.

Table XXIII. gives a notion of the capabilities of various pumps.

TABLE XXIII.

Pump.	Attainable Vacuum.
	mm. Hg.
Mercury vapour (condensation) -	0·000,000,01
Charcoal and liquid air - -	0·000,000,01
Gaede molecular - - - -	0·000,000,2
Gaede rotary (mercury) -	0·000,01
Improved Töpler (mercury) -	0·000,01
Gaede piston - - - -	0·000,05
Geryk (oil) - - - - -	0·000,2
Sprengel (mercury) - - -	0·001
Injector (water) - - - -	7

APPENDIX III.

ELECTRICAL INSULATORS.

Of the available insulators, ebonite, sulphur, amber, sealing wax and fused silica are at present the only ones at all suitable for electroscopic work. With all of these, care should be taken to avoid fingering—grease is fatal to insulation. In testing insulation, it should be remembered that a delicate electroscope may indicate signs of surface electrification for some hours after new insulation has been put in. Such electrification may be dissipated by means of a spirit lamp, or, better, by placing some uranium oxide near the insulator. To reduce the absorption of the electric charge which occurs to a greater or less extent with all insulators,[1] the size of insulating supports should be kept as small as possible in electrometer work.

Ebonite that is really good is difficult to obtain nowadays ; it seems to be regarded by most rubber manufacturers as a convenient means of using up rubber refuse unfit for anything else. Some of its defects are occasionally due to the materials used in polishing. Modern ebonite ages with some rapidity in sunlight, and on damp days may, owing to the film of sulphuric acid which forms on its surface, almost play the rôle of a conductor. In a room which gets much sunshine most modern ebonite usually turns a dirty yellow colour in a few weeks, though some of the ebonite made ten or twenty years ago will exhibit no signs of deterioration. Notwithstanding its defects, ebonite which has had its

---

[1] Paraffin wax, which is an excellent insulator, shows this soaking effect to a marked and objectionable degree.

surface recently renewed is an excellent insulator. Ebonite offers the great advantage of being easily workable.

Sulphur is convenient, in that it can be cast to shape. In this operation the vessels (glass or porcelain) and sulphur used should be clean, and the temperature should be raised but slightly above the liquefying point of the sulphur. In this limpid condition it can, for example, be poured or sucked into clean warmed glass [1] tubing, if sulphur plugs are required. The tubing can be readily slipped off later by slightly warming the outside. For some hours after solidification, sulphur can be turned to size or pared to shape with great ease. The insulating properties improve for some time after setting. There is no better insulator than sulphur, but, after a few months, especially in a room which gets much sunshine, its insulating qualities generally fall off to a considerable extent.

Amber is an excellent insulator, and is almost always reliable. It can, of course, be obtained in the form of pipe stems, which can be mounted in position with sealing wax. The Amberite and Ambroid companies supply amber pressed to convenient shapes and sizes. Amber has the disadvantages of being somewhat brittle and rather expensive.

Sealing Wax is particularly useful in that it combines the qualities of an insulator and an air-tight cement with a very low vapour pressure. The insulating properties depend very much on the quality of the wax. One of the most reliable is "Bank of England." The usual care must be taken to avoid indiscriminate fingering. The insulating ability of the wax will be impaired, if in its manipulation it is allowed to catch fire and carbonise, or if a luminous flame is used. As shellac is hygroscopic, sealing wax as an insulator is somewhat susceptible to damp weather.

Fused Silica yields place to none in its insulating qualities. Its specific resistance has been determined at the National Physical Laboratory to be greater than 2×10^{14} ohm cms. at 16° C. Fused silica is practically independent of atmospheric humidity, and in the form of rod or tubing is particularly convenient as an insulating material. It is the only

---

[1] Not metal, unless lined, say, with paper.

high-class insulator which is unimpaired by moderate heat; it is, however, spoilt if subjected to very high temperatures. Fused silica is now very cheap, but unfortunately the modern furnace methods of production cannot be relied upon to yield a product which possesses the insulating properties of the more expensive silica made by the oxyhydrogen flame. This remark applies alike to the clear transparent variety and the air-streaked satin-like kind. The furnace silica seems to be contaminated in some way, possibly by carbon from the electric furnace. Silica intended for insulation purposes should, of course, be alkali-free.

APPENDIX IV.

TABLE XXIV. THE ELEMENTS IN THE ORDER OF ATOMIC NUMBERS.

International atomic weights for 1922 ; O = 16. The international atomic weights are fixed yearly by an international committee of chemists, consisting at present of Profs. F. W. Clarke (U.S.A.), T. E. Thorpe (Gt. Britain), and G. Urbain (France). The list below comprises 87 elements. For atomic numbers see p. 242.

Atomic Number.	Atomic Weight. O = 16.	Element.	Symbol.	First isolated by	
1	1·008	Hydrogen -	H	Cavendish	1766
2	4·00	Helium - -	He	Ramsay and Cleve [1]	1895
3	6·94	Lithium - -	Li	Arfvedson	1817
4	9·1	Beryllium (Glucinum) -	Be	Wöhler and Bussy	1828
5	10·9	Boron - -	B	Gay-Lussac & Thénard	1808
6	12·005	Carbon - -	C	— Prehistoric	
7	14·08	Nitrogen -	N	Rutherford	1772
8	16·00	Oxygen - -	O	Priestley and Scheele	1774
9	19·0	Fluorine -	F	Moissan	1886
10	20·2	Neon - -	Ne	Ramsay and Travers	1898
11	23·00	Sodium - -	Na	Davy	1807
12	24·32	Magnesium -	Mg	Liebig and Bussy	1830
13	27·1	Aluminium -	Al	Wöhler	1827
14	28·3	Silicon -	Si	Berzelius	1823
15	31·04	Phosphorus -	P	Brand	1674
16	32·06	Sulphur - -	S	— Prehistoric	
17	35·46	Chlorine -	Cl	Scheele	1774
18	39·9	Argon - -	A	Rayleigh and Ramsay	1894
19	39·10	Potassium -	K	Davy	1807
20	40·07	Calcium -	Ca	Davy	1808
21	45·1	Scandium -	Sc	Nilson and Cleve	1879
22	48·1	Titanium . -	Ti	Gregor	1789
23	51·0	Vanadium -	V	Berzelius	1831
24	52·0	Chromium -	Cr	Vauquelin	1797
25	54·93	Manganese -	Mn	Gahn	1774
26	55·84	Iron - -	Fe	— Prehistoric	
27	58·97	Cobalt - -	Co	Brand	1735
28	58·68	Nickel - -	Ni	Cronstedt	1751
29	63·57	Copper - -	Cu	— Prehistoric	
30	65·37	Zinc - -	Zn	Mtd. by B. Valentine 15 centy.	
31	70·1	Gallium -	Ga	L. de Boisbaudran	1875
32	72·5	Germanium -	Ge	Winkler	1886
33	74·96	Arsenic - -	As	Albertus Magnus 13 centy.	
34	79·2	Selenium -	Se	Berzelius	1817
35	79·92	Bromine -	Br	Balard	1826
36	82·92	Krypton -	Kr	Ramsay and Travers	1898
37	85·45	Rubidium -	Rb	Bunsen and Kirchhoff	1861

[1] Janssen and Lockyer (in sun), 1868.

The Elements in the Order of Atomic Numbers—*Continued*

Atomic Number.	Atomic Weight. O=16.	Element.	Symbol.	First isolated by	
38	87·63	Strontium -	Sr	Davy	1808
39	89·33	Yttrium -	Y	Wöhler	1828
40	90·6	Zirconium -	Zr	Berzelius	1825
41	93·1	Niobium (Columbium)	Nb	Hatchett	1801
42	96·0	Molybdenum -	Mo	Hjelm	1790
44	101·7	Ruthenium -	Ru	Claus	1845
45	102·9	Rhodium -	Rh	Wollaston	1803
46	106·7	Palladium -	Pd	Wollaston	1803
47	107·88	Silver - -	Ag	—	Prehistoric
48	112·40	Cadmium -	Cd	Stromeyer	1817
49	114·8	Indium - -	In	Reich and Richter	1863
50	118·7	Tin - -	Sn	—	Prehistoric
51	120·2	Antimony -	Sb	Basil Valentine	15 centy.
52	127·5	Tellurium -	Te	v. Reichenstein	1782
53	126·92	Iodine - -	I	Courtois	1811
54	130·2	Xenon - -	Xe	Ramsay and Travers	1898
55	132·81	Cæsium - -	Cs	Bunsen and Kirchhoff	1861
56	137·37	Barium - -	Ba	Davy	1808
57	139·0	Lanthanum -	La	Mosander	1839
58	140·25	Cerium - -	Ce	Mosander	1839
59	140·9	Praseodymium	Pr	Auer von Welsbach	1885
60	144·3	Neodymium -	Nd	Auer von Welsbach	1885
62	150·4	Samarium -	Sa	L. de Boisbaudran	1879
63	152·0	Europium -	Eu	Demarçay	1901
64	157·3	Gadolinium -	Gd	Marignac	1886
65	159·2	Terbium -	Tb	Mosander	1843
66	162·5	Dysprosium -	Dy	Urbain & Demenitroux	1907
67	163·5	Holmium -	Ho	L. de Boisbaudran	1886
68	167·7	Erbium -	Er	Mosander	1843
69	168·5	Thulium -	Tm	Cleve	1879
70	173·5	Ytterbium (Neo, Yb) -	Yb	Marignac	1878
71	175·0	Lutecium -	Lu	Urbain	1908
72	—	Celtium - -	Ct	Urbain	1908
73	181·5	Tantalum -	Ta	Eckeberg	1802
74	184·0	Tungsten -	W	Bros. d'Elhujar	1783
76	190·9	Osmium - -	Os	Smithson Tennant	1804
77	193·1	Iridium - -	Ir	Smithson Tennant	1804
78	195·2	Platinum -	Pt	—	16 centy.
79	197·2	Gold - -	Au	—	Prehistoric
80	200·6	Mercury - -	Hg	Mtd. by Theophrastus 300 B.C.	
81	204·0	Thallium - -	Tl	Crookes	1861
82	207·20	Lead - -	Pb	Mentd. by Pliny Prehistoric	
83	2080	Bismuth - -	Bi	Mtd. by B. Valentine 15 centy.	
84	—	Polonium -	Po	M. and Mme. Curie	1898
86	222	Radium Emanation (Niton)	Nt	M. and Mme. Curie	1900
88	226·0	Radium -	Ra	Curies and Bemont	1898
89	230 (?)	Actinium -	Ac	Debierne	1898
90	232·15	Thorium -	Th	Berzelius	1828
91	—	Uranium *Y* -	U *Y*	Antonoff	1911
92	238·2	Uranium -	U	Peligot	1841

ATOMIC NUMBERS AND WEIGHTS OF THE RADIOACTIVE ELEMENTS.

Element.	At. No.	At. Wt.	Element.	At. Wt.
Uranium 1 - -	92	238·2	Thorium - 90	232·4
,, 2 - -	92	234·2	Meso-thorium -	228·4
,, X, Y - -	90, 91	230·2	Radio-thorium -	228·4
Ionium - - -	90	230·2	Thorium X - -	224·4
Radium - - -	88	226·0	,, Emanation	220·4
Ra Emanation - -	86	222	,, A - -	216·4
Radium A - -	84	218	,, B, C₁, C₂ 82	212·4
,, B, C₁ - -	82, 83	214	,, D ² - -	208·4
,, C₂, D, E - -	82, 83	210		
,, F (Polonium) ¹	84	210	¹ Probably converted into Pb.	
			² ,, ,, ,, Bi.	

The atomic weight of actinium is probably about 230.

TABLE XXV.—ATOMIC WEIGHTS AND DENSITIES OF THE ELEMENTS.

Element.	Atomic Weight.	Density.	Element.	Atomic Weight.	Density.	Element.	Atomic Weight.	Density.
Al	27	2·70	He	4	0·178 ‡	Rb	85	1·532
Sb	120	6·62	H	1	0·08987‡	Ru	102	12·3
A	40	1·78 ‡	In	115	7·12	Sa	150	7·8
As	75	5·73	I	127	4·95	Sc	44	—
Ba	137	3·75	Ir	193	22·41	Se	79	4·5
Be	9	1·93	Fe	56	7·86	Si	28	2·3
Bi	208	9·80	Kr	83	3·708 ‡	Ag	108	10·5
B	11	2·5 ?	La	139	6·12	Na	23	0·971
Br	80	3·10	Pb	207	11·37	Sr	88	2·54
Cd	112	8·64	Li	7	0·534	S	32	2·07
Cs	133	1·87	Lu	175	—	Ta	181	16·6
Ca	40	1·55	Mg	24	1·74	Te	127	6·25
C			Mn	55	7·39	Tb	159	—
Diamond	⎫	3·52	Hg	201	13·56	Tl	204	11·9
Graphite	⎬ 12	2·3	Mo	96	10·0	Th	232	11·3
Gas carbon	⎭	1·9	Nd	144	6·96	Tm	168	—
Ce	140	6·92	Ne	20	0·9002 ‡	Sn	119	7·29
Cl	35	3·23 ‡	Ni	59	8·9	Ti	48	4·50
Cr	52	6·50	Nb	93	12·75	W	184	18·8
Co	59	8·6	N	14	1·2507 ‡	U	238	18·7
Cu	64	8·93	Os	191	22·5	V	51	5·5
Dy	162	—	O	16	1·429 ‡	Xe	130	5·851 ‡
Er	168	4·77 ?	Pd	107	11·4	Yb	174	—
Eu	152	—	P	31	2·2	Y	89	3·8 ?
F	19	1·69 ‡	Pt	195	21·5	Zn	65	7·1
Gd	157	—	K	39	0·862	Zr	91	4·15
Ga	70	5·95	Pr	141	6·48			
Ge	72	5·47	Ra	226	?	Paper	—	1·0
Au	197	19·32	Rh	103	12·44			

‡ Grms. per litre at 0° C. and 760 mm.

TABLE XXVI. $I = I_0 e^{-\mu d}$.   TABLE CONNECTING I/I_0 AND μd.

E.g. if $\mu d = \cdot 693$, $I/I_0 = \cdot 5$. $e = 2 \cdot 71828$.   (See p. 105.)

(From Kaye & Laby's *Physical Constants*.)

For values of μd from ·0000 to ·0999. — Subtract Differences.

λd	0	·001	·002	·003	·004	·005	·006	·007	·008	·009	·0001	2	3	4	5	6	7	8	9
·00	1·000	·9990	·9980	·9970	·9960	·9950	·9940	·9930	·9920	·9910	1	2	3	4	5	6	7	8	9
·01	·9900	·9891	·9881	·9871	·9861	·9851	·9841	·9831	·9822	·9812	1	2	3	4	5	6	7	8	9
·02	·9802	·9792	·9782	·9773	·9763	·9753	·9743	·9734	·9724	·9714	1	2	3	4	5	6	7	8	9
·03	·9704	·9695	·9685	·9675	·9666	·9656	·9646	·9637	·9627	·9618	1	2	3	4	5	6	7	8	9
·04	·9608	·9598	·9589	·9579	·9570	·9560	·9550	·9541	·9531	·9522	1	2	3	4	5	6	7	8	9
·05	·9512	·9502	·9493	·9484	·9474	·9465	·9455	·9446	·9436	·9427	1	2	3	4	5	6	7	8	9
·06	·9418	·9408	·9399	·9389	·9380	·9371	·9361	·9352	·9343	·9333	1	2	3	4	5	6	7	8	9
·07	·9324	·9315	·9305	·9296	·9287	·9277	·9268	·9259	·9250	·9240	1	2	3	4	5	6	7	8	8
·08	·9231	·9222	·9213	·9204	·9194	·9185	·9176	·9167	·9158	·9148	1	2	3	4	5	6	7	7	8
·09	·9139	·9130	·9121	·9112	·9103	·9094	·9085	·9076	·9066	·9057	1	2	3	4	5	6	6	7	8

For values of μd from ·100 to 2·999. — Subtract Differences.

λd	0	·01	·02	·03	·04	·05	·06	·07	·08	·09	·001	2	3	4	5	6	7	8	9
·1	·9048	·8958	·8869	·8781	·8694	·8607	·8521	·8437	·8353	·8270	9	17	26	34	43	52	60	69	77
·2	·8187	·8106	·8025	·7945	·7866	·7788	·7711	·7634	·7558	·7483	8	16	23	31	39	47	55	62	70
·3	·7408	·7334	·7261	·7189	·7118	·7047	·6977	·6907	·6839	·6771	7	14	21	28	25	42	49	56	63
·4	·6703	·6637	·6570	·6505	·6440	·6376	·6313	·6250	·6188	·6126	6	13	19	26	32	38	45	51	57
·5	·6065	·6005	·5945	·5886	·5827	·5769	·5712	·5655	·5599	·5543	6	12	17	23	29	35	40	46	52
·6	·5488	·5434	·5379	·5326	·5273	·5220	·5169	·5117	·5066	·5016	5	10	16	21	26	31	37	42	47
·7	·4966	·4916	·4868	·4819	·4771	·4724	·4677	·4630	·4584	·4538	5	9	14	19	24	28	33	38	43
·8	·4493	·4449	·4404	·4360	·4317	·4274	·4232	·4190	·4148	·4107	4	9	13	17	21	26	30	34	38
·9	·4066	·4025	·3985	·3946	·3906	·3867	·3829	·3791	·3753	·3716	4	8	12	15	19	23	27	31	35
1·0	·3679	·3642	·3606	·3570	·3535	·3499	·3465	·3430	·3396	·3362	4	7	11	14	18	21	25	28	32
1·1	·3329	·3296	·3263	·3230	·3198	·3166	·3135	·3104	·3073	·3042	3	6	9	13	16	19	22	25	29
1·2	·3012	·2982	·2952	·2923	·2894	·2865	·2837	·2808	·2780	·2753	3	6	9	11	14	17	20	23	26
1·3	·2725	·2698	·2671	·2645	·2618	·2592	·2567	·2541	·2516	·2491	3	5	8	10	13	16	18	21	23
1·4	·2466	·2441	·2417	·2393	·2369	·2346	·2322	·2299	·2276	·2254	2	5	7	9	12	14	16	19	21
1·5	·2231	·2209	·2187	·2165	·2144	·2122	·2101	·2080	·2060	·2039	2	4	6	8	11	13	15	17	19
1·6	·2019	·1999	·1979	·1959	·1940	·1920	·1901	·1882	·1864	·1845	2	4	6	8	10	12	13	15	17
1·7	·1827	·1809	·1791	·1773	·1755	·1738	·1720	·1703	·1686	·1670	2	3	5	7	9	10	12	14	16
1·8	·1653	·1637	·1620	·1604	·1588	·1572	·1557	·1541	·1526	·1511	2	3	5	6	8	9	11	13	14
1·9	·1496	·1481	·1466	·1451	·1437	·1423	·1409	·1395	·1381	·1367	1	3	4	6	7	9	10	11	13
2·0	·1353	·1340	·1327	·1313	·1300	·1287	·1275	·1262	·1249	·1237	1	3	4	5	6	8	9	10	12
2·1	·1225	·1212	·1200	·1188	·1177	·1165	·1153	·1142	·1130	·1119	1	2	4	5	6	7	8	9	11
2·2	·1108	·1097	·1086	·1075	·1065	·1054	·1044	·1033	·1023	·1013	1	2	3	4	5	6	7	8	9
2·3	·1003	·0993	·0983	·0973	·0963	·0954	·0944	·0935	·0926	·0916	1	2	3	4	5	6	7	8	9
2·4	·0907	·0898	·0889	·0880	·0872	·0863	·0854	·0846	·0837	·0829	1	2	3	3	4	5	6	7	8
2·5	·0821	·0813	·0805	·0797	·0789	·0781	·0773	·0765	·0758	·0750	1	2	2	3	4	5	5	6	7
2·6	·0743	·0735	·0728	·0721	·0714	·0707	·0699	·0693	·0686	·0679	1	1	2	3	4	4	5	6	6
2·7	·0672	·0665	·0659	·0652	·0646	·0639	·0633	·0627	·0620	·0614	1	1	2	3	3	4	4	5	6
2·8	·0608	·0602	·0596	·0590	·0584	·0578	·0573	·0567	·0561	·0556	1	1	2	2	3	3	4	5	5
2·9	·0550	·0545	·0539	·0534	·0529	·0523	·0518	·0513	·0508	·0503	1	1	2	2	3	3	4	4	5

For values of μd from 3·0 to 8·9. — Subtract Differences.

λd	0	·1	·2	·3	·4	·5	·6	·7	·8	·9
3	·0498	·0450	·0408	·0368	·0334	·0302	·0273	·0247	·0224	·0202
4	·0183	·0166	·0150	·0136	·0123	·0111	·0101	·0091	·0082	·0074
5	·0067	·0061	·0055	·0050	·0045	·0041	·0037	·0033	·0030	·0027
6	·0025	·0022	·0020	·0018	·0017	·0015	·0014	·0012	·0011	·0010
7	·0009	·0008	·0007	·0007	·0006	·0006	·0005	·0005	·0004	·0004
8	·0003	·0003	·0003	·0002	·0002	·0002	·0002	·0002	·0002	·0001

Mean differences no longer sufficiently accurate.

TABLE XXVII. CATHODE-RAY VELOCITY AND POTENTIAL.

Cathode-ray velocities in cms./sec., corresponding to various voltages. The values are calculated by the formula, $V = 5 \cdot 95 \sqrt{E} \cdot 10^7$, where V is the velocity and E the voltage (see p. 100).

For voltages from 0 to 990. (values $\times 10^9$)

	0	10	20	30	40	50	60	70	80	90
0	0	0·188	0·266	0·326	0·376	0·421	0·461	0·498	0·533	0·565
100	0·595	0·624	0·652	0·678	0·704	0·729	0·753	0·776	0·798	0·820
200	0·842	0·862	0·883	0·902	0·922	0·941	0·960	0·978	0·996	1·014
300	1·031	1·048	1·065	1·081	1·097	1·113	1·129	1·145	1·160	1·176
400	1·191	1·205	1·220	1·234	1·248	1·263	1·277	1·290	1·304	1·318
500	1·231	1·344	1·357	1·370	1·383	1·396	1·409	1·421	1·434	1·446
600	1·458	1·470	1·482	1·494	1·506	1·517	1·529	1·541	1·552	1·564
700	1·575	1·586	1·597	1·608	1·619	1·630	1·641	1·651	1·662	1·673
800	1·683	1·694	1·705	1·715	1·725	1·735	1·745	1·755	1·766	1·776
900	1·786	1·796	1·806	1·815	1·825	1 834	1·844	1·854	1·864	1·873

For voltages from 1000 to 9900. (values $\times 10^9$)

	0	100	200	300	400	500	600	700	800	900
1000	1·88	1·97	2·06	2·15	2·23	2·31	2·38	2·45	2·52	2·59
2000	2·66	2·73	2·79	2·85	2·92	2·98	3·04	3·09	3·15	3·21
3000	3·26	3·31	3·37	3·42	3·47	3·52	3·57	3·62	3·67	3·72
4000	3·76	3·81	3·86	3·90	3·95	3·99	4·04	4·08	4·12	4·17
5000	4·21	4·25	4·29	4·33	4·37	4·41	4·45	4·49	4·53	4·57
6000	4·61	4·65	4·69	4·72	4·76	4·80	4·84	4·87	4·91	4·94
7000	4·98	5·01	5·05	5·08	5·12	5·15	5·19	5·22	5·26	5·29
8000	5·33	5·36	5·39	5·42	5·45	5·49	5·52	5·55	5·59	5·62
9000	5·65	5·68	5·71	5·74	5·77	5·80	5·83	5·86	5·89	5·92

For voltages from 10,000 to 199,000. (values $\times 10^9$)

	0	1000	2000	3000	4000	5000	6000	7000	8000	9000
10,000	5·95	6·24	6·52	6·78	7·04	7·29	7·53	7·76	7·98	8·20
20,000	8·42	8·62	8·83	9·02	9·22	9·41	9·60	9·78	9·96	10·14
30,000	10·31	10·48	10·65	10·81	10·97	11·13	11·29	11·45	11·60	11·76
40,000	11·91	12·05	12·20	12·34	12·48	12·63	12·77	12·90	13·04	13·18
50,000	13·31	13·44	13·57	13·70	13·83	13·96	14·09	14·21	14·34	14·46
60,000	14·58	14·70	14·82	14·94	15·06	15·17	15·29	15·41	15·52	15·64
70,000	15·75	15·86	15·97	16·08	16·19	16·30	16·41	16·51	16·62	16·73
80,000	16·83	16·94	17·05	17·15	17·25	17·35	17·45	17·55	17·66	17·76
90,000	17·86	17·96	18·06	18·15	18·25	18·34	18·44	18·54	18·64	18·73
100,000	18·8	18·9	19·0	19·1	19·2	19·3	19·4	19·5	19·6	19·7
110,000	19·7	19·8	19·9	20·0	20·1	20·2	20·3	20·4	20·4	20·5
120,000	20·6	20·7	20·8	20·9	20·9	21·0	21·1	21·2	21·3	21·4
130,000	21·5	21·6	21·7	21·7	21·8	21·9	22·0	22·1	22·1	22·2
140,000	22·3	22·4	22·5	22·5	22·6	22·7	22·8	22·8	22·9	23·0
150,000	23·1	23·1	23·2	23·3	23·4	23·4	23·5	23·6	23·7	23·8
160,000	23·8	23·9	24·0	24·1	24·1	24·2	24·3	24·3	24·4	24·5
170,000	24·5	24·6	24·6	24·7	24·8	24·9	24·9	25·0	25·1	25·1
180,000	25·2	25·3	25·4	25·4	25·5	25·6	25·6	25·7	25·8	25·9
190,000	25·9	26·0	26·1	26·1	26·2	26·3	26·3	26·4	26·5	26·5

Table XXVIII. Shortest Wave-Length and Potential.

Wave-lengths and frequencies of the "end radiation" are calculated from Planck's relation (pp. 130, 247).

Kilovolts (Peak).	Shortest Wave-Length in A.U.[1]	Highest Frequency.	
10	1·240	2·42 × 10⁻¹⁸	
20	0·620	4·84	,,
30	0·413	7·26	,,
40	0·310	9·68	,,
50	0·248	12·1	,,
60	0·207	14·5	,,
70	0·177	16·9	,,
80	0·155	19·4	,,
90	0·138	21·8	,,
100	0·124	24·2	,,
110	0·113	26·6	,,
120	0·103	29·0	,,
130	0·095	31·4	,,
140	0·089	33·9	,,
150	0·083	36·3	,,
160	0·078	38·7	,,
170	0·073	41·1	,,
180	0·069	43·6	,,
190	0·065	46·0	,,
200	0·062	48·4	,,
210	0·059	50·8	,,
220	0·056	53·2	,,
230	0·054	55·7	,,
240	0·052	58·1	,,
250	0·050	60·5	,,
300	0·041	72·6	,,

[1] A.U. = Angström Unit = 10^{-8} cm.

Table XXIX.   Characteristic γ Rays.

Rutherford and Richardson, *P.M.* 1913 and 1914 (see p. 123).   The absorption coefficients in aluminium may be contrasted with those for X rays on p. 120.

Element.	Atomic Weight.	Absorption Coef. in Al.		Remarks.
		μ	μ/ρ	
		cm.$^{-1}$	cm.-gm. units	
Uranium X_1 -	230	24	8·9	*L* radiation.
		0·70	0·26	Hard rays.
,, X_2 -	230	0·140	0·052	Very hard rays.
Ionium - -	230	1080	400	Extremely soft rays.
		22·5	8·35	*L* radiation.
		0·41	0·15	Very hard rays.
Radium *B* -	214	230	85	Softer than ordinary X rays.
		40	14·7	*L* radiation.
		0·51	0·188	Very hard rays.
,, *C* -	214	0·115	0·0424	*K* radiation.
,, *D* -	210	{ 45	16·5(?)	*L* ,,
,, *E* -		{ 0·99	0·36	Hard rays.
Mesothorium 2	228	26	9·5	*L* radiation.
		0·116	0·043	*K* ,,
Thorium *B* -	212	160	59	Softer than ordinary X rays.
		32	11·8	*L* radiation.
		0·36	0·13	Very hard rays.
,, *D* -	208	0·096	0·035	Hardest γ rays known.
Radioactinium	228(?)	25	9·2	*L* radiation
		0·190	0·070(?)	*K* ,,
Actinium *B* -	212(?)	120	44	Softer than ordinary X rays.
		31	11·4	*L* radiation.
		0·45	0·165	Very hard rays.
,, *D* -	208(?)	0·198	0·073	*K* radiation.

APPENDIX V.

X-RAY AND RADIUM PROTECTION.

THE following memoranda have been issued by the X-ray and Radium Protection Committee, representing various British radiological and other scientific bodies.

The Committee is constituted as follows :—

Chairman—Sir Humphry D. Rolleston, K.C.B. *Members* —Sir Archibald Reid, K.B.E., C.M.G., St Thomas's Hospital; Dr. Robert Knox, King's College Hospital; Dr. G. Harrison Orton, St Mary's Hospital; Dr. S. Gilbert Scott, London Hospital; Dr. J. C. Mottram, pathologist, Radium Institute; Dr. G. W. C. Kaye, O.B.E., National Physical Laboratory; Mr. Cuthbert Andrews. *Hon. Secretaries*—Dr. Stanley Melville, St George's Hospital; Prof. S. Russ, the Middlesex Hospital. *Address*—c/o Royal Society of Medicine, 1 Wimpole Street, W. 1.

MEMORANDUM No. 1 (July 1921).

INTRODUCTION.

The danger of over-exposure to X rays and radium can be avoided by the provision of efficient protection and suitable working conditions.

The known effects on the operator to be guarded against are :—

1. Visible injuries to the superficial tissues which may result in permanent damage.

2. Derangements of internal organs and changes in the blood. These are especially important as their early manifestation is often unrecognised.

T

General Recommendations.

It is the duty of those in charge of X-ray and radium departments to ensure efficient protection and suitable working conditions for the *personnel*.

The following precautions are recommended :—

1. Not more than seven working hours a day.

2. Sundays and two half-days off duty each week, to be spent as much as possible out of doors.

3. An annual holiday of one month or two separate fortnights.

Sisters and nurses employed as whole-time workers in X-ray and radium departments should not be called upon for any other hospital service.

Protective Measures.

It cannot be insisted upon too strongly that a primary precaution in all X-ray work is to surround the X-ray bulb itself as completely as possible with adequate protective material, except for an aperture as small as possible for the work in hand.

The protective measures recommended are dealt with under the following sections :—

  I. X rays for diagnostic purposes.
 II. X rays for superficial therapy.
III. X rays for deep therapy.
 IV. X rays for industrial and research purposes.
  V. Electrical precautions in X-ray departments.
 VI. Ventilation of X-ray departments.
VII. Radium therapy.

It must be clearly understood that the protective measures recommended for these various purposes are not necessarily interchangeable ; for instance, to use for deep therapy the measures intended for superficial therapy would probably subject the worker to serious injury.

I. *X Rays for Diagnostic Purposes.*

(1) *Screen Examinations.*

(*a*) The X-ray bulb to be enclosed as completely as possible with protective material equivalent to not less than 2 mm. of lead. The material of the diaphragm to be equivalent to not less than 2 mm. of lead.

(*b*) The fluorescent screen to be fitted with lead glass equivalent to not less than 1 mm. of lead, and to be large enough to cover the area irradiated when the diaphragm is opened to its widest. (Practical difficulties militate at present against the recommendation of a greater degree of protection.)

(*c*) A travelling protective screen, of material equivalent to not less than 2 mm. of lead, should be employed between the operator and the X-ray box.

(*d*) Protective gloves to be of lead rubber (or the like) equivalent to not less than ½ mm. of lead, and to be lined with leather or other suitable material. (As practical difficulties militate at present against the recommendation of a greater degree of protection, all manipulations during screen examination should be reduced to a minimum.)

(*e*) A minimum output of radiation should be used with the bulb as far from the screen as is consistent with the efficiency of the work in hand. Screen work to be as expeditious as possible.

(2) *Radiographic Examinations* (*"Overhead" Equipment*).

(*a*) The X-ray bulb to be enclosed as completely as possible with protective material equivalent to not less than 2 mm. of lead.

(*b*) The operator to stand behind a protective screen of material equivalent to not less than 2 mm. of lead.

II. *X Rays for Superficial Therapy.*

It is difficult to define the line of demarcation between superficial and deep therapy.

For this reason it is recommended that, in the reorganisation of existing, or the equipment of new, X-ray departments, small cubicles should not be adopted, but that the precautionary measures suggested for deep therapy should be followed.

The definition of superficial therapy is considered to cover sets of apparatus giving a maximum of 100,000 volts (15 cm. spark-gap between points; 5 cm. spark-gap between spheres of diameter 5 cm.).

Cubicle System.

Where the cubicle system is already in existence it is recommended that :—

1. The cubicle should be well lighted and ventilated, preferably provided with an exhaust electric fan in an outside wall or ventilation shaft. The controls of the X-ray apparatus to be outside the cubicle.

2. The walls of the cubicle to be of material equivalent to not less than 2 mm. of lead. Windows to be of lead glass of equivalent thickness.

3. The X-ray bulb to be enclosed as completely as possible with protective material equivalent to not less than 2 mm. of lead.

III. *X Rays for Deep Therapy.*

This section refers to sets of apparatus giving voltages above 100,000.

1. Small cubicles are not recommended.

2. A large, lofty, well-ventilated and lighted room to be provided.

3. The X-ray bulb to be enclosed as completely as possible with protective material equivalent to not less than 3 mm. of lead.

4. A separate enclosure to be provided for the operator, situated as far as possible from the X-ray bulb. All controls to be within this enclosure, the walls and windows of which to be of material equivalent to not less than 3 mm of lead.

IV. *X Rays for Industrial and Research Purposes.*

The preceding recommendations for voltages above and below 100,000 will probably apply to the majority conditions under which X rays are used for industrial research purposes.

V. *Electrical Precautions in X-Ray Departments.*

The following recommendations are made :—

1. Wooden, cork, or rubber floors should be provided ; existing concrete floors should be covered with one of the above materials.

2. Stout metal tubes or rods should, wherever possible, be used instead of wires for conductors. Thickly insulated

wire is preferable to bare wire. Slack or looped wires are to be avoided.

3. All metal parts of the apparatus and room to be efficiently earthed.

4. All main and supply switches should be very distinctly indicated. Wherever possible double-pole switches should be used in preference to single-pole. Fuses no heavier than necessary for the purpose in hand should be used. Unemployed leads to the high tension generator should not be permitted

VI. Ventilation of X-Ray Departments.

1. It is strongly recommended that the X-ray department should not be below the ground level.

2. The importance of adequate ventilation in both operating and dark rooms is supreme. Artificial ventilation is recommended in most cases. With very high potentials coronal discharges are difficult to avoid, and these produce ozone and nitrous fumes, both of which are prejudicial to the operator. Dark rooms should be capable of being readily opened up to sunshine and fresh air when not in use. The walls and ceilings of dark rooms are best painted some more cheerful hue than black.

VII. Radium Therapy.

The following protective measures are recommended for the handling of quantities of radium up to 1 gram :—

1. In order to avoid injury to the fingers the radium, whether in the form of applicators of radium salt, or in the form emanation tubes, should be always manipulated with forceps or similar instruments, and it should be carried place to place in long-handled boxes lined on all with 1 cm. of lead.

2. In order to avoid the penetrating rays of radium all manipulations should be carried out as rapidly as possible, and the operator should not remain in the vicinity of radium for longer than is necessary.

The radium when not in use should be stored in an enclosure, the wall thickness of which should be equivalent to not less than 8 cm. of lead.

3. In the handling of emanation all manipulations should, as far as possible, be carried out during its relatively inactive state. In manipulations where emanation is likely to come

into direct contact with the fingers thin rubber gloves should be worn. The escape of emanation should be very carefully guarded against, and the room in which it is prepared should be provided with an exhaust electric fan.

Existing Facilities for Ensuring Safety of Operators.

The governing bodies of many institutions where radiological work is carried on may wish to have further guarantees of the general safety of the conditions under which their *personnel* work.

1. Although the Committee believe that an adequate degree of safety would result if the recommendations now put forward were acted upon, they would point out that this is entirely dependent upon the loyal co-operation of the *personnel* in following the precautionary measures outlined for their benefit.

2. The Committee would also point out that the National Physical Laboratory, Teddington, is prepared to carry out exact measurements upon X-ray protective materials, and to arrange for periodic inspection of existing installations on the lines of the present recommendations.

3. Further, in view of the varying susceptibilities of workers to radiation, the Committee recommend that wherever possible periodic tests, *e.g.* every three months, be made upon the blood of the *personnel*, so that any changes which occur may be recognised at an early stage. In the present state of our knowledge it is difficult to decide when small variations from the normal blood-count become significant.

MEMORANDUM No. 2 (December 1921).

In view of the widespread uncertainty and anxiety as to the efficacy of the various devices and materials employed for the purposes of protection against X rays, the X-ray and Radium Protection Committee strongly advises that the Heads of X-ray Departments of hospitals and other institutions should safeguard themselves and their staff on this score by recommending to the Hospital Authorities the adoption of the following precautions :—

1. The various protective appliances should be inspected and reported on by the National Physical Laboratory

(N.P.L.), Teddington. In the event of an adverse report, early steps should be taken to carry out the recommendations of the Laboratory. The Laboratory is prepared, wherever possible or expedient, to engrave (or otherwise suitably mark) the N.P.L. monogram and year of test on such appliances as provide the full measure of protection laid down in the Preliminary Report (July 1921) of the Protection Committee. It should be pointed out that, in the case of materials which may deteriorate, *e.g.* lead rubber, such inspection should be periodic, say every twelve months.

2. Within the Committee's recent experience, the working conditions of X-ray Departments, *e.g.* lay-out of installations, degree of scattered radiation, ventilation, high-tension insulation, etc., are often unsatisfactory. It is recommended that such conditions be inspected by the N.P.L., and that early steps be taken to give effect to such alterations as may arise out of their report. It is advised that, in the planning of new radiological departments, advantage be taken of the facilities available at the N.P.L.

3. Manufacturers of X-ray apparatus are also invited to assist in reassuring the public by actively co-operating with the Committee in its recommendations. It is suggested that protective materials or equipment should not be sold or incorporated into an installation unless accompanied by a specification based upon an N.P.L. certificate or report stating, in terms of the equivalent thickness of lead, the degree of protection afforded.

In the interests of both the trade and profession, it is urged that manufacturers should put themselves into a position to be able to guarantee that their apparatus complies completely with the recommendations of the Committee.

4. The Committee recommends that the various instruments dealing with the measurement of current (ammeters and milliammeters) and voltage, be standardised by the N.P.L. With reference to the measurement of secondary voltage, the Committee recommends that every installation should be provided with adequate means for enabling this to be easily effected, *e.g.* by kilovoltmeter, sphere-gap voltmeter, or the like.

5. The Committee would further urge that Heads of X-ray Departments should insist upon complete N.P.L. inspection of imported materials and apparatus.

APPENDIX VI.

X-RAY AND ELECTRO-MEDICAL NOMENCLATURE.

THE following list of terms, restricted to those of physical application, includes those approved by the British Engineering Standards Association :—

I. X RAYS.

Absorption Coefficient.—The ratio of the distance-rate of change of intensity of a particular quality of X rays at a point in a specified material to the intensity at that point.

Anode.—The positive (or the incoming-current) electrode in a discharge tube.

Anticathode.—The target on which the cathode rays are focussed in an X-ray tube, and which forms the source of emission of the X rays.

Auto-Transformer.—A static transformer, consisting of a primary winding (on an iron core), the winding having a number of tapping-off wires at various points for obtaining a gradation of voltages.

Brush Discharge (Corona).—An intermittent hissing discharge due to local ionisation of the air by voltages insufficient to produce a true spark discharge. The effect is emphasised in the regions of points, sharp corners, etc.

Cathode.—The negative (or the outgoing-current) electrode in a discharge tube.

Cathode Rays.—A stream of negatively charged electrons emitted with high velocity from the cathode or its neighbourhood when an electric discharge is passed in an evacuated tube.

Cathode or Crookes' Dark Space.—A non-luminous region which envelops and follows the outline of the cathode in a discharge tube at moderately low pressures.

Characteristic X Rays.—X rays which are wholly peculiar to, or characteristic of, a particular element.

Condenser.—A device possessing electrical capacity which works in conjunction with an induction coil and mechanical interrupter. Normally constructed of tin foil and paraffined paper.

Coolidge Tube.—A type of hot cathode tube.

Crookes' Tube (Vacuum tube; Discharge tube; Geissler tube).—An electric discharge tube provided with electrodes and exhausted to a low gas pressure.

Dosemeter.—A device for determining the exposure when using X rays for treatment purposes.

Electrometer (Electroscope).—An instrument for measuring potential differences by electrostatic means.

Electron.—The fundamental carrier of unit negative electric charge.

Fluorescent Screen.—A screen coated with a finely divided substance which fluoresces under the influence of the X rays.

Gas Tube.—An X-ray tube which depends for its action on the presence of the residual gas in the tube, and in which the anticathode is usually connected electrically to the anode.

Hardness of X Rays.—The quality, penetrating power or wave-length of X rays. The "harder" the rays, the shorter the wave-length.

Hardness of X-Ray Tubes.—The degree of vacuum in an X-ray tube. The "harder" the tube the higher the vacuum.

Hot-Cathode Tube.—A tube in which electrons are produced by an electrically-heated cathode. The vacuum is so high that the residual gas plays no active part. The anticathode serves also as the anode.

Induction Coil (Ruhmkorf Coil).—An open-core, high-tension, static transformer, with independent interrupter.

Influence or Static Machine.—A high-potential generator, which depends for its action on electrostatic means.

Intensifying Screen.—A thin screen coated with a finely divided substance which fluoresces under the influence of the X rays, and which is mounted in close contact with the emulsion of a photographic plate or film for the purpose of reinforcing the image.

Intensity of X Rays.—The X-ray energy per unit area of a receiving surface placed at right angles to the rays.

Interrupter (or Break).—An apparatus for mechanically interrupting the primary current of an induction coil.

Ion.—A molecular or atomic aggregate consisting of one or more molecules or atoms, which carries either a positive or negative electrical charge. At low pressures the negative ion exists as the electron.

Ionisation.—The temporary conductivity imparted to a gas by the presence of ions produced by X rays, radium rays, etc.

Ionisation Chamber.—An apparatus for measuring the degree of ionisation in a gas.

Negative Glow.—The luminous glow which envelops the cathode at moderately low pressures in a discharge tube.

Oscilloscope.—An accessory discharge tube in which the

length of the negative glow indicates comparatively the amount of current passing.

Peak Voltage.—The maximum voltage corresponding to the peak or crest of the potential wave in alternating or pulsating current.

Penetrometer (or Qualimeter).—An instrument for measuring the penetrating power or quality of X rays.

Positive Rays.—A stream of positively charged atoms which travel mainly away from the anode when an electric discharge is passed in an evacuated tube.

Quantum Limit.—The short wave-length boundary to a spectrum of general X rays. Its position is definitely related by Planck's quantum relation to the maximum potential on the X-ray tube.

Radiograph (Radiogram, Skiagraph, Skiagram : in America Roentgenogram).—The image produced on a photographic plate or film by the action of X rays.

Radiography.—The production of X-ray photographs.

Radiology.—The science and practice of X rays, radium rays, etc.

Radiometallography.—The radiography of metals.

Rectifier.—A device, either mechanical or of valve-tube type, for suppressing or inverting the "non-useful" half of an alternating or pulsating current wave.

Spark-Gap.—The maximum sparking distance between point, spherical, or other electrodes, the degree of separation being a measure of the applied voltage.

Target.—See Anticathode.

Transformer.—A static, closed-core, high-tension transformer, for converting alternating low-voltage current to high-voltage current of the same frequency.

X Rays (Röntgen Rays).—Electro-magnetic waves of very

short wave-length, which are set up when electrons have their velocities altered.

X-Ray Crystallography.—The study of the arrangement of the atoms in a crystal by " reflecting " X rays from the several faces of the crystal.

X-Ray Spectrum.—The spectrum produced by splitting up a heterogeneous beam of X rays by means of " reflection " at a crystal face.

X-Ray Tube.—An electric discharge tube of appropriate gas pressure in which a stream of cathode rays falls upon a metal target with the resultant production of X rays.

II. ELECTRO-MEDICAL.

Diathermy.—The therapeutic use of high-frequency, sustained and undamped oscillations of comparatively low voltage and relatively high amperage. The term is used in recognition of the marked heating effect produced throughout the tissues.

Faradism.—The therapeutic use of the interrupted current from an induction coil, usually from the secondary though occasionally from the primary. The object is the stimulation of muscles and nerves.

Galvanism.—The therapeutic use of direct current.

" High-Frequency " Treatment (D'Arsonvalism). — The therapeutic use of very high-frequency intermittent and isolated trains of heavily damped oscillations of very high voltage and relatively low amperage.

Medical Ionisation or Ionic Medication.—The therapeutic use of an electric current for the purpose of introducing the ions of soluble salts into the tissues.

Radiotherapy.—The treatment of disease by radiation.

Sinusoidal Current.—A single-phase alternating current of sine wave form and of a periodicity adapted to the purpose in hand.

Static Breeze (Static Brush).—The therapeutic use of the brush discharge.

Static Induced Current.—The current which passes through a " patient " connecting the outer coatings of two Leyden jars, the inner coating of one of which is connected to the positive terminal of an influence machine and the inner coating of the other to the negative terminal, the two inner coatings being periodically discharged

Static Wave Current.—The current resulting from the periodic sudden discharging of a " patient " periodically raised to a high potential by means of an influence machine.

INDEX.

Printed in Great Britain at THE DARIEN PRESS, *Edinburgh.*